Fertility decline in a traditional society: The case of Bali

Kim Streatfield

Indonesian Population
Monograph Series No. 4
Department of Demography
The Australian National University

First published in Australia 1986

National Library of Australia
Cataloguing-in-Publication entry

Streatfield, Kim
    Fertility decline in a traditional society: the case of Bali

    Bibliography
    ISBN 0 86784 711 5

    1. Fertility, Human - Indonesia - Bali. 2. Birth control -
    Indonesia - Bali. I. Australian National University.
    Department of Demography. II. Title. (Series: Indonesian
    population monograph series; 4).

304.6'32'095986

Printed in Australia by The Australian National University
Printing Service, for the Department of Demography.

Distributed by BIBLIOTECH, ANUTECH Pty Ltd., GPO Box 4, Canberra,
ACT 2601, Australia.

To Jan and Claire

FORWORD

Almost a decade has passed since the appearance of the first
publication in the Indonesian Monograph Series of the Department
of Demography, Australian National University.   Attention has
previously been given to Java, Sumatra and Sulawesi, and, with
the present work, the fourth in the series, Bali joins that list.

The Department of Demography has had close relations with
Indonesia for over twenty years, and over 40 Indonesians have
studied in Canberra for graduate degrees in demography.   Ten
staff members of the Department of Demography have been seconded
to Indonesian Institutions for long periods, and non-Indonesian
graduate students of the Department have also carried out their
research in Indonesia.   Appropriately, Indonesia has become the
most important focus of the Department's research and teaching
outside Australia.

The present monograph draws together several of those strands.
Kim Streatfield was an Australian student who lived in Bali and
undertook his Ph.D. research there; he later joined the academic
staff of the Department of Demography and was seconded for two
years to the Population Institute of Gadjah Mada University in
Yogyakarta; later still he returned to work with the Department
in Canberra.

This monograph explores a question of the greatest importance.
Bali has preserved much of its traditional society, and its rural
population has remained relatively poor.   Yet fertility has
declined steeply.   Kim Streatfield concentrated on one rural
area, employing both standard demographic and participant
approaches, to explore the reasons for this change as well as the
mechanisms.   He unravels a complex story which is of great
importance both to Indonesians and to the world beyond.

> John C. Caldwell
> Head
> Department of Demography
> Australian National University

PREFACE

This monograph is based on the writer's doctoral dissertation which was submitted to the Department of Demography, Research School of Social Sciences, Australian National University. It is based on work undertaken in Canberra and Bali between 1979 and 1982.

Bali is such a fascinating society that I consider myself very fortunate to have had the opportunity to reside and carry out fieldwork there. For this opportunity I am indebted to the Australian National University, in particular the Department of Demography whose Head, Professor J.C.Caldwell and other members provided support and encouragement throughout the study period. The assistance given by my departmental supervisors, Dr. Valerie Hull and Dr. Peter McDonald, was invaluable and underscores the benefits of selecting good supervisors! I also wish to thank other staff, Dr. T.H. Hull, Bernadette Derrick, Jenny Widdowson, Pat Mooney, Liz Baker, and Pat Quiggin in the library. Special thanks go to Wendy Cosford, who, with the steady hand of a microsurgeon, excised countless floating participles from the original draft. I am very grateful to Daphne Broers-Freeman who has put considerable editorial effort into transforming the text from thesis to publication standard.

Many thanks are due to those in Indonesia who were involved in this project. I am grateful to the Indonesian Institute of Science (LIPI), the official Indonesian sponsor of the research project. I am particularly indebted to my counterpart, Dr.N.T. Suryadhi of the Medical Faculty, Udayana University; to Dr.I.B. Tjitarsa, the Dean; to Dr. D.W. Wirawan who helped rescue the fieldwork from impending disaster at one stage; and to Drs. K.S. Astika of the Anthropology Section in the Faculty of Arts.

The staff of the Bali Family Planning Program, Dr. I.B. Astawa, Pak P. Gourde, and Dr. Inne Susanti were very helpful, as were Government officials in the offices of the Bureau of Statistics, and at the village administration level. Anak Agung Niang took my family and myself into her home and provided a warm and cheerful living atmosphere, and a wealth of information about all things Balinese.

Finally, I am especially grateful to my wife, Jan, for her encouragement, interest, and patience during a demanding time. Our infant daughter, Claire (Putu Ratna Wati), unknowingly added another dimension to the rewarding experience of living in rural Bali.

Kim Streatfield
Canberra
April 1986

TABLE OF CONTENTS

	Page Number

LIST OF TABLES

LIST OF FIGURES

MAPS

MAP OF THE PROVINCE OF BALI

KARANGASEM

Gunung Agung ▲
Gunung Seraya ▲
Karangasem ●

● Besakih

NUSA PENIDA

Klungkung ●
KLUNGKUNG

BANJARANGKAN

Gunung Batur ▲
Lake Batur

BANGLI

Bangli ●

I

GIANYAR

Gianyar ●

BADUNG

Sanur ●

Den Pasar ●

BUKIT

Singaraja ●

Gunung Pengelengan ▲
Lake Bratan

Gunung Batukau ▲

L

A

TABANAN

Tabanan ●

BULELENG

B

Pulukan ●

JEMBRANA

Negara ●

xvii

1.1 BACKGROUND

In 1969 the Indonesian government established a Family Planning Program which was implemented initially on the islands of Java and Bali, containing between them about two-thirds of the country's population.

Since that time, data on numbers of family planning acceptors and on fertility levels have suggested a substantial decline in fertility coinciding with the operation of the program. The changes have been particularly dramatic in the case of Bali.

Before the introduction of the Family Planning Program, the level of marital fertility in Bali was the highest of the six provinces which make up Java and Bali. In the late 1960s, the crude birth rate was estimated at around 40 per 1,000, (Table 1.2), the total fertility rate at 5.8 (Table 1.3), and there was little evidence of much use of either modern or traditional birth control. By 1976, the World Fertility Survey data indicated that some 39 percent of Balinese married women of childbearing age were using contraception, that the crude birth rate had fallen some 10 percentage points to about 29 per 1,000, and the total fertility rate had fallen by about one third to 3.8.   This latter figure was obtained by Sinquefield using the current pregnancy status method.[1] If this figure proved to be correct, then Bali's fertility would have been the lowest of any province in Indonesia; however there was some doubt cast on the figure, not only by criticisms of the method itself, but also by the alternative figure of 4.9 for 1975 calculated by Hull using the 'Last Birth' method on data from the 1976 Intercensal Survey (Supas II) (see Section 1.2.1).   'Last Birth' data from the 1980 Census showed a TFR of 3.5 for Bali in 1980 (Dasvarma, et al.,1984).

From 1976 onwards, the provincial office of the National Family Planning Coordinating Board (BKKBN) was releasing contraceptive prevalence figures based on fieldworker reports from their newly introduced community based Sistem Banjar distribution system. These figures were usually somewhat higher than the figures from the central office of BKKBN in Jakarta based on contraceptive distribution data (see Chapter 4), and threw some doubt on the validity of the prevalence levels of current use being claimed by the provincial office of BKKBN in Bali. For example, at the time of this study, BKKBN Bali claimed a contraceptive prevalence rate for Bali of 75.0 percent compared to the estimate of 50.8 percent from the BKKBN head office.   Since the 1978-9 Socioeconomic Surveys (SUSENAS), there had not been any surveys against which the figures could be checked.

1.1.1 Claims for success of Family Planning Program in Bali

Both the fertility level data and the family planning prevalence data seemed to be accepted almost without question by many observers, and gave rise in the mid to late 1970s to a number of extremely optimistic articles, particularly in the more popularised population journals (see Panel 1).

PANEL 1

(a) the International Fertility Research Program's publication
<u>Taking Family Planning to the World's Poor</u>:

(the Family Planning Program in Bali) ...may well be the most
successful in any part of Asia. Fifty-four percent of all eligible
couples now use some contraceptive method (Potts,<u>et al</u>., 1977: a-1).

(b) in the Ford Foundation publication, <u>Cycle</u>:

(Bali) happens to be the setting for one of the most exciting and
demographically successful family planning programs in the world
(Piet and Piet,1977-8:1).

(c) the IPPF's journal, <u>People</u>:

Within just eight years, Bali has neatly stepped out of the vicious
circle of poverty and overpopulation (Harrison,1978:14).

(d) and <u>International Family Planning Perspectives</u>:

...a behavioural and demographic transition of remarkable proportions
seems to be emerging (Meier,1979:63).

Regardless of whether or not all of these claims were justified,
especially when compared with countries like Taiwan, Korea and Singapore,
there can be little disagreement that up to the end of the 1970s the
results, in terms of prevalence rates and apparent fertility decline, had
been quite impressive.

The apparent achievements of the National Family Planning Program in
Bali were viewed, understandably, with some pride by the Bali provincial
Family Planning Program office. They pointed out that in March 1977,
compared to the national average of 35 percent of eligible couples using
some kind of contraceptive, the level in Bali was 56.5 percent. The head of
the program in Bali, Dr. I.B. Astawa noted that this was nearing the
national target for family planning acceptors of 60 to 70 percent for the
year 2000 (1977:28). The latest figures available from BKKBN head office
indicate that in August 1985 Bali still has the highest contraceptive
prevalence rate, at 74.5 percent, of all provinces. This is after the
reassessment of the monthly statistics which saw the national prevalence
rate reduced from 62.6 percent in March to 50.4 percent in June 1985. By
August the national prevalence rate had risen to 52.2 percent. More
detailed discussion of the BKKBN monthly statistics can be found in
Streatfield,1985.

1.1.2 <u>Levels of Development in Bali</u>

The success of the program in Bali was seen as boding well not only
for the rest of Indonesia, but also for other poor, rural developing
countries. The reason for this optimism was that in Bali, unlike the
modernising countries of East Asia, the decline in fertility had
occurred without accompanying signs of major economic development. Per
capita income, investment and levels of small business activity, often

2

taken as indicators of economic modernisation, remained relatively low in Bali.

Such a situation where fertility falls in the absence of major social and economic change is not entirely new. Recent decades have produced evidence which show the classical demographic transition theory of Notestein as not being capable of defining a precise threshold of modernisation which would enable the making of reliable predictions as to when the fertility of a population would be ready to fall. Although development variables such as industrialisation, urbanisation and education usually appeared to play an important role preceding fertility decline, there were sufficient exceptions throughout the Western world to undermine the place of these variables as essential precursors. The only feature that did seem to be common to most examples of fertility decline was a shift in economic, social and political functions from the family to larger, specialised (non-familial) institutions.

The magnitude and rapidity of fertility declines in some developing countries in recent times have further illustrated the deficiencies of the demographic transition theory. The patterns of development variables at the time fertility started to fall have been so varied (and different from the variations seen earlier in the West) that it has been very difficult to isolate the important factors. For example, while all these developing countries have had a Family Planning Program in operation for varying periods of time prior to the decline, some have been well on the way to becoming industrialised at the time fertility started falling (e.g. Taiwan, Korea). In others the government had introduced strict measures to discourage high fertility (eg., China, Singapore). Some had near universal literacy (e.g. Barbados). In some (often islands) the economy was heavily dependent on one or two vulnerable exports (eg., Mauritius). In many the social and economic position of women was unusually good (e.g. Thailand), conversely, where the position of women was not good (as in many Muslim countries) fertility has not fallen markedly. In virtually all transitional countries however, mortality had fallen from the traditionally high levels prior to the fertility decline and in some (e.g. Sri Lanka) mortality had declined very steeply.

To make more difficult the task of understanding recent fertility declines using classical demographic transition theory is the fact that the circumstances of present day pre-transition societies differ from Western pre-transition societies. Today most societies have mass media and communication networks as well as modern, Western-style education systems of varying degrees of coverage and, through these, exposure to Western lifestyles and technology. These countries also have the opportunity to avail themselves of Family Planning Programs with a wide range of modern contraceptives. However, researchers continue to try to identify those social and economic variables which appear to be related to the onset of fertility decline. Recent studies have implicated some variables which appear to be inversely related to fertility levels (Adelman and Morris, 1966; Kasarda, 1971; Ekanem, 1972; and Mauldin and Berelson, 1978). These variables usually include education, per capita income, urbanisation, industrialisation or degree of modernisation.

Variable	Level in Bali
EDUCATION	
(a) Adult Literacy	Males (10+)=62%
	Females (10+)=34%
(b) School Enrolments:	
-Primary (7-12)	Males-64%
	Females-49%
	Total-57%
-Secondary (13-18)	Males-35%
	Females-16%
	Total-25%
HEALTH	
(c) Life Expectancy (birth)	About 50 years
(d) Infant Mortality Rate	(i) Late 1960s =127 per 1,000
	(ii) Early 1970s =100 per 1,000
ECONOMY	
(e) % Adult Males in Non-Agricultural Labour	26.7% of total labour force
(f) GNP Per Capita	US$100-140 (1971)
URBANISATION	
(g) % Popn. in Cities of 100,000+	5% (Capital city only)

Sources: (a),(b),(e),(g) - 1971 Census
          (c) - McDonald,(1979)
          (d)   (i) - McDonald,(1979)
              (ii) - Gardiner,(1979:4)
          (f) - Astawa et al.,(1975:86)

However, if we examine the seven variables chosen by Mauldin and Berelson in their detailed attempt to elucidate the 'Conditions of Fertility Decline in Developing Countries, 1965-75', the island of Bali scores rather poorly in virtually all of them. The seven variables were chosen for their ability to satisfy simultaneously 'the two criteria of substantial relevance and substantial availability' (Mauldin and Berelson, 1978:99) and are listed in Panel 2 with levels in Bali around 1971.

The levels of each of these variables, with the possible exception of education, are indicative not of a modern but a traditional society. Demeny has generalised that these two types of society are readily distinguished in that 'in traditional societies fertility and mortality are high. In modern societies fertility and mortality are low. In between, there is demographic transition' (1968). While Bali, at the time the Family Planning Program began, certainly fell into the former category it is useful to look at a broader definition of a traditional society, such as that used by Coale (1973:64). The levels for Bali in 1971 are enclosed in parentheses in the following definition: 'A society was traditional if less than 30 percent of its population lived in urban settlements of more than 20,000 persons (6 percent), if fewer than 50 percent of females 6 to

13 were enrolled in school (42 percent), and if more than 60 percent of the labour force was engaged in agriculture, fishing or forestry (67 percent of total). High fertility and mortality could be defined as a total fertility of over 5.0 (5.8 in 1967-70), and an expectation of life at birth for women of less than 60 years (about 50 years)' (1973:64). The character-istics listed above firmly categorise Bali as demographically 'traditional' at the time the Family Planning Program was introduced in 1970.

The question of whether Bali would have been classified in the 1960s as traditional in an anthropological sense involves examination of the changes in social, economic and political structure that have occurred during this century.

While anthropologists are reluctant to give an all-encompassing definition of a traditional society, it is possible to list certain features which might be expected to distinguish traditional and modern societies. These are family structure; community structure and networks of support and obligations; political structure, in particular the role of the royal families; and the nature of employment opportunities. In reference to Bali, Hildred Geertz stated that 'present-day Balinese social structure has one very general property which affects political processes in certain crucial ways: it is essentially traditional in form and function' (1959:24), but she goes on to emphasise that while traditional, 'Balinese social structure has a great deal of flexibility in adapting to the modern world' (ibid, 24). These matters will be discussed in some detail in Chapter 2 where it will be argued that with the possible exception of the political structure, Balinese society in the 1960s was still traditional in a functional sense.

1.2   MACRO-LEVEL DEMOGRAPHIC EVIDENCE FOR FERTILITY DECLINE

This section will examine the available data upon which claims for a substantial fertility decline in Bali have been based. Before examining the recent (macro-level) demographic evidence for a fertility decline it is necessary to look briefly at rates of population growth in the past. The population estimates from the nineteenth century and early twentieth century vary considerably (see Table 1.1a) and could not be considered very reliable.

The earliest systematic population estimate (for 1815) was that of Sir Thomas Stamford Raffles who used the unusual, and very dubious, method of extrapolating the total population from the number of males who had had their teeth filed (Raffles,1830:App.K.,ccxxxii).[2] The resulting figure of about 800,000 was about one sixth of the estimated population of 5,000,000 for Java at that time (Nitisastro,1970:19), and was not inconsistent with other estimates of the period (Table 1.1a). The Java figure, on the other hand, was probably too low at that time. In 1980 Java's population of around 91 million was about 36 times greater than that of Bali.

Throughout the nineteenth century other observers, both British (Moore) and Dutch (Helms, Van Eck and Van Eijsinga), estimated the popu-lation of Bali as between 700,000 and one million. Even by the mid nine-teenth century, Bali was considered to be densely populated. Crawfurd

5

concluded that even low estimates of Bali's population size:

> ...makes the relative population half again as much as Java, or near 480 to the square mile, being the greatest density of population throughout the whole Malayan and Philippine Islands (Crawfurd,1856:197).

TABLE 1.1a
POPULATION ESTIMATES AND CENSUS COUNTS, BALI, 1815-1980.

YEAR	POPULATION	SOURCE
1815	800,000	Stamford Raffles,Sir Thomas
1830	700,000	Moore,J.H.
1849	892,500	van Eck
	988,000	van Eijsinga
	1,000,000	Helms
1908-28	1,000,000	Dutch Administrative Records
1914	1,207,030	Dutch Administrative Records
1920	947,233	Dutch 'Census' Report
1930	1,101,393	Dutch Census
1940	1,321,114	Dutch Official Figure
1945	1,430,975	Dutch Official Figure
1949	1,540,834	Dutch Official Figure
1961	1,782,529	National Census
1971	2,120,099	National Census
1980	2,469,731	National Census

Sources: (1815) Raffles,1983; (1830,1849) Hanna,1971

TABLE 1.1b
RATES OF POPULATION GROWTH, BALI.
(Calculated from figures in Table 1.1a)

PERIOD	RATE (Percent per annum)
1920-1930	1.51%
1920-1961	1.56%
1930-1961	1.58%
1961-1971	1.67%
1971-1980	1.70%

Nevertheless, in spite of the relatively high density of population, village records indicate that at the beginning of the twentieth century, the average peasant family owned approximately one hectare of good land, irrigated or dry (Hanna,1975:97).   However by 1978 the population was just under 2.5 million and:

> ...this has resulted in the average Balinese family's farmland holding of one hectare in 1900 shrinking to perhaps 0.3 hectare today (Poffenberger and Zurbuchen,1980:24).

In 1930, the first official Dutch census of Bali gave a figure of 1,101,393 suggesting a relatively slow rate of population growth up to that time (1.5 percent per annnum between 1920 and 1930). Indeed, thereafter the rate of growth did not increase greatly (see Table 1.1b), reaching a maximum of 1.7 percent per annum between 1971 and 1980, although some writers have suggested otherwise:

> ...between 1930 and 1971 the rate of population growth in Bali took a sharp upswing, ...the control of endemic and epidemic diseases such as smallpox, cholera, malaria, and others had a major impact on mortality levels throughout the island, as did the growing availability of modern medical treatment (Poffenberger,1981:12).[3]

Poffenberger went on to suggest that:

> the rate of population growth increased continuously, keeping pace with Java, and reaching approximately 2.35 percent per annum in 1971 (1981:13).

Despite claims to the contrary, the Bali population has in fact grown steadily at a relatively low rate throughout the present century. Unfortunately it is not possible to determine whether or not fertility and mortality levels have changed within this period as there is reliable data only for 1961 onwards (see Table 1.2), however this period covers the introduction and operation of the Family Planning Program.

1.2.1 Fertility Estimates

The data presented in Table 1.2 show some consistency for the late 1960s, with different sources giving a crude birth rate of around 41 per 1,000. However, for the 1970s there is considerable variation with source. For the first half, the figure from SUPAS I (37.6 for 1971-75) is close to the figure from the World Fertility Survey (SUPAS III) of 36 per 1,000 for 1972-73, but for 1976 the figures given vary greatly depending on the assumptions made about changes in marriage patterns and marital fertility. The most likely scenario is one in which marriage patterns have remained constant (at 1971 Census levels) but marital fertility has fallen. This produces an estimated crude birth rate of 29 per 1,000 which does not seem unreasonable considering the prevalence rate of contraceptive use was estimated at 39 percent currently using in 1976, although it does imply a rapid decline in the preceding two or three years.

As might be expected, data on total fertility rates also show a decline, and indeed it is these figures which have been the basis for the claims of a dramatic fertility decline in Bali. An estimated total fertility rate of 3.8 was obtained for Bali,1976,from the World Fertility Survey data by Jeanne Sinquefield (Table 1.3).

There are serious doubts however, about the accuracy of the current pregnancy status method. In addition, the size of the WFS (SUPAS III) sample for Bali was rather small at 893 women. The'Last Birth' method estimate by Hull, was based on the larger sample from SUPAS II but this method is also open to error of recall of exact date of birth of the child.

TABLE 1.2
ESTIMATES OF CRUDE BIRTH RATES, Late 1960s to 1976,Bali.

Period	Source	CBR (per 1,000)
1965-70	1973 F-M Survey	41
1967-70	1971 CENSUS	42
1971-75	1976 SUPAS I	37.6
1967-71	1976 WFS	39
1972-73	1976 WFS	36
1976	a)constant marital fertility, changing marital patterns	37-38
	b)changing marital fertility, constant marriage patterns	29
	c)changing marital fertility, and marriage patterns	28

Sources: Sinquefield and Sungkono,1979:46
          For SUPAS I, CHO et al.,1979:21

Note: CBRs are calculated using appropriate ASFRs and estimates
          of population.
      CBRs for the late 1960s use 1970 estd. popn. figures.
      CBRs for 1972-73 use 1973 popn. estimates.
      and CBRs for 1976 use 1976 popn. estimates.

      1976:
      a)   1967-71 ASMFR estimates and 1976 Supas I proportions
           currently married to generate ASFRs (constant fertility).
      b)   1976 est. of ASMFRs and 1971 Census estimates of proportions
           currently married to generate ASFRs (constant marriage).
      c)   1976 est. of ASMFRs and 1976 Supas I est. of proportions
           currently married to generate ASFRs
           (changing marriage patterns and marital fertility).

     In conclusion then, Bali has undergone an increase in the rate of
population growth during the twentieth century, although this rate has been
kept below 2 percent per annum by relatively high mortality rates, and
late age at marriage restraining overall fertility levels.

     Nevertheless the available evidence suggests that fertility was high
before the beginning of the Family Planning Program around 1970, and has
dropped markedly, though the actual extent is uncertain. Consistent with
this situationhas been a dramatic increase in the prevalence of use of
modern contraceptive methods, although again, there are inconsistencies in
the levels according to different sources.

TABLE 1.3
ESTIMATES OF FERTILITY FOR BALI.
TOTAL FERTILITY RATES

Period	Source	TFR
1965-70	F-M SURVEY	5.9
1967-70	CENSUS 1971	5.8
	SUPAS I	5.8
		(5.7)*
	SUPAS II	5.6
1971-75	SUPAS I	5.1
		(4.9)*
	SUPAS II	5.3
1972-73	SUPAS III	5.2
1975	SUPAS II	
	(Last Birth)	4.9
1976*	SUPAS III	
	(Curr.Preg.)	3.8
	SUPAS III	
	(Linear Proj.)	4.3 $
1975-80	CENSUS 1980	4.0
1976-79	CENSUS 1980	4.0
1980	CENSUS 1980	3.5

Source: Freedman et al.,1981:4 and Sinquefield and Sungkono,1979:45
for ( )* figures. Census 1980 figures from Dasvarma et al.,1984.

$: Projected linear decline based on estimates from 1976 IFS for
1967-71 and 1972-73. The figure is a December 1976 estimate,
to match the pregnancy status estimate.

1.3 RECENT ATTEMPTS TO EXPLAIN THE BALI FERTILITY DECLINE

A number of writers have searched for the social and cultural
factors unusual to Bali which might help explain why the National Family
Planning Program had been more successful there than elsewhere, at least
until recently, when some other provinces have attained similar prevalence
levels of current use of contraception.

The factor which was most often picked out and presented as being the
key to success was the role of the unit of subvillage or hamlet organisation known locally as the banjar (see Chapter 2.1.1 for description).
This was around the time when community-based Contraceptive Distribution
Programs were demonstrating in countries such as Thailand, Sri Lanka, Korea
and Colombia, that non-clinic based Family Planning Programs could achieve
wider coverage successfully if they utilised existing social networks.
Paul Harrison wrote in the IPPF publication, People:

The banjars of Bali... have become the principal vehicle for
family planning. Their astonishing success is an object in how to
integrate family planning with key social institutions (1978:14).

The specific role of these social units in family planning acceptance

9

The specific role of these social units in family planning acceptance remains unclear. Is it that the banjar simply provide a grass roots level distribution system or is it that the banjar can apply social pressure to its members as implied in the statement by Freedman and Berelson: 'the village (banjar in Bali) has a corporate character facilitating collective action on common grounds' (1976:28). If the latter, were the banjar council members who issued the instructions responding purely to Government orders, indeed could they? Does this show a proper understanding of the role and limitations of the banjar council and leader? Or was family planning viewed as beneficial in itself, to the banjar or the village, as suggested by Piet and Piet:

> ...the Balinese have obviously decided that family planning is a serious matter and that population limitation is beneficial not only to individual families but also to the community as a whole (1977:8).

The former view is closer to that suggested by McNicoll in his paper on 'Institutional Determinants of Fertility Change', where he claims that one consequence of the communist uprising in the mid-sixties was that members of the military and others who came across from Java to re-establish order, produced a strengthening of the administrative system which enabled easier implementation of government programs at the village level:

> this (local) administrative system emerged greatly strengthened, a major contributor to this strength being its capacity to mobilise and work through the constituent hamlets ... free of significant countervailing political or social interests (1980:10).

McNicoll later qualified this with '...and low fertility clearly enough served the community's (qua community) own economic interests' (1980:11).

This implication of strong administrative and political pressures on couples to accept family planning in Indonesia has received support recently from a report by Murdijanto Purbangkoro on the 'special drives' in three villages of East Java in 1977. While he states 'that a majority of special-drive acceptors in all villages but Tulungrejo perceive that coercion was employed is important' he qualifies that with 'unfortunately, the term coercion is not easily defined', referring to the view of many poor people in fatalistic cultures, that they are very much subject to the forces of destiny or fate. In this context being forced to take an action does not necessarily imply pressure by another individual or institution (1978:67-8).

There is no doubt, however, that pressure to accept family planning has been applied fairly directly in some parts of Indonesia at certain times, although as Freedman , et al., point out 'a possible socially coercive element in the program could not be so successful if there were not latent, if ambivalent, motives for family limitation in the situation' (1981:11).

It is a little ironic that some writers, while on one hand emphasising the importance of social and cultural factors unique to Bali in explaining the Bali experience could readily be extrapolated to other, quite different societies. Harrison, for example, concluded his description of the 'success story' with 'It spells hope for Asia, showing that ANY POOR RURAL SOCIETY can adopt a small-family norm even before it begins to develop in other ways' (1978:14) - (This writer's emphasis).

Fortunately there were, at the same time, some rather more detailed examinations of the factors which appeared to be of importance in explaining the program's success in Bali. The notable studies were that by the program's head in Bali, Dr.I.B.Astawa and others (1975), and that by Hull, Hull and Singarimbun in 1977, followed by a detailed examination in 1978 by T.H.Hull.

There has been a tendency to simply compile a list of characteristics of Balinese culture and society which distinguish Bali from other places, particularly Java, without really attempting to evaluate their relative importance in explaining events in Bali. Thus it is one of the aims of this study to try to determine which factors have been of importance in the context of family planning acceptance and fertility decline in the study population.

The factors given greatest prominence by Astawa et al., tended to be, understandably, those implicating the well organised structure of the Family Planning Program, sensitively tuned to its social environment.

The factors emphasised by Astawa were:

(a) the ratio of population to clinics is somewhat lower in Bali than in the other provinces at 2,253 persons per clinic, (see Hull et al., 1977:26);

(b) the program has heavily emphasised the IUD as the method of choice, and this method has considerably better continuation rates than, say, the pill which is the main method used in Java;

(c) the budget for the program has been higher in Bali than in other provinces in terms of expenditure per eligible couple;

(d) information has been disseminated through a great variety of different bodies ranging from women's organisations, religious organisations, down to the banjar organisation which has apparently played such an important role in the uptake and use of family planning in Bali;

(e) apart from its role in informing the community members of the benefits of using family planning, the banjar was also used as a community level infrastructure to distribute contraceptives; to monitor performance of the banjar members use of contraception, and to encourage those who were not using but were eligible, to accept family planning;

(f) a system of fieldworkers was instituted to identify eligible couples and to motivate them to accept family planning, also to maintain the record keeping system. There were 231 fieldworkers for all Bali, an average of one for each four or five villages.

Astawa also mentioned a number of cultural factors, in particular religion, suggesting that Bali Hinduism is more receptive to family planning than Islam. Also Balinese women are traditionally industrious, often working outside the home in farming or labouring jobs, therefore they are expected to be more receptive to arguments about the practicality of having fewer children. Other factors implicated were: the traditional naming system, whereby most Balinese children are given a birth order name taken from a repeating cycle of four; the land tenure system, whereby most farming families receive directly the benefits of their work and thus feel a greater degree of control over their lives than if sharecropping; the fact that birth attendants have traditionally been male in Bali, thus minimising the embarrassment often felt by women when being examined by a male doctor, e.g., for IUD insertion; and finally, there is a widespread openness in discussion of reproductive matters.

Astawa's emphasis on the effect of program effort is also supported, to a degree, by the data of Freedman et al., who found, in their analysis of factors related to contraceptive practice in Java-Bali, that region (province) was the most important predictor of modern contraceptive use (1981:9). While recognising that regions may 'differ culturally in ways that affect fertility independently of the other demographic and social variables considered in this and other studies' (p.14), they also point to the fact that program effort has varied throughout Indonesia, and that such effort together with mobilisation of local leadership to recruit acceptors, has been quite strong in Bali (p.14). Although these are unsatisfactory measures of program effort, the fact that the rank order of clinic availability matches the rank order of contraceptive prevalence levels, with Bali topping both, is consistent with the claim that program effort plays an important role.

A more recent study by Khoo using the same combined data source examined the role of program effort indicators in greater detail (1981:15). These indicators were numbers of clinics, doctors, midwives, administrative personnel and fieldworkers per 1,000 ever-married women. Khoo concluded that while 'Region still appears to be important as a factor affecting both program input and contraceptive use, ...regional differences remain even after controlling for community-level differences in the number of program clinics and workers relative to population' (1981:15).

In their 1977 Population Bulletin article on Indonesia's Family Planning Program, Hull et al., in trying to explain the high latent demand for contraceptive services, also touched on two cultural characteristics. These were the 'high proportion of Balinese women who work outside the home at laborious jobs, including construction and roadwork'; and the fact that 'much agricultural land is worked collectively for the benefit of all members, thus there is little need for a nuclear family to increase its "labour force" through childbearing' (1977:28).[4]

The examination of cultural factors was extended by Hull in his 1978 paper entitled 'Where Credit is Due'. In this paper he listed five points that 'call into question the notion that Bali was, in the late 1960s, either a child-centered or an intensely traditional society. Instead the culture put little stress on the need to achieve economic, social or personal goals through childbearing. In contrast to virtually all other ethnic groups in Indonesia, Balinese could attain economic security and a large measure of personal fulfilment without children because of the effectiveness of non-familial groups'. These points were:

Firstly, that individuals belong to a wide range of groups organised for work, religious observance, or recreation, and membership of such a variety of groups gives the individual a substantial amount of flexibility and allows individual initiative.

Secondly, Bali has a tradition of marriage by capture, or elopement (see Section 2.2.1), interpreted by Hull to indicate that the initiation of proceedings, and partner selection, is done by the young people themselves, rather than by the older, parental generation. Hull suggests that this situation allows a more rapid change (delay) in age at marriage. There is not much evidence, however, to indicate what mean age at marriage was in earlier times, and what changes had been taking place (see Section 5.1).

Thirdly, the Balinese child is not raised as the precious possession of its parents, but as a small member of the extended family so the 'costs' and 'benefits' of childbearing are distributed among the members of the family compound, and hence do not fall solely on the shoulders of the biological parents.

Fourthly, population pressure is now more acute than in most other parts of Indonesia, with little prospect of intensifying cropping further, and with poor job prospects outside of agriculture. Young people are concerned about their futures, and that of their children.

The fifth and final point is the effect of the 'rapid pace of social change' reflected in the introduction of Western-style schooling; modernisation of transportation and communication; the penetration of the central government into the community; and of course the introduction of artifacts of modern society, such as radios, rice hulling machines, plastic housewares etc.

The conclusion was that 'the environment encountered by the Family Planning Program in 1969 was thus highly conducive to a remarkable success'(Hull,1978:5).

He goes on to say :

Who deserves credit for the fertility decline? It is obviously not sufficient to cite the government's policies and program, for while these provided the very necessary contraceptive supplies, they did not create the demand to restrict fertility. Small family norms were rather a product of Bali's unique traditional institutions which structured productive and family relations, and the modernising forces of education, and economic and political change (Hull,1978:6).

In their discussion of the patterns of use of contraception throughout Java-Bali, Freedman et al., also emphasise a number of the same points as Hull but they differentiate between the relative importance of different factors on the various strata of the society:

modernisation may work to increase contraceptive use among higher status groups; sheer Malthusian pressure coupled with aspirations arising out of access to outside influences including the information and services of the family planning program may increase contraceptive use among the poor (1981:15).

The concept of Malthusian pressure, also implied in Hull's fourth point, raises the issue of 'island status' as an explanatory factor. This is a notion that a community required to live within a restricted space is more aware of 'having nowhere to go', i.e., of its physical limits, and thus tends to exert a special control over fertility. However, Mauldin and Berelson (1975:11) point out that such a response may not derive from island residence as such, but from the population density associated therewith, for islands are on average relatively densely populated.

In a study of island states in the Caribbean and the Pacific, Cleland and Singh (1980:969) found 'modest' support from the Caribbean data for the view that island status is linked to an early demographic transition, independent of intervening, socio-economic factors, but for the Pacific the situation was the reverse, with high fertility persisting despite improved standards of living. It should be noted that Bali is not an island state, and there is the possibility of transmigration to other provinces of Indonesia, even if such a prospect is not viewed favourably by many Balinese.

Hull (in his fifth point mentioned above) is the only writer to really emphasise the possible role of 'modernisation' in the social sense rather than the fertility behaviour of Western style education, increased communications, mass media and consequent exposure to different value systems. This is an area which will need to be discussed in some detail in later chapters, particularly in the light of the timing of the fertility decline. In other words, even if there did long exist a number of cultural factors conducive to a fertility decline, as Freedman and Berelson point out 'it is not clear why they should operate at this time' (1976:28), that is, at the precise moment the Family Planning Program came into effect.

Thus the situation is that a poor, rural society, showing few signs of economic development and other changes often considered prerequisite for fertility decline, has demonstrated an apparent rapid and widespread acceptance of family planning and subsequent dramatic fertility decline.

Up to this point attempts to examine the reasons for this somewhat unexpected situation have dwelt, on the one hand upon aspects of the vigorous family planning program, and on the other hand on a variety of special social, cultural and economic conditions in Bali at the time the program commenced. Thus the purpose of this monograph is to investigate, and try to evaluate, the relative importance of these and other factors in explaining the fertility decline.

While national censuses and large scale surveys are useful and necessary in determining how widespread is any change in fertility, and National Family Planning Program data can show certain characteristics of those using contraception, neither type of data can be used to devise anything but speculative explanations for such changes as they usually do not gather adequate data on what motivated the respondents to act as they did. It is necessary to have available from individual respondents, detailed, reliable data on fertility and family planning (past and present), particularly reasons for acceptance of family planning, education, occupation, economic status, aspirations for children, etc., if any satisfactory examination of such a decline is to be carried out, and any advance made in refining current theories of fertility.

This monograph will be concerned with determining past and present levels of fertility and contraceptive use for a village population in rural Bali. Thereafter the role of contraceptive use as a factor in the fertility decline will be examined, in comparison to other possible factors. Finally, there will be an exploration of reasons why a predominantly poor, rural society such as that in Bali should accept family planning to such an unexpected degree.

CHAPTER 2
BALI'S SOCIAL AND ECONOMIC SITUATION, PAST AND PRESENT

This chapter is concerned with the setting in Bali into which the Family Planning Program was introduced. One of the questions arising from the rapid decline in Balinese fertility since 1970 is whether a latent demand for the means of family limitation existed before the introduction of the program, or whether the program itself changed people's attitudes toward children and changed their family size norms in a few short years. If there was a latent demand for family planning, was it a consequence of recent social or other changes, or had it long been present, remaining latent either because the available means of birth control were considered unsatisfactory or because the concept of birth control was not yet present in society? Also, was the faster pace of fertility decline in Bali compared to most parts of Java due to factors in the setting or to differences in implementation of the Family Planning Program? While this background information does not claim to be a full ethnography, it provides detail which will be drawn upon in following up the above questions in later chapters.

Any attempt to examine these questions requires a familiarity with social and economic organisation in Bali, both past and present; any changes being examined in the light of their possible effect on attitudes to childbearing and family limitation. As Bali is still primarily an agricultural society, the relationship between the people and the land is of particular interest here. This relationship will be seen to underlie a number of aspects of social, economic and political organisation in Bali.

2.1 BALINESE SOCIAL STRUCTURE

There has been some disagreement amongst Bali scholars about the form of the 'traditional Balinese village'. Some writers have suggested that the few remaining pre-Hindu villages (eg., Trunyan and Tenganan) have preserved the true form which has elsewhere undergone marked changes since the arrival of the Hindu aristocracy in the exodus of Javanese nobles, priests, soldiers and artisans that followed the collapse of the kingdom of Majapahit in the early sixteenth century. The prevalent view has been that the state, composed largely of descendants of the Javanese royal families, was superimposed upon the 'patriarchal communism' of the existing, self-contained village. This imported state structure was pictured as parasitic and exploitative, often trying to impose its influence upon the unwilling inhabitants of the autonomous dorpsrepubliek (village republic).

The accuracy of this 'oriental despotism' view has recently been challenged by Geertz in a detailed elucidation of the symbiotic relation between the precolonial negara, (the Balinese state), and its subjects. Geertz argues that while the above view of the state would have been very comforting to the colonial Dutch who had just displaced the indigenous aristocracy in the early part of this century, in fact the negara was neither a tyranny nor a hydraulic bureaucracy, nor even very much of a government. It was instead an organised spectacle, a theatre state designed to dramatise the ruling obsessions of Balinese culture: social inequality and status pride (see Geertz,1980:25).

Whatever the true relation between the state and its subjects, there were locally based political forms, to a large degree independent of the state, which played a predominant role in (1) the ordering of the public aspects of community life, (2) the regulation of irrigation facilities, and (3) the organisation of popular ritual. For each of these tasks there were separate (though not unrelated) institutions specifically directed toward their fulfilment : the hamlet (banjar), the irrigation society (subak),and the temple congregation (pemaksan) (Geertz,1980:47). Together with these major forms were a number of organisations also with specific functions and normally non-political: kin groups (dadia), voluntary organisations (seka), and so on. The result is not a territorial corporate unit coordinating most aspects of life, as peasant villages have commonly been described, but a compound of overlapping and interlocking distinct corporate groups, each based on a different principle of social affiliation. It is this multiple, composite nature of Balinese village structure which makes possible its high degree of variation while maintaining a general format (see Geertz,1959:991).

2.1.1 The Banjar

The hamlet, or banjar, is basically a residential unit. The members of one hamlet live side by side with each other, although it is not uncommon for some members of another hamlet from the same village to have their houses interspersed amongst those of the first. The hamlet is, however, much more to its members than just shared residence. It is a public corporation regulating a wide range of community activities. In those areas for which it is responsible it has virtually total power; whereas in other areas it has no power.

The banjar is closely involved in most aspects of a person's life, virtually from the time of birth until his spirit finally departs from this earth.

The functioning of each hamlet is regulated by a council (krama banjar) to which membership is compulsory for all 'adult' males residing in the hamlet. Adulthood however, is defined differently in different areas across the island, but generally comes with marriage. The unit of banjar membership is the kuren (hearth or kitchen), or household, which is usually a conjugal family as there is need of both males and females for the various temple duties. Within a houseyard there may be only one household or several, residence therein and the duty to worship in the houseyard temple being transmitted by the principle of patrifiliation: from father to son. That is, the heads of the component households in a houseyard live there because their fathers lived there before them, not just because they are all members of a patrilineage.

The banjar council usually holds a meeting (Sangkep) once every thirty five days on an auspicious day of the calendar, although some banjar meet as infrequently as once a year. At these meetings decisions are normally arrived at by consensus or unanimous agreement, under the guidance of the headman, the Kelian Banjar. Non-attendance at banjar meetings is met with a fine, and persistent refusal to fulfil banjar obligations can be dealt with by social ostracism which is viewed by most Balinese as a fate worse than death.

In the 1975 book, Kinship in Bali Geertze and Geertze wrote that the Perbekel, or headman of the government village, was the lowest rung of the central Indonesian government administration. Since then, however, there has been a process of what might be called 'Dinasisation' in which the vast majority of banjar have not only a traditional headman, the Kelian Banjar, but also have an administrative headman, the Kelian Dinas. The latter receives a regular salary from the government (Rs. 17,500 (A$25) per month in 1980) although he is still elected by the banjar members, while the Perbekel is not. The primary function of the Kelian Dinas is not the arranging of traditional duties (cremations, etc.) but rather the administrative procedures of the hamlet, such as passing on to members information about new government programs, and the consequent monitoring of those programs. The program of most interest in this context being the Family Planning Program introduced to Bali in 1969. Data on registration of births and deaths, and in- and out- migration from the hamlet is also supposed to be recorded by the Kelian Dinas.

The membership of the banjar usually numbers between 50 and 100 heads of households, averaging about 80 to 90. If the banjar grows much larger than this it may fragment into several smaller banjar, or it may less frequently become a fully fledged village (desa).

2.1.2 Subak (Irrigation Society)

One of the most important aspects of Balinese life fell outside the jurisdiction of the banjar: wet rice agriculture. The membership of these irrigation societies or subak is composed of all individuals who own, or rent, or have sharecropping rights to plots of wet rice land (sawah) which receive water from the same source (usually a dam and its canal). Three typical subak in the vicinity of the study villages comprised around 100 hectares each and had around 350 to 400 members. Records go back to the first millennium A.D. of kesuwakan, the forerunner of the present day subak.

The functions of the subak are to build and maintain a major dam and sluice on a river along with its set of canals, tunnels, aqueducts and lesser sluices. Another function, of special importance when water is scarce in the dry season, is the control of timing of the planting and other steps in the cultivation process, which require the allocation of water. Finally, and perhaps most important in the eyes of its members, each society is responsible for the religious rituals and observances in the various agricultural temples of the subak, which are necessary for the success of the crop.

Because the subak is based purely on the fact that its members own (or use) adjoining plots of land (fed by the same source) then the members may well reside in different villages, and indeed an individual may well be a member of several different subak simultaneously. The subak is, and always has been, quite separate from the village level government structure in Bali.

2.1.3 Temple Congregation

The third politically important institution in the desa system is the temple congregation, or pemaksan. Usually this group consists of a

18

number of cooperating congregations which support together a set of related temples. The temples of the <u>desa adat</u> are known collectively as the <u>Kahyangan-Tiga</u>.[5] The three temples concerned in any particular locality are the <u>Pura Puseh</u>, or origin temple, theoretically the temple built at the time of the first settlement of the area; the <u>Pura Dalem</u>, or graveyard temple for the spirits of the local dead; and the <u>Pura Bale Agung</u>, or 'great council temple' (council of the gods), dedicated primarily to maintaining the fertility of the surrounding rice fields. However it must be cautioned that 'whatever the Balinese village may or may not be, it is not simply definable as all people worshipping at one set of <u>Kahyangan-Tiga</u>, because people so obligated to worship commonly form a group for no other social function - political, economic, familiar, or whatever' (Geertz, 1959:993).

Another definition which distinguishes an 'administrative' village from a 'real' village, or <u>desa</u>, is that a 'real' <u>desa</u> is one 'which possesses an "<u>adat</u>": a body of customary law, usually unwritten and derived from "historical" memory, which serves to define not only the relations between segments of the village but the village itself' (Lansing,1974:2). Hence,although the <u>desa adat</u> has a most important religious significance for its members, it does not generally hold a great deal of social importance, in terms of social obligations among members, as do its components the hamlets or <u>banjar</u>. Consequently the government village or <u>desa</u> usually consists of parts of several <u>desa adat</u>, and any single <u>desa adat</u> will be distributed among several government <u>desa</u>. At this time in Bali there are 564 government <u>desa</u> (under a <u>perbekel</u>), but about 1,456 <u>desa adat</u>.

For the sake of completeness, it is necessary to briefly describe the non-political, voluntary organisations or clubs, the <u>seka</u>.

2.1.4   <u>The Seka</u>

The Balinese have considerable skills when it is necessary to perform some task or function requiring more than a few people. It is in this context that the <u>seka</u> or club (<u>seka</u> meaning 'to be as one') comes into being. It is composed of people who have a common task or duty to perform, and the life of the <u>seka</u> is usually only sufficiently long to complete the task, thereafter the <u>seka</u> will be disbanded. In certain cases, e.g., a <u>gamelan</u> orchestra, the <u>seka</u> may exist for quite a long period of time.

Examples of the <u>sekas</u> one might find in a village are those concerned with music, dance and drama; those concerned with the cultivation of rice; those which arrange the all important cockfights; as well as those for thatching roofs or protecting crops from rodent attacks.

2.1.5   <u>Social Stratification</u>

In earlier discussion of the state, the role of the aristocracy was briefly mentioned. It is appropriate at this stage, to examine more closely the nature of social stratification, and the relationship between the aristocracy and the commoners. Balinese society is notable for its stratification into ranked descent groups, or <u>penaksaan</u> which are commonly classified into four <u>wangsa</u> (literally: colours) - <u>Brahmana</u>, <u>Satria</u>, <u>Wesia</u> and <u>Sudra</u> - according to an ideology similar to the Indian caste system,

with a formal division of spiritual and political authority between
Brahmana and Satria respectively.

Gentry (i.e. high castes) and commoners live side by side, although
there are some hamlets which are composed exclusively of one or the other.
Everyday social intercourse between gentry and commoners is usually
unaffected by prestige differences, as long as the forms of etiquette
(mainly use of the appropriate language level) are observed.[6] However, in
certain respects the attention of the gentry is turned outward and away
from the village, toward the affairs of gentry in other villages or in the
court, while commoners' interest is turned inward onto strictly local
matters. In many areas gentry do not participate in hamlet council
decisions or projects, but hold themselves aloof (Geertz and Geertz,1975:
22).

The members of the hamlet council (krama banjar) are, so far as
legal rights are concerned, all absolutely equal citizens, decisions are
only taken after reaching unanimous agreement, and their leaders are never
considered to be more than representative of the common will. Thus, to be
a member of the hamlet council places the gentry in a difficult situation,
for their title reflects a claim, however weak, to political and social
superiority, a claim to membership in an exalted and nonlocalised aristo-
cratic community above and outside the hamlet (Geertz and Geertz,1975:
90).

2.2   MARRIAGE AND REPRODUCTION

2.2.1   Marriage

Covarrubias claimed that: 'a Balinese feels that his most important
duty is to marry as soon as he comes of age and to raise a family to perpetuate his line' (1937:122). Data on proportions remaining unmarried
would seem to support this view, marriage being almost universal.

Ngerorod (Marriage by kidnapping or elopement):
This method (known as kawin lari or 'marriage on the run') remains
popular amongst Balinese, partly because of the opportunity for a
melodramatic, but usually unsuccessful, pursuit by the girl's father and
friends. A more fundamental reason for this practice is the conflict set
up by the existence of numerous subcastes amongst the commoner (Sudra)
caste or title group.

Masakapan:
This is the ceremony that will take place to legitimise a marriage by free
choice, or one by kidnapping after the various families concerned have
adjusted to the situation. It must take place on a propitious day, be
conducted by a priest, either high priest (pedanda), or village
priest (pemangku), and of course the appropriate offerings must be made,
and the established procedure followed.

2.2.2   Age at Marriage

The first menstruation of a girl (nyacal) is regarded as a significant
stage in the life cycle of a female, worthy of a ceremony, and for a high

caste girl it indicates that she is now of marriageable age. This is not to say that she will be married off immediately, although there is often concern that she may fall into the hands of a commoner and disgrace her family and herself.

The adolescent period between coming of age and the time of marriage (<u>teruna</u>) is described as 'that age of virginity' (Mershon, 1937:137), but in fact this may well not be the case. Apart from the high castes, the average Balinese do not consider virginity to be of great importance. There is often premarital sexual activity, although this should not be considered as promiscuity because the penalties for pre-marital or extramarital births can be severe. If a woman has an illegitimate child, she will be fined, but if the parents are living together the child (known as <u>Astra</u> or <u>Bebinyat</u>) may go to the temple; if however, the father does not live with the mother the child may not go to the temple, a very severe sanction. Normally the couple may live together in what is viewed as a trial marriage (<u>gendak</u>), the marriage being later legitimised before the public and the gods.

Age at marriage in Bali is quite late relative to some other parts of Indonesia, for example Java. Covarrubias states (without source) that at the time of writing (1936) the average marriageable age was eighteen for boys and sixteen for girls. According to the 1971 Census the average age at marriage for girls in Bali was 21.8, and according to the Indonesian Fertility Survey of 1976 the mean age for girls was 22.4 (Hull, Hull and Singarimbun,1977:27). Both these figures are substantially higher than the median age for females of 18.9 years obtained by the 1978 Marriage Survey.[7] As discussed in Chapter 5, available data does not indicate unambiguously any change in age at marriage in recent times in Bali.

In 1974 a new Indonesian marriage law was promulgated, establishing strict controls on polygamy; minimum age at marriage; consent and divorce. A 1978 review of the effects of this law suggested that in Bali the effect on age at marriage of raising the minimum marriage age to 19 years for men, and 16 years for women, had been negligible as Balinese generally married later than these ages (Katz and Katz,1978:314). A somewhat different explanation of the absence of an effect of the new marriage law in Bali is that presented by McDonald and Kasto who state that the experience gained from their 1978 Marriage Survey suggested that the marriage law was not being implemented in Bali:

> As marriage in Bali is adequately controlled by the <u>banjar</u>, ... it is felt that registration of marriage is unnecessary except for government officials (1978:1).

They also state a further reason for ineffectiveness:

> ...in respect of awareness of the law in the villages surveyed, we can state unequivocally that knowledge of the existence of the law is, with the exception of village leaders, almost zero (1978:2).

Finally, there is the problem of lack of official proof or record of birth for a large proportion of the population, though this is less of a problem among contemporary adolescents than formerly.

2.2.3 Polygyny

In the past polygyny was believed to be relatively common amongst royal families, but Covarrubias claims that even in 1936, the great majority of Balinese - about ninety five percent - had only one wife. This is supported by data from the 1930 Census which indicated that 3.8 percent of married men had more than one wife at that time (Volkstelling,1930). Commoners are said to have believed that polygyny constituted a violation of custom and religion, usually practising it only for humanitarian reasons such as the provision of a father for the children of a widow (Kusuma,1976: 48). But it was certainly not uncommon for members of the nobility (who comprised only 5 to 10 percent of the population) to have had many wives. Indeed the present Kelian Desa Adat of Banjarangkan, Klungkung, indicated how the situation has changed when he described, somewhat wistfully, how his grandfather had had two hundred wives, his father had had seventeen but he could only manage five. In the past, as now, the number of wives a man had reflected his wealth as it was usual to house the different wives in different houses, or different parts of the same houseyard.[8]

A significant change that came with the marriage law is that the husband must obtain the approval of his current wife (wives) and a court before taking another wife. Nevertheless the present Dewa Agung of Klungkung has some forty five wives in his Puri (palace), this regency probably being the most traditional in Bali. For all Bali, however, the prevalence of polygyny is probably no higher than it was in 1930. The most recent data, from the 1973 Fertility-Mortality Survey are presented in a different form, namely the proportion of women stating that their husbands hadat least one other wife. For Bali in 1973 the figure was 6.8 percent, but this naturally includes some double counting of polygynous husbands. Depending on the average number of wives per polygynous husband, the prevalence of polygyny was probably about 3 percent in 1973, that is only slightly less than in 1930. This absence of change was also suggested by Katz and Katz, 'the new law, therefore, has made very little difference in Bali regarding polygamy' (1978:312).

Polygyny is not only a simple reflection of a man's ability to support a number of wives, but probably more commonly is the result of an inability of the first wife to bear children. The general attitude in these cases is that the woman is the cause of the infertility and a second wife may provemore fruitful. In many cases the first wife will involve herself in the selection of the second wife, in fact this may be a relative such as her younger sister.

2.2.4 Divorce

The old laws relating to divorce were uncomplicated and fairly liberal. Writing in 1936, Covarrubias said: 'a man may claim divorce if his wife is sterile, quarrelsome, or lazy, but a woman has also the right to divorce an impotent man, or one who has some occult illness, is cruel to her, or fails to support her'(1937:158). A woman who wanted a divorce simply left her husband's home, although he may have tried to bring her backby force. The divorce was performed by the village authorities (in whose judgement the case rests) by minor ceremonies. Since the new marriage law, however, men as well as women must petition the court for a

22

divorce, and both sexes are required to give 'sufficient reasons' supporting this petition.

Within Indonesia, however, divorce is least common in Bali of all the
provinces, as can be seen from the 1971 Census, the 1973 Fertility-
Mortality Survey, and the 1976 Indonesian Fertility Survey. Although the
divorce laws are relatively simple, there are complicating factors which
may account for the relative infrequency of divorce in Bali. These
factors include the type of marriage, the presence of dowered land, and the
existence of offspring. A barren wife who was captured from outside is
simply sent home, if her family will have her. The children of a divorced
outsider-wife belong to the husband's group, but any such rule is subject
to many qualifications which vary across local spheres of customary law.
Divorce in a group-endogamous marriage would place great strain on the
collateral bond; ordinarily, the husband continues supporting his family
spouse and takes a second outsider-wife (see Boon,1977:96). In other
words, there are numerous social reasons why divorce is strongly dis-
approved of in Bali, and these ensure a low rate of divorce regardless of
the divorce laws.

Another practice which presumably reduces the pressures for
divorce in cases where a couple is childless, is that of adoption or
'borrowing' of children from, usually, another branch of the family.
Also where a couple have a daughter but no sons, they may arrange for the
man who marries their daughter to live in their houseyard and fulfil the
duties of a natural son (sentana marriage).

2.2.5 Conception

Questions concerning sexual and reproductive matters are discussed
freely and from an early age children naturally become familiar with
such matters. Covarrubias found that most of the people he talked to had
a correct idea of the physiology of reproduction, or at least of conception: 'they said that the man's seminal fluid (semara, named after
the god of love), coming in contact with the "female semen", turns into
blood in the womb, forming a ball which, fed by the woman's own blood,
eventually takes human form and develops into a child'(1937:123).

A similar, though different concept is presented by Jane Belo in 'The
Balinese Temper' whereby the woman is supposed to have within her
a manik (or 'gem'), which upon being repeatedly 'hit' during sexual intercourse, grows larger and larger until it becomes a child (Belo, 1970:102).
After the birth of the child she will get a new manik. This view implies a
triggering function for the sperm of the man, but does not imply any
contribution of characteristics from the male side.[9] However both these
concepts, along with that described by Weck (1937) whereby the egg is
entered by both Buta and Tuhan (demons and gods) simultaneously at the
time of conception, imply that the child comes into being at the time of
conception. This is consistent with the feeling that induced abortion even
at a very early stage is salah (against the laws of the gods; sinful). As
in many places, menstrual regulation is not considered to infringe these
laws because there is still doubt as to whether conception has taken place.
One member of the staff of the Bali Family Planning Program explained that
the conceptus does not become a living being until it has undergone a
number of cell divisions, and it is during this very early period that

menstrual regulations are performed.   This is a modern, scientific view not held by all Balinese of course.

2.2.6 Menstruation

In the past the time of menstruation involved the powerful taboo of pollution (sebel) whereby the woman was forbidden to go to the temple, into the ricebarn or the kitchen, or to the well. She was not permitted to prepare food and most certainly not offerings. In a commoner household there would often be a separate room for the woman to sleep in, away from her husband, or else the husband would sleep at a friend's house during this time. In the house of a nobleman the wife would be required to sleep far from her husband. This aversion to menstrual blood apparently stems from the belief that a man can be bewitched, losing his will to a woman who can anoint his head with menstrual blood, thereafter he will be perpetually henpecked by the woman.

The present day situation seems less rigid with regard to such domestic activities as cooking and fetching water, although the taboos on making offerings, and against entering any temple including the houseyard temple are still strictly enforced. This particular taboo is of some importance when evaluating the common side-effects of IUD use, namely longer menstrual periods, and breakthrough bleeding.

2.2.7 Naming System

As Geertz explains in some detail in 'Person, Time and Conduct in Bali', 'there are six sorts of labels which one person can apply to another in order to identify him or her as a unique individual: ...(1) personal names; (2) birth order names; (3) kinship terms; (4) teknonyms; (5) status titles (usually called 'caste names' in the literature on Bali); and (6) public titles. ...These various labels are not, in most cases, employed simultaneously but alternatively, depending upon the situation and sometimes the individual' (1966:13).

In this context we were interested primarily in Birth Order names for the purposes of completing the pregnancy history section of the survey questionnaire.   Also the use of kinship terms can result in difficulties in matching individuals with their 'official' names on, for example, the records of the Family Planning Program, partly because people may not be known in their own banjar by that name, and are therefore difficult to locate.

The first type of name or label is that which is automatically bestowed on a child (even a stillborn child) from the moment of birth according to whether it is the first, second, third, fourth, etc., member of a sibling set. The usual names for Sudras (male or female) are Wayan (meaning eldest) for the first born; Made (or Nengah, meaning middle child), Nyoman (meaning youngest), and Ketut (meaning literally 'follower' or extra). For fifth born the cycle starts again with Wayan, sixth born, Made, and so on. For high caste children there are also names which follow the caste (status) title but cannot be so readily related to a particular order. For example, a first born high caste boy might be called Cokorda Gede or Cokorda Raka; if the former, the second born might be Cokorda Raka, if the latter, the second born may be Cokorda

Rai. Names for lower birth orders include Anom and Alit but are used for both third or fourthborn depending on what names have already been used for older siblings.

Once a Sudra couple give birth to a live-born child their birth order names cease to be used outside the immediate family (and the Government registers) and are replaced by the practice of teknonomy. Parents take the title 'Father/Mother-of-first child's name' (in fact the personal name of the child, which otherwise is rarely referred to). Hence if the firstborn child's personal name is Sukrig, his or her father's name will become Pan Sukrig, and the mother will be known as Men Sukrig, these names being retained after the births of later children - at least until grandchildren appear, usually even if the child dies at a very early age.

With high caste parents the system is very often different, at least for members of the Satria and Wesia castes. The mother will drop her birth order name and take the title Biang, meaning simply 'mother', but without the name of the child being included. Naturally she continues to use her caste title at the beginning of the name. When she becomes a grand-mother, the name Biang will change to Niang. The high caste male will usually not change his name to indicate parenthood, or grandparenthood, although Aji is sometimes used.

When a Sudra couple become grandparents, they are entitled to use for grandfather the word Pekak (often abbreviated to Kak), and for grandmother the word Dadong (abbreviated, to Dong). Both great-grandparents and great-grandchildren are known by the term Kumpi. This change is sometimes delayed in practice, because it is at the level of Pan and Men that individuals are generally active in community politics.

Other circumstances where names may be changed are sickness, ill-fortune and marriage. If a child has died it is not uncommon for that birth order name to be skipped for future children. In some areas of Bali, especially in the east, both the man and woman may change their names at the time of marriage.

2.3 POLITICAL STRUCTURE

As mentioned above, the arrival of the aristocracy from Java resulted in the division of Bali into eight kingdoms each under the control of a king, or raja. The kingdom was divided into territories, each under a local prince or lord. The political system,with the raja at the top, was linked to the individual villagers through the Perbekel system. The perbekel was the state official responsible for ensuring implementation of the lord's instructions to the villagers, amongst other duties.

This system remained virtually unchanged until the conquest of south Bali by the Dutch in 1908. Thereafter the power of the indigenous ruling families was reduced gradually, first by the imposition of a 'rationalised' colonial administration, and later by the limitation of land holdings under the Indonesian Land Reform Laws in 1960. However despite these changes, the aristocracy still maintain their hold on power through public office in many areas.

Although the Dutch rationalised the administrative system, in effect they basically renamed many of the former subdivisions, with the exception of the village. The former kingdoms became local administrative centres, kabupaten, and each kabupaten was divided along more or less pre-existing lines, into kecamatan, perbekelan, and banjar; although the groupings of banjar to form a village were in a number of cases reorganised according to proximity, rather than by taking traditional allegiances into account. However the Dutch administrative policy towards the Balinese was generally lighthanded, indeed they went to some lengths to ensure that there was as little interference as possible from outside Bali. Foreign commercial ventures and Christian missionary activity were not permitted. Nevertheless the system had been altered, and it was altered even more after the Revolution which saw the expulsion of the Dutch and the growth of an independent Indonesian nation. During this post-Revolution period, villages were further reorganized in the attempt to ensure that the leaders at all administrative levels could be depended upon to carry out the designs of the national government of President Sukarno.

The 1950s and early 1960s, however, saw increasing fragmentation and politicisation of communities, with the growth of parties from both ends of the political spectrum. The attempt to satisfy the various and competing demands, and the enthusiasm for rapid change that often follows independence, resulted eventually in the bureaucracy being unable to function satisfactorily, and the President resorted more to stirring rhetoric than sound administrative guidance (Emmerson,1978:88ff).

Late 1965 saw an attempted coup, apparently by the Communists, which resulted in a murderous backlash by the military and Islamic extremists. In Bali the violence was particularly savage, with estimates of 40,000 to 80,000 killed. At the end of this confrontation, the now somewhat smaller Communist party was banned; President Sukarno was no longer in office; and one of the generals involved in suppressing the coup (Suharto), took over as head of the 'New Order' military government.

The 'New Order' government acted quickly to restore a functioning administrative system. It did this by making considerable use of active or former members of the armed forces in all levels of government down to village headmen. Hull and Singarimbun state that by 1973, 84 percent of the regency heads in Indonesia's most populous province, East Java were military appointees (1982:30). In Bali, according to McNicoll:

> The military and members of Muslim youth organizations coming across from East Java took a prominent role in the island's local administration over succeeding months. With slowly returning normality, this administrative system emerged greatly strengthened, a major contributor to this strength being its capacity to mobilize and work through the constituent hamlets ...free of significant countervailing political or social interests (1980:10).

The situation after 1965 was, then, significantly different from the earlier period in that the government, having power firmly in its grasp, could implement its plans effectively down to the sub-district and village level. President Suharto also differed from his predecessor in turning for advice and guidance to outside aid agencies and international organisations such as the United Nations.

It also happens that this was the period of great growth of population programs in the developing world. Substantial increases in population growth rates had awakened considerable concern regarding the prospects for developmentof many of the world's poorer nations. The development of the oral contraceptive pill a short time earlier made the prospect of effective national population control programs appear feasible. It was in these favourable circumstances that the Indonesian National Family Planning Program came into being (see Chapter 3).

2.4 ECONOMIC STRUCTURE

As we have seen, Bali is a small island, densely populated by a people for whom agriculture is the main occupation. Normally there is sufficient rice produced for local consumption as well as some for export to other islands. A key question, however, is whether or not food production can continue to increase at a rate sufficient to support a growing population. This implies either intensification of production on currently available land or an increase in the area of land under cultivation, or both. This section will examine this question.

2.4.1 Agriculture

The most striking element of the Balinese landscape is the ever present irrigated ricefield, the sawah. One has the impression that virtually every available piece of ground to which it is possible to bring water, is utilised to grow rice. These irrigated terraces have yielded rich harvests of rice since at least the ninth century A.D.

In fact the Balinese landscape varies considerably from region to region. A mountainous ridge of volcanic origin crosses the island from east to west. To the south is a gentle decline towards the Indian Ocean - the densely populated territory, known as central Bali to the Balinese, where the art and culture of Bali flowered. In the north, there is a sharp drop to the narrow strip of fertile land which nourishes the regency of Buleleng. The area of central Bali, cut through by many river valleys running from north to south, is a fertile sawah region. Over four-fifths of agricultural households cultivate sawah, and half of these cultivate less than 0.5 hectares. Though agriculture has been declining in importance, both in terms of labour force (67 percent in 1971 down to 61 percent in 1976) and of regional income (66 percent in 1971 down to 53 percent of Gross Regional Domestic Product in 1976), it is still the mainstay of the economy of Bali (Bendesa and Sukarsa,1980:32).

2.4.1.1 Changes in Irrigated Land

In 1950, some 30 percent of Bali's land area comprised unproductive wasteland and large tracts of inaccessible forest reserves, mainly in the western end of the island. Of the remaining 70 percent of the surface which was under cultivation at that time, only 26 percent (96,000 hectares) consisted of wet ricefields, 41 percent of non-irrigated fields (about one-third of them planted with maize, one-third with beans and tubers, and one-seventh with rice), 7 percent of coffee gardens, and 17 percent of coconut groves (Swellengrebel,1960:10), (see Table 2.1).

27

TABLE 2.1
LAND USE IN BALI ca.1950 AND 1970.

Land Use	1950 Hectares	%	Land Use	1970 Hectares	%
Sawah	96,000	17	Sawah	74,500	13
Dry land agric. and annual crops	178,300	32	Dry land agric. and annual crops	152,200	27
Estates	89,100	15	Estates	124,800	24
Forests	123,700	23	Forests	81,000	14
Other land	74,500	12	Other land	112,200	20
TOTAL	562,000	100%		548,400	100%

Source: Daroesman,1973:33

The figure obtained by the Udayana University research team of 74,500 hectares of sawah for 1970 (Table 2.1), suggests a substantial decline in the twenty years to 1970. Daroesman acknowledges that encroachment of urban areas and extension of village land needed for housing could account for some loss of sawah, along with the 1963 eruption of Mount Agung, which covered more than 7,000 hectares of sawah and nearly ten times that area of dry land with volcanic debris,[10] and also damaged irrigation works to other areas. However other data throw doubt on this decrease of over 20,000 Hectares. The alternative sources suggest that the area planted to sawah remained fairly steady at around 100,000 hectares per year (Daroesman,1973:34). Indeed, figures from the Central Bureau of Statistics show that the total area of sawah in Bali in 1978 was 98,269 hectares (BPS,1980:24).

If the figure of 100,000 hectares is accepted, the area of sawah had apparently not decreased but also it had not increased, leading Ravenholt to remark on the population pressures:

Balinese farmers are affected critically by the fact that the present area of sawah, or irrigated rice fields, totalling about 96,000 hectares is only slightly larger than it was in 1930, judging by available accounts (1973:119-220).

This concern is supported by the fact that population density per hectare of sawah increased by some 50 percent, from about 16 persons per hectare in 1954, to about 24 persons per hectare in 1970.

These figures may be misleading however, as although the area of sawah appears to have stayed fairly steady at around 100,000 hectares per year since 1940 (Daroesman 1973:33), the area of sawah that can be double-cropped has increased considerably as a result of irrigation projects that, up to 1978 had increased the supply of water available during the dry season (May-October) so that almost half the sawah had semi-technical irrigation. The additional irrigation has made possible the planting of a second rice crop on three-quarters of the sawah during this dry period, when the _sawah_ would otherwise be fallow or planted with secondary crops.

This raises the question of ways of improving productivity from the _sawah_ which is not currently double-cropped. At present, there is no _sawah_ with full technical irrigation, and the irrigation system in its present state does not have the potential for supporting a major expansion of irrigated land (_sawah_). The customary irrigation systems, excellent for the time when they were constructed, are now inadequate, even with the improvements that followed the coming of the Dutch administration in 1908. Nearly all are constructed as 'run of the stream' diversion dams although the mountain sides are sculptured into innumerable deep ravines. Almost none of these has been dammed to provide storage capacity for the dry season months from late April through October. There is a problem resulting from the fact that the ravines fall so steeply. Even a large, high-wall dam will have only a short backwater, thus relatively little storage capacity. On the other hand, there appears to be potential for irrigation involving pumping water up from the subterranean water-table.

Ravenholt has pointed out that the numerous springs which flow year-round at various points, usually below the lower escarpment on the island's profile, hint at the water resources within the mountains behind. As most of these springs are too low to feed into the irrigation channels they are not used currently. However it does seem that the underground water-table, fed by the 2.5-3 metres of precipitation that falls annually on the mountain tops, might well provide the potential for a considerable increase in water available for irrigation 'and allow the main rice granary in south Bali to produce probably two or even three rice crops where now water is sufficient often only for one good crop' (Ravenholt, 1973:220). The potential increase in rice production from such improvements would, naturally, depend on their extent, although figures for elasticity[11] of rice yield with respect to irrigation show Bali as being markedly ahead of other major rice growing areas of Indonesia (Mears, 1980:45). Mears notes, however, that the efficiency of the traditional management system, the _subak_, accounts for much of the difference between Bali and, say, Java. Daroesman also emphasises the potential benefits of sinking a few deep wells, equipped with pumps and storage tanks, particularly in the dry western parts and the north-east coast of the island (1973:46).

The importance of water in increasing rice production is illustrated by the experience of those increasing numbers of farmers who are having to turn to cultivating the marginal uplands. In 1969, upland rice - unirrigated - was planted on 13,758 hectares yielding about 1.3 tons of stalk _padi_ per hectare on the average. This can be compared to per crop yields of harvested, undried stalk _padi_ from _sawah_ in 1969 which averaged over 3 tons per hectare.

2.4.1.2 Prospects of Increasing Food Production

In the history of pre-mechanised agriculture few societies have ever achieved the high levels of productivity characterised by wet rice farming in Bali, which in itself is one of the most efficient and productive forms of agriculture known to man. With traditional technology the Balinese

29

peasant could produce twice as much rice on his land as his neighbour the Javanese farmer (Hanna,1976:96), whose techniques are by no means unsophisticated.

How have the Balinese done it? It appears that four factors are central to their traditional success as rice farmers. These include the fertility of the volcanic soil; a highly complex technology and corresponding knowledge which allows the Balinese to make maximal use of environmental systems and resources; an organizational system (subak) capable of coordinating use of manpower and resources; and genetic strains of rice selected over thousands of years for their disease resistance, productivity and appearance. As it happens these strains of Beras Bali tended to be largely non-photosensitive, allowing planting and harvesting at all seasons of the year. This is in contrast to most of Asia where the predominantly photosensitive varieties of rice must be planted in the appropriate season in order to flower, hence the farmers are locked into seasonal cycles thereby being more vulnerable to fluctuations in rainfall.

Hence, before the introduction of the new high yielding varieties of rice, predictability of yields from the system of year round wet-rice cultivation in Bali had buffered the populations against the famines that can result from crop failures in other parts of the world.

a) BIMAS - It is in the area of rice strains that the most noticeable changes have taken place over recent years, certainly as far as the individual Balinese is concerned.

Prior to 1970, there was a certain amount of construction of new dams and other irrigation works, mainly by the Government, but also by local groups. This was an attempt to increase the productivity of the land, resulting from the concern that production was not keeping pace with population growth. In 1966/67 the government began to intensify its program to increase agricultural production (BIMAS or 'mass guidance'). The program was based around the introduction of new high yielding varieties (HYV's) of rice developed initially at the International Rice Research Institute in the Philippines.

Because of the nature of these new HYV's the changeover involved the introduction of petrochemical fertilisers, insecticides and other pesticides for application during the preparation and growth stages of the rice and use of Japanese-made, rubber rollered hulling mills. These are capable of recovering some 68 percent milled, polished rice (beras) from dried unhusked grain (padi), compared to about 50 percent recovery when milling is performed by hand pounding with a wooden mortar and pestle, which however is more nutritious than polished rice as it retains some of the bran (Ravenholt,1973:220).

Another factor which has been necessary for the implementation of the program, has been the making available of credit to farmers to purchase the new inputs necessary for the successful growth of the new varieties. The area of both irrigated sawah and unirrigated land over which agricultural credit is available has expanded from 15,200 hectares in 1968/69 when some 39,000 hectares of sawah were under the BIMAS program, to 135,300 hectares in 1978 when approximately two-thirds of the 100,000

hectares of <u>sawah</u> in Bali were under the program (S.Foley, personal communication).

As a result of this program, average rice production per hectare
increased from 3.3 tonnes per hectare in 1961 to 4.0 tonnes/hectares in
1969, and to 4.8 tonnes/hectares in 1973 (Soedjatmiko <u>et al</u>.,1976). In the
following year, a prolonged drought and the explosion of the <u>wereng</u>
disease (leaf hopper pest) reduced overall production, bringing to light
two of the vulnerable aspects of the new HYV rice strains.

b) MECHANISATION - Agricultural labour in Bali has always been, and
largely still is, hand labour, although ploughing is performed with cattle
or water buffalo, and reliance on only the simplest of tools. In 1972
Hanna stated that 'since Bali suffers from an excess rather than a surplus
of labour, there is no plan to introduce mechanisation even to the degree
which is possible on the minute holdings into which the land is divided'
(1972:8). This, however, seems not to be the case a few years later.

Hull cites an example from the Rural Dynamics Project in Bogor, Java,
where it was found that tractors already sold or on order under an
ambitious plan by a tractor import firm, would provide the capacity to
cultivate far more than the total arable land of Bali (Hull,1978:4). In
1977 there were already 268 of the two-wheel tractors, and 3 of the four-
wheel tractors in Bali (Purwadi <u>et al</u>.,1979).

This replacement of the traditional cattle-drawn ploughs (<u>bajak</u>) by
hand-tractors is discussed in Astika's article on effects of the new rice
technology in which he states that:

> ...in 1975, privately-owned hand-tractors were introduced for
> the first time and by 1977 were used by 20% of the farmers (in
> his sample of 108 in Abiensemal, Badung) in place of the
> traditional cattle-drawn plow (sic.) (1978:48).

Astika also made the interesting point that they were only used for
ploughing in preparation for the dry-season crop, not the wet, when
preparation of the soil for a second crop must take place as quickly as
possible. Presumably for reasons of cost,these tractors were being used
primarily by the larger land owners, as is the case in Java. Despite the
plans of the importers, and the rapid acquisition of tractors for use on
rice lands outside Java and Bali, their introduction has met considerable
social resistance in Bali (see Mears,1981:320 re Sinaga). Such resistance
is mainly due to an awareness that there is no shortage of agricultural
labour in rural Bali, as was the case, for example, in Taiwan and South
Korea when they were industrialising. Because there is little alternative
employment for rural workers, agricultural labourers' wages have remained
low, but even so there is a concern that such 'tractorisation' will
replace many more jobs as the tractors can prove more economical for the
farmer just as mechanical rice hullers have replaced many jobs formerly
performed by women. Cain estimates that 1.2 million jobs inJava alone
have been lost to these hullers (1980:134).

The tractors threaten the jobs of the men, and Sinaga has
calculated that the introduction of one tractor in normal use (65 hectares

per year) replaces 2,210 man-days of human labour per year if replacing cultivation by hoe, or 650 man-days per year if replacing a combination of plough and hoe. This represents a potential shift of more than Rp.1 million per tractor per year away from the pockets of labourers (Sinaga,1978:104). One of the advantages that the tractor has over its human counterpart is its capacity to prepare an area of land considerably quicker, and this is becoming of increasing importance as pressure is put on farmers to follow the kerta-masa system of synchronised planting over a short period in order that large areas of rice are at the same stage of growth at the same time. The purpose is to try to prevent the wereng (leaf hopper) pest from finding suitable breeding sites in the rice stems. However this requires a limited cultivation period of only 15 to 21 days, compared with 21 to 75 days in the past with the traditional varieties of rice (Hamid,1980:21).

The trend to double cropping also aggravates the seasonal nature of demand for agricultural labour as at the time when the sawah should be cultivated for dry season crops, the labourers are still completing the wet season harvest.

To put the effect of tractorisation in Bali into perspective, if the 271 tractors (see above) in 1977 each displaced 650 man-days of agricultural labour this would be equivalent to about three or four labourers per tractor, minus the one who operates the tractor, thus about 550 to 800 jobs being replaced out of an agricultural labour force estimated at 568,000 in 1976 (Bendesa and Sukarsa,1980:32), or about 0.1 percent of total agricultural labourers. At the macro-level this is clearly a negligible displacement effect, even though it may not be seen as such by agricultural labourers.

c) OTHER CROPS - As farmers steadily push their fields up the unstable slopes, growing corn and other annual crops on slopes where in a few years erosion will have washed away much of the top soil, there is concern with the decline in the area of forest reserve, ravines and wastelands. The combination of forest clearing for agricultural purposes, for supplying wood to wood-carvers making artefacts for the growing numbers of tourists, for firewood used in cremations, and as fuel for the increasing number of lime kilns which supply the booming construction business in the tourist areas, resulted in a decrease in the area of forest from some 123,700 hectares (23 percent of total land area) in 1950 to 81,000 hectares (14%) in 1970 (this figure includes 27,721 hectares devoted to coffee crops) (Daroesman,1973:33).

The effect of this is not yet clear but scientists at Udayana University in Bali have calculated that the area of forest cover should be doubled to 30 percent of the island to restore the earlier moisture pattern upon which the productivity of the sawah is so dependent (Ravenholt,1973:222).

d) RICE CONSUMPTION - In his 1972 article 'Population and Rice', Hanna claimed that conditions were deteriorating in Bali as: 'prior to 1945 Bali exported 8,000-12,000 tons of rice each year; today (1972) it seeks to import 8,000-12,000 tons. The provincial government therefore calls upon the central government for the 'injection' into the Balinese market of about 1,000 tons of rice per month in order to keep the retail price below

Rp.45 per kilogram' (1972:1). Bendesa and Sukarsa, however, claimed that Bali in 1980 was self-sufficient in rice since only one to three thousand tonnes were imported annually for purposes of price stabilisation (1980: 41). This latter statement appears to be the more reliable as Mears indicated that in the period 1974/75 to 1978/79 annual imports of rice averaged only 847 tonnes, and this was affected partly by the need to assist in overcoming the poor harvest which occurred in 1977, (Mears, 1981:32). In fact, during that period Bali began exporting rice again. Starting in 1974/75 with 6,300 tonnes, by 1978/79 it was sending 35,300 tonnes to other provinces, in particular Jakarta and Kalimantan. This statement must be qualified, however, by the point that:

> although 'self-sufficient' in rice, many Balinese cannot afford to eat rice all year round, as can be seen from the estimates of productionof cassava and maize. Especially since 1973 cassava has been an important food crop; its quite high production in 1974 and 1975 was probably due to the the relative decline of the rice in those years because of the wereng problem. Bendesa and Sukarsa,1980:41).

By 1978, local production minus exports to other provinces left sufficient rice (376,822 tonnes) for about 160 kilograms per person per year in Bali. This is not substantially less than the 500 grams per day per person considered ideal by the Balinese, according to Hanna (1972:1).

In summary, rice production in Bali seems to be roughly keeping pace with population growth. Even though total area of wet rice growing land does not appear to have increased to any extent over the last forty years, there have been increases in production through increased irrigation and through use of high yield varieties (HYV) of rice.

Regarding prospects for the future, the present irrigation system appears to be operating at close to the limit of its capacity, although there is the prospect of tapping underground water sources using wells and pumps. It is probable that increases in available water, particularly in the dry season, would be reflected in increased rice production. It is also the case, however, that much of the gain in production as a result of a switch from traditional to HYV rice occurs in the first ten years, thereafter further production gains are considerably more difficult to obtain. Bali now seems to be at that stage where further rice yield increases will be much more elusive than in the past decade.

2.4.1.3 Outmigration

An obvious outlet for landless Balinese unable to obtain land, would be outmigration to a part of Indonesia where agricultural land is plentiful. The government transmigration program offers transmigrantsan area of two hectares of arable land of which 0.25 hectare is supposed to be already cleared for a house. Such an area, if suitable for wet rice production, would provide a very satisfactory existence for the average Balinese farmer. Indeed there are stories of farmers who have done well enough in Sulawesi or Kalimantan to be able to fly back to Bali at regular intervals. There are also less positive tales of uncleared land, lack of water, no housing, etc. But on the whole the Balinese have not responded enthusiastically to the transmigration program.

According to the 1980 Census, the total number of Balinese living in other Indonesian provinces was 117,828 or 4.7 percent of the total Balinese population. This is equivalent to just over one year's natural population increase. While part of the explanation is the limited capacity of the transmigration program to transport large numbers, and to prepare land adequately, there are also cultural factors inhibiting movement away from Bali.

In a study of Balinese transmigrants to Parigi in Central Sulawesi, Gloria Davis noted that Christians were overly represented largely because of a difference in attitude compared to the Hindus:

> ...nine-tenths of the families to move to Parigi were Christian. Hindus viewed migration as an alternative only if all others had failed, Christians viewed migration as an opportunity for improvement (1976:170).

In characterising the dichotomy noted by the Balinese themselves, that the Hindus were knit into traditional communities which they could not, or would not, leave, while the Christians were experienced migrants who characterised themselves as open to change, Davis listed some of the characteristics of the Hindus (1976:169), as follows:

(1) Conventional (afraid of the unknown);
(2) Only know traditional ways;
(3) Identify with their villages and village <u>adat</u> (law);
(4) Tied to one place, physically, socially, spiritually, dislike change;

(5) Subscribe to traditional temples and kin relationships - discouraged from leaving them;
(6) Little experience outside natal villages.

Another factor is the practice of the religion. When the first group of twelve families were imported to Parigi by the Dutch in 1905 in the hope of inspiring the locals to increased crop production, the Balinese were under Dutch protection and could preserve their religious rituals and traditional attitudes and practices. But after the war and revolution they no longer had such protection and had to make considerable adjustments to local conditions, including some marriages to non-Balinese, use of a different language, and a change from traditional law to government regulation (Davis,1974:2). Similar fears are held today by potential Balinese transmigrants, although the precedent of numbers of satisfied fellow Balinese has reduced their apprehension somewhat.

2.4.2 <u>Socio-Economic Change</u>

2.4.2.1 Roles of, and Value of Children in Balinese Society

The role of very small children is reflected in the fact that Balinese believe that the child is 'a god' or at least is guided in its actions by a god within him. For this reason he is not responsible for his actions and treated very leniently, with few obvious signs of discipline from elders.

This apparent disinterest by the parents is a reflection of the view that even children are individuals as are adults, just needing a little more care until they become independent. And in fact as soon as they are old enough to walk they will often be left to the care of older children, especially older sisters. When they are three or four years commonly they will spend the day roaming the village with friends, in what Covarrubias called the 'childrens' republic' (1974:132). This leaves both parents free to work, the women often working outside the household. This should not be viewed simply as neglect of the children in order for mothers to return to the workforce, but as a reflection of the general attitude to the independence of children from an early age. That is, even amongst 'non-working' mothers this pattern is observed.

This early independence does not mean that children are not expected to contribute to the work of the household, indeed it is usual for girls to be given the care of their younger siblings at quite an early age. They will also help their mothers with cooking, carrying, selling in the market, fetching water, and washing clothes. Slightly older girls may often be seen performing jobs in their own right, this being compatible with a schooling system that operates in shifts so that children attend either mornings (7am-11am) or afternoons (1pm-5pm).

From quite an early age boys will be given responsibility for family animals, shepherding ducks to and from the rice fields, taking the cattle or water buffalo to be washed at the river at sunset. If the father is a craftsman, the sons may become apprentices. Children of both sexes assist in jobs such as weeding of the rice fields. However the major aspects of rice cultivation such as field preparation, planting and harvesting are all performed by adults, usually groups from the banjar of the parents, although the children are permitted to follow the harvesting team and keep for themselves any rice grains missed by the harvesting team. These activities are, naturally, similar to those listed by White in his study of the economic activities of Javanese village children (White, 1975:136).

In later life children are expected to contribute in various ways to the running of the household. For example, if they have work they may give cash to the parents, particularly towards ceremonial and educational expenses for younger siblings. They may also be called upon to fulfil some of the banjar obligations, in place of the father, or with the father. The girls, at least until they marry and leave home, will spend a considerable amount of their time making the various offerings both for the housetemple and for the variety of banjar and village temples at which the family worships.

The sons also have a role in the arrangement of the parents' cremations, a most important duty to be performed according to Hindu belief. The banjar may take much of the responsibility for this, such that a couple without sons will normally be sure of being cremated in the appropriate manner. These roles will be discussed in greater detail in Chapter 7, however as the concern of this chapter is social and economic change, it is essential to describe some of the changes that have occurred in education, particularly over the last decade.

2.4.2.2 Education

In Bali in 1971, the proportion of 7 to 12 year olds attending school was 57 percent, but by 1980 this figure was up to 87 percent.[12]   This proportion was nearly double that of 44 percent recorded in the 1961 Census for Bali, Nusatenggara and Maluku combined.   This was in accordance with the aim of the second five-year plan (REPELITA II) to have 85 percent of children in this age range in school by 1979.

The attitude of the Balinese to the value of education and literacy is not straightforward. In the past, the stores of written knowledge were kept in the form of palm-leaf books called <u>lontar</u> or <u>rontal</u>, which were preserved and copied by the owning families over generations.   These texts contained the Hindu myths such as Ramayana, as well as 'mantras and other ritual formulae, (as well as the outlines of a theology that, based on the worship of Siwa as manifested in Surya the sun god, could be regarded as monotheistic)' (Forge,1981:3); also the genealogies of royal families and histories of kingdoms (<u>Babas</u>), and the various calendars so essential to Balinese ritual. As Forge points out, the superiority of the Brahmanas was based not just on birth but also on their possession of, and ability to read and understand these texts (1981:3). And to a degree, the power of the Satria kings was supported by their patronage of the Brahmana high priests (<u>Pedandas</u>), and their ownership of such texts, even if they could not read them personally.   Thus there was a situation where a small group of select individuals kept a strong hold on the stores of the society's written knowledge. The fact that they not only did not encourage but actually discouraged the masses from gaining direct access to it, has been interpreted as reflecting a low regard for schooling:

> The emphasis on literacy and schooling were contrary to the
> values of traditional Balinese religion, which as Geertz has
> emphasized is primarily concerned with orthopraxy rather than
> orthodoxy (Forge,1981:3).

In fact this emphasis was contrary to the interests of the Balinese priests, rather than to Balinese religion[13] as has been demonstrated by the growth of a body, Parisada Dharma Hindu Bali (PDH Bali), concerned with the preservation of Balinese religion and culture. This body evolved through the fears of the Balinese Hindus that their religion would be classed as a 'religion of ignorance' together with some of the animist religions of Eastern Indonesia, leaving only Islam and Christianity as acceptable to the (new) Ministry of Religion. PDH Bali has published many books and pamphlets on religion and generally this movement towards wider availability of religious writings brought about a change of attitude among many Balinese (especially in the towns) to the benefits of literacy. It must be said that in the past the strength of the oral tradition was such that there was little need to be literate. The Hindu epics were all well known to the illiterate villagers through the dances which most would have attended dozens, if not hundreds of times. To some degree this situation still holds. There is no suggestion that the effect of movements such as the PDH has been mainly to encourage people to read the sacred texts, but rather to make them aware that literacy is within the grasp of those other than members of the Brahmana caste.

Thus it is only recently that education has become a realistic possibility for the majority. Apart from changing attitudes, the availability of schools has also been a major factor, and it is only since the revolution that these facilities have become widespread. The Dutch in the period of their administration, did not build schools in Bali to the extent that they did in Java, thus it should not be surprising that in 1980 the literacy rate in Bali (62.1%) was lower than that for Indonesia as a whole (71.1%). Table 2.2 shows how recent is widespread literacy, where older age groups have very much lower rates than younger people. In 1980, while 78 percent of Balinese aged 20 to 24 were literate, only 21 percent of 50 plus year olds were literate.

TABLE 2.2
PROPORTIONS LITERATE, BOTH SEXES, BALI, 1980

Age	% Literate
15-19	83.0
20-24	78.0
30-34	62.8
40-44	45.4
50 +	21.2

(Source: BPS, Ser. S, No.16, p.42)

TABLE 2.3
NUMBERS OF SCHOOLS, PRIMARY AND SECONDARY, 1971 AND 1979/80.

School Type	1971	1979/80
PRIMARY	1,240	1,830
JUNIOR SECONDARY	162	237
SENIOR SECONDARY	60	107
TOTAL	1,462	2,174

(Source: Statistik Persekolahan SD, Propinsi Bali
Department of Education and Culture.

Clearly, large numbers of Balinese children are now obtaining some schooling, at least at primary level. As mentioned above, the proportion of 7 to 12 year olds attending school has risen from less than 50 percent 1961, to 57 percent in 1971, and up to 87 percent by 1980. The number of primary schools grew from 1,240 in 1971 to 1,830 in 1979/80, many (551) of the new schools having been built under the instructions of the President (INPRES schools) during that period. During the same period, the numbers of both junior and secondary schools increased by 50 percent (see Table 2.3). The primary (SD) schools are virtually all government operated, although it is not uncommon for local communities to have contributed to their construction. There are no tuition fees although there are other expenses including books and writing materials, and uniforms.[14]

Tuition fees for junior secondary schools (SMP), at which tuition fees are charged at a rate of about Rs.150 per month (US$0.25) for a government school, or Rs.750 per month (US$1.25) in a private (Swasta) SMP, of which there are many, just as there are many senior secondary schools, tertiary academies and universities.   The tuition fees at senior secondary school (SMA) are about Rs.500 (US$0.85) per month at a government school, and Rs.1,500 per month (US$2.50) at a private (Swasta) school.

In a discussion of the effects of schooling, Hull and Hull point out that not only does schooling demand some of the child's time which would otherwise be used in work at home or in productive employment, but schooling leads to changes in the relationship between children and adults, particularly when the parents are illiterate (1977:872). Hull and Hull also pointed out that the content of the schools' teaching program and the mass media project images of comfortable, middle-class families where the 'women are shown as housewives rather than traders or labourers' (1977:873) and children are shown as 'seldom doing anything other than "standard" housework like washing, carrying water and caring for younger siblings.   The realities of lower class village life are seldom portrayed' (ibid.).

It is not only the aspirations of the educated children that are changing, there have also been changes in the aspirations of adults resulting from increased availability of, and demand for consumer goods.   These range from modern versions of old implements such as plastic buckets for carrying water, aluminium cooking pots replacing fired clay pots, to quite new items such as battery cassette recorders, radios, motor cycles and Western style clothes. As well as household goods there have been major changes in access to distant areas, especially cities. The growth in numbers of vehicles used for transport of both goods and people has been extraordinary.   In 1971,the number of registered pick-up trucks in Bali was 506; by 1977 the number was 3,627. In the same period the number of motor cycles increased from 5,053 to 40,777 (Bali, Kantor Sensus dan Statistik,1978:90).   Such reasonably priced transport facilities have introduced many rural dwellers to the city environment which previously they may never have been able to visit.

There is no doubt that such changes in availability of goods involves a shift of the production process from the individual family, or neighbouring artisans, to factories located some way away.   There is some doubt though, at least in the case of Bali, that the suggestion of Hull and Hull that changing tastes or values are 'pushing people to abandon traditional relationships and ways of doing things for the sake of entry intothe modern world'(1977:878).   This will be discussed further in the final chapter.

2.4.2.3 Tourism

It should be clear from the examination of the agricultural situation (section 2.4.1) that for the majority of families, prospects for the next generation do not look promising in agriculture.   Yet children are still looked upon as the most likely reliable source of support for parents in old age, and education is viewed as a means toward that end. Thus the question arises as to where these educated children are going to find employment.

The economic situation in Bali has been well reviewed in articles by Daroesman (1973) and Bendesa and Sukarsa (1980). The data they present very much emphasise the growth of the tourist industry and associated services as the most promising source of employment in the foreseeable future, although other sectors of the economy such as industry and trade now occupy substantial numbers of workers (see Table 2.4).

While agriculture still occupied the majority of the work force in 1976 (61 percent) the growth in absolute numbers was only 16 percent in the five years since 1971,[15] compared to growth rates of 172 percent in industry, 62 percent in services, and in transport and trade 56 and 43 percent respectively. One area of manufacturing that Bendesa and Sukarsa emphasise as a potential growth industry for females is textile manufacture (1980:46). This increased quite markedly over the decade of the 1970s despite strong competition from Japanese manufacturers. It is worth noting that while many women in Bali are economically active and often play a pivotal role in small scale trading, in fact they are precluded from a number of the areas opening up in the growth of the tourist industry. Traditionally, Balinese women may not become woodcarvers, painters, metal-smiths or musicians, and this has not changed. There are, of course, many other aspects of the tourist industry which are open to them.

TABLE 2.4

INDUSTRIAL DISTRIBUTION OF THE LABOUR FORCE, BALI, 1971 and 1976.

Industry	1971 ('000)	%	1976 ('000)	%
Agriculture	489	67	568	61
Mining	---	-	4	-
Industry	42	6	117	13
Electricity,gas,water	-	-	-	-
Construction	18	3	24	3
Trade	77	11	110	12
Transport	9	1	14	2
Finance	1	-	1	-
Services	61	8	99	11
Other	35	5	-	-

Sources: Biro Pusat Statistik, 1971 Population Census, Bali;
Sakernas (Labour Force Survey),1976.
From Bendesa and Sukarsa,1980:32.

The tourist industry is certainly viewed by many Balinese as a possible source of employment for educated young people, particularly if they speak English. Many youngsters who consider that education has entitled them to higher status work than in the fields, gravitate to the capital city and nearby tourist areas in hope of obtaining suitable employment. Not only Balinese, but also other Indonesians, particularly Javanese hawkers continue to swell the numbers searching for work in the tourist industry, despite the Balinese government's 'closed island' policy introduced in 1973.

The potential of the tourist industry is somewhat uncertain. A government commissioned report by a French consultant team in 1969, the SCETO Report, or 'Master Plan', made numerous estimates of numbers of tourists and hotel rooms up to 1984. Based on this, the government (in 1973) expected that by 1984, 750,000-1,000,000 foreign tourists should be visiting Bali annually, ten times the 1973 flow. However, in 1979, the actual number of tourist arrivals was only about one quarter of the expected 467,000 (SCETO estimate), although the number of available rooms was close to the projected 4,000. Assuming full room occupancy (clearly too optimistic), and using the estimate that hotels employ about 2-2.5 persons per room, the number of persons employed in hotels would be 8,000-9,000. Including smaller hotels, the total might come to 12,000. Inflating by 50 percent Daroesman's estimate of 12,000-16,000 occupied in 1973 in tour and travel agencies, restaurants, artshops, as professional artists and in the handicraft industry (1973: 60), we arrive at an estimated number of 30,000-36,000 employed directly in the tourist industry. The SCETO Report assumed that indirect employment generated by tourism was expected to be in a ratio of 3:1 to direct employment. This yields a total figure 120,000-145,000 in direct and indirect employment generated by the end of the 1970s. Assuming that 75 percent of this employment is in Badung (as did Daroesman in her 1973 article), this accounts for 50 to 70 percent of the Badung work force, but only 3-5 percent of the work forces in the other seven kabupaten (regencies). It is relevant to note that a 1979 report from the Bali Governor's office gave an estimate of about 7,000 persons employed directly in the tourist industry at that time, rather fewer than the 30,000 plus estimated earlier (Bendesa and Sukarsa, 1980:38).

Thus in terms of actual employment opportunities, tourism really affects only Badung and the slow down in tourist arrivals during the 1970s casts some doubt on future capacity to absorb substantial numbers of workers.

The potential negative effects of large scale tourism have been given considerable attention by Bali scholars. While agreeing that there have been changes in certain aspects of life for those involved in tourism, McKean argues persuasively that 'traditional roles have not been entirely replaced or substituted with those found in the capitalistic West. ... Some social units have gained greater cohesion while simultaneously profiting from the tourist industry' (1978:98).

In proposing that culture is not the static entity that many anthropologists - and tourists - assert, McKean suggests that, in the light of the absence of local resources and with little prospect of successful industrialisation, 'it appears that economic prosperity might be based on cultural production - the establishment of a truly "post-industrial" service industry, which is at least in part what tourism offers' (p.101). While admitting the dangers of becoming a hypocritical 'fake culture', he argues that Balinese society might well be able to adapt to such a role with minimal dislocation and without greatly sacrificing traditional social bonds.

2.5 CONCLUSION

In summary, the examination of Balinese social structure shows no evidence that there has been any significant change in social relations, either at the family or village level. While it must be said that there is a serious lack of in-depth source material in the area of family structure, there is no indication of marked increases in family nucleation, nor in changes in patterns of marriage, both of which might be considered as indicators of social change and modernisation. There has, however, been a dramatic increase in educational facilities and in literacy, particularly for girls.

Economic changes refer mainly to agriculture, and there is no indication of either marked improvement or deterioration in economic circumstances at the individual level, rather there seems to be an equilibrium where increases in rice production are roughly keeping pace with population growth, at least for the moment. Even taking into consideration the rapidly growing, but localised tourist industry, there seems little prospect of major growth in employment opportunities in the immediate future.

CHAPTER 3
FAMILY PLANNING IN BALI

3.1 INTRODUCTION

Until the early nineteen fifties, the concept of family planning using modern contraceptives and services was virtually unknown in Indonesia. The 'Old Order' government (prior to 1965) associated national strength with large numbers of inhabitants, and indeed held a pronatalist policy based on the view that the country could cope with a population of 250 million. It was believed that any excess of population on Java and Bali (with two-thirds of the people on seven percent of the land), could readily be accommodated by transfer of people to the outer islands, mainly Sumatra and Kalimantan. In the period between 1950 and 1965, fewer than half a million people were moved to other islands. The population of Java grew by around eighteen million during that period. The necessary infrastructure simply did not exist to transfer sufficient numbers of people to keep pace with the growth of Java's population (Nitisastro,1970).

In addition to the pronatalist attitude of the government in the 1950s, the term 'birth control' had something of a negative connotation in the public mind, as being contrary to basic human rights. So it was with some caution that several groups of concerned women and doctors established small organisations aimed primarily at the improvement of the health of mother and child, but also including the possibility of contraception. In December 1957 the Indonesian Planned Parenthood Association (IPPA or in Indonesian, PKBI) was established by members of the Indonesian Physicians' Association.

In 1966 the 'New Order' government came into being under the leadership of President Suharto, and with this change came a new attitude to family planning. Partly as a consequence of the fact that growth of the Gross National Product had just kept pace during the 1960s (2% per annum) with population growth (1.9% per annum), the President issued a Decree in 1968 instructing the Minister of Welfare to establish the National Family Planning Institute (NFPI) as a semi-governmental body to promote and coordinate family planning activities. Family planning was also included in the first national five year development plan (REPELITA I) in 1969, and the following year the President issued a new Decree assuming full responsibility, and the National Family Planning Institute was replaced by the National Family Planning Coordinating Board (NFPCB or BKKBN in Indonesian).

The objectives of the National Family Planning Coordinating Board Program were to:

* bring about a 50 percent decrease in the total fertility rate of Indonesian women by the year 2000, compared to the level of 5.6 children per woman in 1971;

* recruit in the first five year plan (beginning in the fiscal year 1969-70) 6 million new acceptors with the goal of averting 1.7 million births;

* decrease in the same 5 years the growth rate of Indonesia by 0.8 percent, from the level of 2.6 percent to 2.8 percent believed to prevail in 1970.

The Minister, Dr. Suwardjono Suryaningrat and his assistants (in particular Dr. Haryono Suyono) decided that Java and Bali were the two strategic areas which must be tackled first, as they contained two-thirds of the population. For the first five year plan their strategy was to mount a large scale information campaign among various social and religious groupings; to mount a large scale distribution campaign of contraceptives through family planning operations in the field; and finally, to prepare and train an adequate number of family planning fieldworkers (PLKB in Indonesian).

In the second five year plan (REPELITA II) beginning 1974, ten additional provinces joined the six from Java and Bali in the program. In REPELITA III, starting 1979, the remaining eleven provinces were brought into the program so that it covered the entire nation.

Further details of the structure of the national BKKBN program can be found in the Technical Report Series published by the BKKBN central office in Jakarta.

3.2 HISTORY AND ORGANISATIONAL STRUCTURE OF THE NATIONAL FAMILY PLANNING PROGRAM IN BALI.

The earliest organised family planning activities began in 1961 with the establishment in Bali of a branch of the Indonesian Planned Parenthood Association (PKBI). From this time until the National Family Planning Institute was set up in 1969, this private organisation (PKBI) was the only source of family planning services. Because of limited resources the PKBI's success was not great in terms of numbers of acceptors. It is estimated that during this entire period less than 9,000 acceptors were recruited in Bali (about 3 percent of the eligible population) (Astawa, 1980). A West German gynaecologist working in the Department of Obstetrics of Sanglah Hospital, Denpasar, introduced the metal Grafenberg ring (IUD) in the late fifties, but only about fifty women accepted this method. In 1963, the PKBI introduced the Lippes Loop as a pilot project at Sanglah Hospital. In the two years of the project, 1963-65 there were 325 IUD insertions, the acceptors consisting mostly of paramedical personnel and local women.

After the reorganisation of the PKBI and the NFPI in 1970 to form the BKKBN, the situation changed somewhat in response to the involvement of the government. The BKKBN in Bali now coordinates the activities of four government and four private agencies (implementing units). In addition to the Health Ministry which has primary responsibility for providing clinical services, and the Information Ministry which was given principal responsibility for providing information and motivational inputs, the government implementing units include the Armed Forces (for military personnel and dependants) and the Ministry of Religious Affairs (for motivational efforts directed toward religious leaders). The private agencies consist of the PKBI, which maintains some clinics and assists in training; and three religious organisations - Dharma Dutta (Hindu), the Indonesian Council of Churches (Christian), and Muhammadiyah (Muslim) - which serve

43

to involve religious leaders and facilities in the program. Also, in the private field, an important contribution to family planning in Bali has been the practice of menstrual regulation by some private medical practitioners (Astawa, 1980:7).

In 1975, Dr. I.B. Astawa, Head of BKKBN, Bali, stated that 'the two most important components of the program are clinical services and information/motivation activities' (1975:87). At that time the program maintained 150 clinics in Bali (one for every four villages or 2,200 eligible couples) most of which were staffed by one trained midwife (bidan), one assistant midwife (pembantu bidan), and one clerical worker. Also at that time there were only 109 physicians in Bali, and about 70 of those were living in the capital city, Denpasar, and thus were not readily available for work in the village clinics. Because of this situation, the Family Planning Program employed only 45 doctors, of whom four were women. The majority of IUD insertions and prescriptions of oral contraceptives are carried out by the nurses, all of whom are trained in IUD insertion.

During 1972-73, each clinic was open for family planning services for an average of 67 hours per month (about three hours per day). Doctors were available for only about a quarter of this time; the remainder of the clinic staff, however, were on duty during all clinic hours (Astawa et al., 1975:87).

3.2.1 Village Family Planning

By 1974 there was some concern about maintaining program momentum, and increasing program activity in lagging areas. Discussions between Jakarta and the provincial BKKBN offices concluded that:

> ...the program would have to move out of the clinic if it were to avoid the supposed 'plateauing' that has bedevilled other large national family planning programs. In order to attract younger, lower parity women into the program, services would have to made more convenient, more readily available and integrated into the way of village life (Suyono et al., 1976:13).

Part of the motivation for this change of emphasis away from the clinic was 'to simplify contraceptive resupply in order to prolong contraceptive use with the pill and the condom' (ibid., 13). However, as the Bali program is largely an IUD program, less emphasis has been placed on contraceptive resupply, and more on recruiting new acceptors and maintaining those already in the program.

Bali's system was planned somewhat differently from the village family planning systems on Java. In Bali it revolves around the banjar, or the sub-village unit of which there are over 3,700 with an average population of some 670. The banjar family planning system included not only contraceptive resupply, but also a registration and mapping system in which family planning users were supposed to be followed up monthly and their status noted on a prominently displayed banjar map.

Also in 1974 the provincial BKKBN began training fieldworkers and banjar heads in family planning tactics at the local level. As Hull, Hull and Singarimbun described the aims:

As they became more aware of birth control issues, it was hoped
banjar members would help each other to deal with side effects,
identify potential acceptors, and, through community pressure,
encourage non-users to accept birth control. ...The contraceptive
situation is discussed at each monthly meeting of household
heads. If an apparently fertile couple are not trying for a
pregnancy and are also not contracepting, the husband will be
questioned (1977:25-28).

3.2.1.1 Village Contraceptive Distribution Centres (VCDCs)

This addition to the program was established in 1975 and is the most
recent of BKKBN's efforts to overcome the problem of 'plateauing' which
eventually confronts all Family Planning Programs. Thus the contraceptives
are sent out from the clinic to the village contraceptive depot. The depot
is either in a villager's home or a village administrative office and is
run by a volunteer or a member of the village administrative staff. This
person is linked to the clinic with the assistance of the fieldworker, and
the depot's job is to ensure that contraceptives are available to eligible
couples in the village, as well as to provide information about family
planning. The supply route was through the clinic in order that the flow
of contraceptives, and data on acceptors, would be kept within the clinic's
service statistics system so that activities could be monitored and controlled.

In December 1975, there were some 1,800 such VCDCs at the banjar
level, as well as the 152 family planning/health clinics. By December
1976, all 3,708 banjar were said to have a VCDC operating, and all were
reporting quarterly to the provincial BKKBN office. As the VCDCs took
more of the family planning load the number of family planning sessions in
the clinics declined somewhat from 1,949 (9,472 hours total) in December
1973, to 1,304 (6,973 hours total) in December 1976. During this period
the number of clinics stayed constant, though by December 1981 there were
159 clinics operating throughout the island.

3.2.1.2 Fieldworkers

Fieldwork is administered separately from clinic services. In Bali in
1980 the total number of fieldworkers was 231, one for every 1,250 eligible
couples. This number had stayed constant since 1975. They are grouped
into 51 teams of four or five workers, each team (one team per
kecamatan or district) being supervised by a group leader (Pemimpin
Kelompok or PK). The group leaders are in turn assigned to eight regency
supervisors, and the regency supervisors are in turn directed by one provincial coordinator.

Fieldworkers are not required to work fixed hours, instead each is
given a monthly quota of new acceptors. They must travel their allotted
territory by bicycle or on foot in search of potential new acceptors.
These may be women who have just given birth to their first child, or
women with children who have recently moved into the area. They are also
expected to visit all eligible couples in the registers about once in three
months to check their current status, and remotivate them if they have
dropped out. Originally, their task was basically to refer interested

couples to the clinic, or to make appointments for the next visit of clinic staff to a convenient place such as the banjar hall, or kelian banjar's house. However, over recent years the fieldworkers have been given responsibility to distribute contraceptives directly to couples, i.e., condoms and foam tablets, and to resupply oral pills.

Although the fieldworkers are usually working in their own area, there can be difficulties. They may be perceived as government officials coming to pressure the couples into accepting family planning when they don't want it. The system of targets of acceptors may put the fieldworkers in a situation of conflict with the regional administration who may not understand the particular circumstances of the couples in the area. Some consider their area is excessively large compared to other fieldworkers, access to couples varying greatly with the terrain. Sometimes they are called upon for advice regarding contraceptive side-effects, which they are ill-equipped to give, owing to limited training.

Most fieldworkers (79%) are married men, about half are aged 20-24 years, the remainder being somewhat older, and most have finished high school (Astawa et al.,1975:87). Fieldworkers are recruited from the local village and are required to have completed at least junior high school, and be a minimum age of eighteen years. The training of fieldworkers is done in the Provincial Training Centre and goes on for three weeks (two weeks theory and one week in the field). Morale, however,has often been low resulting in a rapid turnover, about 30 percent per annum in 1981, and some difficulty in finding new recruits largely because of the government's continued reluctance to upgrade their status from temporary workers to that of permanent civil servants, with its accompanying job security and retirement benefits (see Hull et al.,1977:9). As of July 1981 field-workers throughout Indonesia have achieved permanent civil servant status, and hopefully this will alleviate some of the problems.

3.2.1.3 Sistem Banjar

The Bali office of the National Family Planning Program incorporated the subvillage unit, the banjar, into the program for several reasons. Firstly, to try to institutionalise the small family norm into the community, using the banjar meeting and leaders as the medium. Secondly, the banjar system was needed to accumulate the statistics for recording acceptors and current users each month. Thirdly, the system was an ideal supply route for contraceptives throughout the rural areas, where the 150 clinics could not possibly have been adequate.

When Sistem Banjar began it took some time to organise reporting from all the banjar. In the first quarter of 1976 only 1,848 banjar were surveyed and of those 1,690 (or 91.5%) returned reports. But by the fourth quarter of that year all 3,708 banjar were surveyed and all reported.

The system operates by each banjar head (Kelian Dinas) completing a register (Elco-Register) of names and other details for each 'eligible couple' in his banjar.

The information included in the register is:
- ..Name of woman
- ..Age of woman
- ..Name of husband of woman
- ..Date on which she accepted FP
- ..Number of children ever born alive (total)
- ..Number of children still living (male and female)
- ..Number of new-born children within the current year (M/F separate)
- ..Contraceptive status for the current month
  specifying method used; not yet accepted; pregnant; or dropped
  out.

Normally this Elco-Register would be kept by the banjar head and updated when he hears of some change of status occurring to a couple in his banjar. At the end of each quarter the family planning fieldworker will take the register to his office (usually at the local health clinic if there is one) and write up the quarterly report (Laporan Triwulan). This is sent to the Group Leader for the kecamatan for summarising and forwarding to the provincial office where the reports are published, data being aggregated to kecamatan level.

3.2.1.4   Program Infrastructure

A paper by Khoo using the integrated SUPAS II and III data from the 1976 Intercensal Survey (SUPAS) of Indonesia (see Freedman et al.,1981:3), examined the role of factors such as different program strength in the various provinces of Java-Bali in relation to levels of contraceptive use (Table 3.1). This analysis showed that, of the six provinces, Bali had, in 1976, the most favourable situation in regard to numbers of clinics, mid-wives, fieldworkers and program administrative personnel per 10,000 ever married women (EMW). Bali was second only to Yogyakarta in numbers of doctors per 10,000 EMW.

TABLE 3.1
VARIOUS MEASURES OF FAMILY PLANNING PROGRAM EFFORT
FOR RURAL REGENCIES, BALI and JAVA-BALI, 1975-76.

Measure of Program Effort:	Number Bali	Java-Bali
Clinics/10,000 EMW	4.3	1.8
Doctors/10,000 EMW	1.3	0.7
Midwives/10,000 EMW	4.4	1.8
Administrative Personnel/10,000 EMW	4.2	1.6
Fieldworkers/10,000 EMW	6.4	4.2

Source: Khoo, 1981:Table 2.

It is of interest, however, that Khoo concluded from this analysis that:

> There is no strong relation between contraceptive use and
> program input as measured by the number of clinics and workers...
> regional differences remain even after controlling for community-
> level differences in the number of program clinics and workers
> relative to population (1981:15).

This question of the role of the program infrastructure will be examined in
more detail later in the monograph.

3.2.2 Results of the Family Planning Program

The most relevant measure of the program's effectiveness in
promoting contraceptive use in Bali is the increase in the prevalence rate
over time.

The sources of such data are primarily the Service Statistics Reports
from the Bureau of Research and Evaluation of BKKBN central office in
Jakarta, and, since the establishment of Sistem Banjar in 1976, the
quarterly reports from the BKKBN provincial office in Bali. It can be
seen in Table 3.2 that these two sources present rather different rates
for Bali for the same periods. The reasons for these differences are
partly the different systems involved in estimating current users, and
partly in the definition of the eligible population. This will be
discussed further in Chapter 4. The figures from the Jakarta office are
based on numbers of pill cycles, condoms, vaginal tablets distributed,
numbers of IUDs inserted, tubectomies performed, etc., with assumptions
being made about continuation rates for pill and IUD users. On the other
hand, the BKKBN Bali figures are intended to reflect current use levels
derived by the fieldworkers actually asking the current status of the
eligible couples at regular intervals, with updating through couples notifying their Kelian Dinas of changes of status between fieldworker visits.

In the 1970s, there have also been three major surveys in Bali which
have inquired about use of contraception. These were the Fertility-
Mortality Survey in 1973, the World Fertility Survey in 1976, and the 1979
Socio-Economic Survey (SUSENAS). The 1980 Census also asked two questions
about past and current contraceptive use. The prevalence rates for
currently married women aged 15-44, using program methods, are presented in
Table 3.2 for comparison with the BKKBN figures for the same time.

The prevalence rates from the surveys are consistent with the
levels estimated in Jakarta for the same periods. However the level of
73.5 percent from the Bali BKKBN office for third quarter 1979 is much
higher than the 46.0 percent of eligible couples using a program
method, or the 48.5 percent currently using, from the 1979 SUSENAS survey.
Because the levels from the Bali BKKBN office are derived by questioning
eligible couples about current family planning status, they can include
users of modern methods obtained outside the program, although in Bali
this is quite a small number, whereas the levels emanating from central
office in Jakarta concern use of program methods only.

TABLE 3.2
PREVALENCE RATES OF PROGRAM CONTRACEPTIVE USE
FROM DIFFERENT SOURCES, BALI, 1971-1985

Fiscal Year	BKKBN Source		Survey/Census
	Jakarta BKKBN	Bali BKKBN	
1971-72	6.6%		
1972-73	15.3%		19.4 % -- FMS(15-44)
1973-74	22.3%		
1974-75	27.1%		
1975-76	32.0%		33.3 % -- WFS(15-44)
1976-77	35.5%		
1977-78	42.8%	61.4%	-------------- (Jul-Sept.1977)
1978-79	46.0%	73.5%	-------------- (Jul-Sept.1979)
			48.5% -- (SUSENAS,Early 1979)
1979-80	49.8%	75.9%	-------------- (Mar.1980)
1980	51.8%		48.8% Census (Oct. 1980)
1980-81	53.7%	76.3%	(Oct-Dec.1980)
1985	74.5%		

Note: The Jakarta data are for the end of each financial year,
          eg., the figure for 1975-76 is for March 1976.

Sources: Jakarta data - Bureau of Reporting and Documentation
                        Monthly Statistics, BKKBN, Jakarta.
         Bali data   - Provincial Office Quarterly Reports,
                        BKKBN, Denpasar.
         FMS data   - FM Report,1974:50
         WFS data   - BPS, Vol.II,Tables 2.3.3A
         Susenas data - BPS,1980, Vol.I and II,Table 9.1.1
                        Calculated by subtraction of Java
                        from Java-Bali figures.
         Census data - BPS, S16, Table 20, 1982:79.

Leaving aside the differences between rates from the two BKKBN sources, the more conservative Jakarta office figures show a dramatic increase in levelof current use from less than 5 percent in 1971 to 53.7 percent ten years later, and almost 75 percent after fourteen years.

3.2.2.1 Methods Used

Before the introduction of the Family Planning Program in 1970, there appears to have been very little use of traditional contraception. The levels of current use of 'folk' and traditional methods[16] combined, were 2.2 percent in the 1973 FM survey, 0.8 percent in the 1976 WFS (no 'folk'), and 1.0 percent in the 1979 SUSENAS survey (half 'folk' and half traditional) (calculated from Table 3.3). While there is always the likelihood that these methods are often underreported in such surveys, the levels appear to be low. It is not possible to deduce more about levels in the past as there are no published data from any of these surveys on ever-use of these methods. There are, however, a number of unsupported claims that traditional methods, in particular abortion, have been widely used by Balinese women in the past. Jacobs, writing in 1883 stated confidently:

> Every woman knows a number of abortifacients and there is no doubt that they are often used. Hence it happens that so few illegitimate children are born (although most of the daughters of this very voluptuous tribe practise prostitution). And not only unmarried women have recourse to these specifics.
> (Cited in Ploss et al.,1935:498)

Jacobs went on to describe the Chinese medicine (called pengeret) that was to be drunk if a woman fell pregnant.

Another, more recent unsupported reference comes from Poffenberger: '...there is evidence that the Balinese practised delayed marriage and induced abortion to some degree' (n.d.:10). On the other hand, there are some data from Edmondson, an anthropologist who worked for 22 months in east Bali (a similar area to Poffenberger), which suggest that of a closely studied sample of 94 ever-married women, about one quarter (n=23) had undergone a traditional abortion at some time in their lives. About 5 percent (n=5) claimed to have had an abortion in the previous 12 months. Edmondson states that 'the major traditional method of fertility control used in the village is uterine massage... used in conjunction with herbal medicine' (n.d.:8). This type of massage abortion is widely known throughout parts of Southeast Asia, particularly Thailand and Malaysia.

Whether this high incidence of abortion can be extrapolated to all Bali is another matter as such practitioners are often few in number but known over a wide area. For example, one informant of this writer had, some years ago, travelled from the town of Ubud in central Bali to a village in eastern Bali (close to where Edmondson has worked) in order to be aborted. She stated that there was a reputable abortionist in that area, and it was preferable to travel a considerable distance to obtain the services of an 'expert' than to risk an 'amateur' operation. In this case the abortion was performed by insertion of a piece of thin branch from the sirih bush (the leaves chewed with betel nut and lime) into the cervix. This method is said to bring about uterine contractions within about 24 hours, resulting in expulsion of the contents of the uterus. That such caution was probably wise is illustrated by an incident in 1979 where an old man was imprisoned in Denpasar for causing the death of a young woman whom he had attempted to abort using a bicycle wheel spoke. The spoke had perforated the uterine wall of the woman. The fact that the old man was blind may have contributed to the tragedy.

There is, however, anecdotal evidence from one of Bali's leading obstetricians that such 'backyard' abortions are on the decline. This doctor has, for some time, been responsible for attempting to repair the consequences of these operations, although he does not perform abortions himself, nor does he permit them to be performed in the provincial hospital in Denpasar. He has noted a marked decrease in the numbers of such botched abortions since the ready availability of family planning, although this has also coincided with the introduction of facilities for menstrual regulations on the island. At the time of the survey there were at least three doctors in Denpasar regularly performing menstrual regulations. One of these doctors estimated that about 3,000 or more such operations were being performed annually by himself and his colleagues. This was despite the illegality of the operation in the eyes of the Islamic authorities in Jakarta. Some doctors in the regency hospitals also performed menstrual regulations on Family Planning Program users who had fallen pregnant.

While it is extremely difficult to state with any certainty that abortion was probably not widespread in the past, (the extravagant nature of Jacobs' remarks must cast some doubt on his claims), and that other traditional and folk methods do not appear to have been used to any substantial extent, that must be the conclusion drawn from the examination of the limited available literature and from anecdotal evidence. This conclusion is also supported to some degree by the very high rates of marital fertility which existed prior to the 1970s as indicated by Hull et al.: 'reluctance to use such traditional birth control methods as abstinence or abortion kept fertility high right up to the advent of modern contraceptive methods' (1977:28).

TABLE 3.3

PERCENT DISTRIBUTION OF CURRENT-USERS BY METHOD USED,
FOR MARRIED WOMEN AGED 15-44 YEARS, BALI.

Source-Year	Pill	IUD	Condom	Other Modern	Total Tradl.	Prevalence Any (Program) Method
FMS-1973	12.0	77.0	1.4	-u-	9.5	23.0% (19.4%)
WFS-1976	14.1	70.3	10.9	3.1	1.6	39.3% (33.3%)
BKKBN-1976	9.4	85.5	2.6	2.4	N.A.	(32.0%)
SUSENAS-1979	16.1	64.9	3.0	4.3	1.1	(48.5%)
BKKBN-1979 July	9.1	82.2	3.6	4.9	N.A.	(46.0%)
CENSUS - 1980	12.4	63.8	4.9	18.9	N.A.	48.8%
BKKBN-1981 July	8.1	82.2	3.3	6.4	N.A.	(53.7%)

N.A.: not applicable, only program methods recorded.
-u- : unavailable

Sources: as for Table 3.2

To move on to modern contraceptives, the figures for 1976 for prevalence rates of program methods are very similar from BKKBN (32.0%) and the WFS (33.3%), though the method mixes are noticeably different. This is also true of the 1979 SUSENAS survey and the 1979 BKKBN figures. Table 3.4 shows method mixes for new acceptors and for current users for the same points in time. As the proportion of current users having an IUD is greater than the proportion accepting an IUD, and for pill users less than for pill acceptors, it is clear that BKKBN Jakarta assume considerably higher continuation rates for IUD acceptors than for pill acceptors.

Indeed, this is acknowledged to be the case and is an important reason why the Bali provincial office of BKKBN chose to 'push' the IUD over other methods (Astawa, et al.,1975:95). However, the comparison of proportions using each method can be seen (Table 3.3) to vary considerably between the survey figures and the BKKBN monthly statistics, even though the overall prevalence levels match. This suggests that the assumptions used by BKKBN Jakarta, regarding method continuation rates, tend to overestimate the actual IUD continuation rates and underestimate actual pill continuation rates (see Streatfield,1985).

TABLE 3.4

PERCENT DISTRIBUTION OF NEW ACCEPTORS AND CURRENT-USERS, BY METHOD, DIFFERENT YEARS, BALI.

New Acceptors	Pill	IUD	Condom	Foam Tabs.	Inj	Other	Total
March 1976	33.7	42.6	21.9	0.3	---1.6---		100%
September 1976	21.0	61.3	13.7	0.5	0.1	3.5	100%
March 1981	17.5	63.5	-- 10.7 --		2.7	5.3	100%
Current Users							
March 1976	10.9	82.2	5.0	0	0	1.9	100%
September 1976	9.4	85.5	2.6	0	0	2.4	100%
March 1981	8.1	80.9	3.8	0	0.5	6.4	100%

Source: BKKBN Jakarta Monthly Statistics

3.2.2.2   New Acceptors

The differences between the distributions of new acceptors according to method for March and September 1976, illustrates one of the problems which beset a program which has targets for the number of new acceptors obtained within a fiscal year. The pressure of provincial offices to attain their particular target tends to result in a marked increase in numbers of acceptors in the month or two before the end of the year (see Figure 1, Hull et al.,1977:16).

In the five years from September 1976, the prevalence rate has risen from 32.4 percent to 57.2 percent, but through that period the distribution of new acceptors and current users according to method has changed very little, apart from the annual fluctuations described above. Also the number of monthly acceptors has changed little, usually being between three and four thousand.

There has been a modest increase in the proportions accepting IUDs from around 50 percent of acceptors in 1973 and 1974, to around 64 percent in 1981. This shift has been occurring as mean age and mean parity of acceptors has been declining, that is, younger women are being gradually drawn into the program. The median age of new acceptors in 1971 was 29.6 years but by late 1976 this median had declined by two years. In early 1979 the median age was still 27.5 years (Table 3.5, column A). The shift to younger acceptors is also reflected in the increasing proportions under 30 years of age (Table 3.6, row A). In the early days of the program, about half of the acceptors fell into this category, but by the late 1970s the proportion under 30 had increased steadily to 66 percent (1978-79).

If age at marriage has not substantially increased (see Chapter 5.1), and family planning is not generally available to nulliparous women, it would be expected that as median age of new acceptors decreases, so would median parity. That this is the case is demonstrated by the data in Table 3.5 which show that median parity has fallen by about one child, from 3.8 in 1971 to 2.9 in 1979. This decline is again reflected in the proportions of new acceptors having two or less children. This proportion increased from 28 percent in the early 1970s to 52 percent in early 1979 (Table 3.6, row B). The explanation for the decline in mean age of users is that the program initially attracted the older, high parity women wanting to limit births. Later, younger women wanting to space pregnancies were also attracted to use family planning. There can, of course, also be an effect of declining completed fertility in that women wanting no further births will tend to be, on average, younger and of lower parity when fertility levels have dropped.

TABLE 3.5

MEDIAN AGE AND PARITY OF NEW ACCEPTORS
OF FAMILY PLANNING, 1971-79, BALI.

Period	(A) Median Age	(B) Median Parity
1971 (Apr-Jun)*	29.6	3.8
1973 (Oct-Dec)*	28.7	3.2
1976 (Oct-Dec)**	27.5	2.6
1979 (Jan-Mar)***	27.5	2.9

Sources: *   - Astawa, et al., 1975:89, Table 4.
     ** - Soetedjo and Parsons, 1977, Table 7, page 14.
    *** - Ulusan Singkat Ciri-Ciri Akseptor, BKKBN, Jakarta.

TABLE 3.6
CHARACTERISTICS OF NEW ACCEPTORS OF FAMILY PLANNING,
1971-72 TO 1978-79, BALI.

	1971 -72	1972 -73	1973 -74	1974 -75	1975 -76	1976 -77	1977 -78	1978 -79
A) % LESS THAN AGE 30 YEARS	51	53	55	58	61	62	63	66
B) % 2 OR LESS CHILDREN	--	28	--	35	37	48	46	48	52
C) % LESS THAN 6 YEARS SCHOOL	66	70	71	63	63	64	N.A.	67
D) % HOUSE HEAD OCCUPATION: FISHING,FARMING, LABOUR, UNEMPLD	79	85	87	82	85	87	N.A.	87

Source: Ulusan Singkat Ciri-Ciri Akseptor, BKKBN,Jakarta,
          1971-72 to 1977-78.
          Soetedjo and Parsons,1977,Table 10, for FY 1978-79.

        In regard to the education of acceptors, the data in Table 3.6, row C
indicate little change in the proportions of new acceptors having less than
six years schooling during the 1970s, though there was an upward fluctua-
tion during 1972-74.   It was during this period that an 'Extra-Drive' was
made by the Family Planning Program to bring the less accessible and more
'resistant' couples into the program (Astawa et al.,1975:89).   Acceptor
drives of this kind were soon found to result in shorter continuation rates
(Tjitarsa et al.,1975) and were not repeated.   Thus by 1977-78 the proportion of women with less than completed primary education was two-thirds,
as was the case in 1971-72.   The proportion (64%) was markedly higher
than the 52 percent for the general population in 1976-77.   This pattern is
also reflected in the occupational category of the head of household.
While in the first year or so there was an increase in the proportion from
manual occupations (fishing, farming and labouring), this proportion
remained steady at around 85 percent from 1972-73 through until 1978-79.
The reason for the initial change was that in the early years of the
program, the acceptors were more likely to come from the more elite
groups and government employees who could more easily be reached through
existing information channels.   Later years saw an expansion of the
program network through the introduction of fieldworkers, travelling
medical teams and village contraceptive distribution centres which have
made information and supplies more accessible to the less well-off social
groups and those in more remote villages.

        It should be clear from the above description that the implementation
of the National Family Planning Program in Bali has been multi-faceted with
an early recognition that the clinic infrastructure with its relatively
limited coverage needed to be supplemented by establishing supply routes
and depots of contraceptives in villages and hamlets.

54

On the administrative side, the Sistem Banjar approach provided rapid flow of current prevalence data both upward to kabupaten and province administrative levels, and down to the fieldworkers and village headmen. This feedback of current status was cleverly augmented by appealing to the Balinese penchant for competition among banjar with rewards for the village headman of the most successful banjar, in terms of contraceptive prevalence.[17] In fact the program was promoted quite openly as being Balinese rather than national, with family planning posters not only written in the Balinese language but depicting scenes, such as a woman feeding pigs, which are peculiar to Bali. There has been considerable pride taken in the belief that Bali had consistently maintained the highest family planning prevalence levels of any province, until East Java and Yogyakarta displaced it temporarily.

The decision by BKKBN, Jakarta to allow provincial offices considerable flexibility in designing and operating the Family Planning Program in their areas has undoubtedly facilitated this parochial but successful promotion of the concept that the program is 'by Balinese, for Balinese', even if there have been non-Balinese working within it. This appears to have successfully forestalled any substantial negative reaction from the populace who may otherwise have viewed such a program as external interference. As mentioned in Chapter 1, religious minorities at times view Family Planning Programs introduced by the majority as a possible attempt to gradually eliminate them. This suspicion seems to have been avoided in the case of the Bali Hindus.

The Bali office of BKKBN did go to some lengths to reassure the people that family planning was not forbidden by the Hindu religion. This was done by encouraging the local Hindu authorities, (Parisada Hindu Dharma), to pass judgement on the matter then publish booklets such as Agama Hindu Tidak Melarang Keluarga Berencana (The Hindu Religion Does Not Forbid Family Planning) (Oka,1971). The program also emphasised cultural factors such as the four birth-order name cycle implying that this legitimised the small family size norm (Astawa et al.,1975:93).

The process whereby the Balinese apparently came to rapidly accept the concept and practice of family planning is of major importance in this study, and will be examined in greater depth in the final chapter.

CHAPTER 4
COMMUNITY LEVEL STUDY

4.1 SURVEY METHODOLOGY

4.1.1 Study Population

In order to have a sufficiently large study population for obtaining reliable fertility estimates for the past as well as present it was considered necessary to survey about 1,000 respondents, the definition of which was any ever-married woman between the ages of 15 to 54 years. The purpose of including the five year age group beyond the normally accepted reproductive span is to include some women who had completed most of their childbearing before the introduction of the Family Planning Program. As the Family Planning Program Registers indicated that the villages of Banjarangkan, Tusan and Bakas contained 932 currently married women aged 15 to 44 years it was considered that the addition of widowed and divorced women, and women aged 45 to 54 years would bring the total to around 1,000 women.

The purpose of the study was not primarily to estimate fertility levels or contraceptive prevalence levels for the province of Bali, but rather to investigate the reasons for the rapid acceptance of family planning (see Chapter 1). For these reasons, it was decided that a sample survey of the whole province was not the most appropriate approach. Rather a survey which could be complemented by further in-depth interviews, or micro-studies, would be more useful. Such an approach could only be undertaken by a single individual through a village study which provided an opportunity to observe the workings of village life over a reasonably long time, and at close hand.

4.1.2 Life History Matrix

Two aspects of the questionnaire which may be of particular interest were the use of the Life History Matrix approach to record information on marriage, pregnancy history and family planning history, and the Balinese system of recording dates of birth in terms of a variety of overlapping cyclical calendars of different periods. The Life History Matrix approach has been described in some detail in Perlman (1976:265-7) and Lauro (1979:134ff).

The system of recording events in columns against 'Year of Event' proved to be a very easy method for interviewers to learn and to operate successfully. This was particularly the case where they were required to fill in the respondent's family planning history for each birth interval. With usual pregnancy history forms, such as used in the World Fertility Survey, important data of this kind can easily be missed. It was also very obvious to the interviewer if stated birth intervals were inexplicably long (four years or more), whereon the interviewer was to enquire further as to the reason. As the birth order name was also being recorded it was possible for the interviewers to detect a number of occasions where the respondent had failed to report the birth of a child who had since died. This was particularly the case for the early births of older women.

After the Life History Matrix (LHM) was complete, if there were any children born during the last five years (i.e. since mid-1975) the interviewer was required to turn to the 'Last Five Years' chart under the LHM and complete the details for these 'under-fives'. The aim was to utilise the local calendar systems to try to obtain very accurate data (to the day) on the date of birth of these children. This was done by first inquiring the current age of the child in terms of Balinese otons (each of 210 days or six 35-day months) and Balinese months. Next to this 'current age' in column 1, information on the day of birth according to the seven-day week and the five-day week was noted, then the name of the week according to the Wuku calendar of thirty weeks (see Streatfield,1982). It is this system of noting day of birth that is used by the Balinese for determining when the various life ritual ceremonies of the child should take place. The dates are remembered for quite some time after birth as these ceremonies are observed rigorously for the first three otons (roughly two calendar years), and sometimes after that.

4.2   SELECTION OF THE STUDY AREA

For reasons explained in detail in Streatfield (1982:Chapter 4.1) the regency chosen was the regency of Klungkung, which in many ways is typical of traditional Bali. It is often said to be the most conservative regency and it still has a strong, close-knit Puri headed by the Dewa Agung (who would formerly have been the Raja or king). Many of the royal family are now ensconced in government administrative positions, the old royal family networks being maintained in the attempt to retain power under the new system of national government. The town of Klungkung is visited by many tourists wishing to see its famous old courthouse, and although it is on the route both to the mountains and to the eastern end of the island, it has not been affected in the same conspicuous ways that Badung and Gianyar have. Klungkung town has good access to the capital, Denpasar, the 45 kilometre trip taking about 45 minutes by bus. Being one of the larger regency centres it has a large hospital, numerous schools and a number of administrative offices (see Map 1).

4.2.1   Kecamatan Level

An important factor in the selection of Klungkung was the fact that there were some data available on fertility levels for one of the four kecamatan or subdistricts, for the period 1974 to 1977. This was the result of the Sample Vital Registration Project (SVRP) run by the Central Bureau of Statistics in ten project centres throughout Indonesia. Of the fifty one kecamatan in Bali, the only one included in the SVRP study was Banjarangkan in Kabupaten Klungkung. Banjarangkan contained thirteen villages and about 28,000 inhabitants at the time of the project. The SVRP data indicated that fertility was quite low in Banjarangkan at that time (TFR = 3.3 in 1977), and the marriage data from that project indicated that changes in marriage patterns did not explain the low fertility; marriage patterns were similar to those for all Bali. This was considered important because it was necessary to choose an area where

57

MAP OF THE STUDY VILLAGES, BANJARANGKAN, TUSAN AND BAKAS

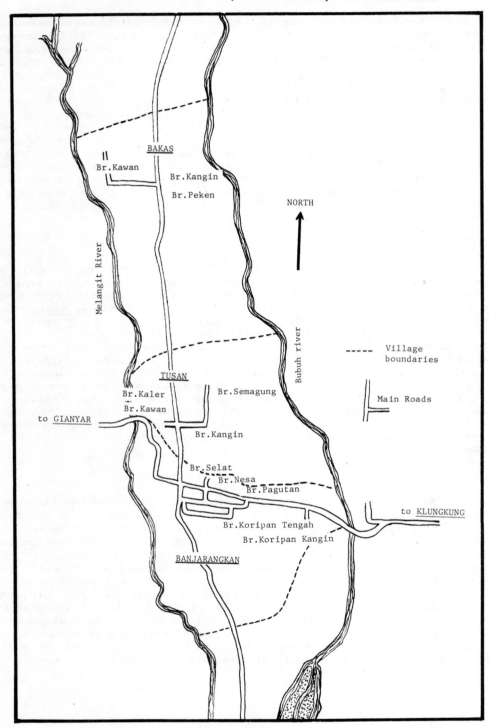

fertility had definitely declined in order to investigate the causes
underlying such a decline.

The kecamatan of Banjarangkan was quite typical of all Bali in terms
of its family planning usage according to the data from BKKBN, Denpasar,
which showed that 75.2 percent of all eligible couples were currently
using family planning, compared to the all-Bali level of 75.9 percent, for
the first quarter of 1980. The method composition was slightly different
with greater reliance on the IUD and less on the pill in Banjarangkan
than over all Bali. Apart from the data which were available from the SVRP
project, it was hoped that birth certificates would still be available for
the births which occurred during the three years of the project. It was
intended that these certified dates would be compared to the answers given
by mothers according to their recollections of birth dates for their children born during the same period, as a method of assessing accuracy of
recall of dates by mothers. This was of interest because an attempt was to
be made to determine exact (to the day) dates of birth for all children
under five years using the overlapping calendar system so important in
Balinese ritual and ceremony. The SVRP also provided a means to cross-
check data on infant mortality for the period 1974-77.

The question arises whether the low level of fertility in
kecamatan Banjarangkan was a recent phenomenon or the result of some
long entrenched factors. Evidence from the national Censuses of 1961, 1971
and 1980 suggests that while the annual growth rate of the population was
lower than that for Bali as a whole, it was considerably higher during the
period 1961-71 than for the period 1971-80 (see Table 4.1). Part of
this decrease in annual growth rate may, of course, have been due to outmigration, although apparently that has not been great.

TABLE 4.1
POPULATION and GROWTH RATES, 1961-1980, KLUNGKUNG, BALI

Year	Kabupaten Klungkung	POPULATION Kecamatan Banjarangkan	Study Villages	All Bali
1961	127,814	27,716	6,638	1,782,529
1971	139,307	31,038	7,459	2,120,091
1980	148,746	32,705	8,117	2,469,724

GROWTH RATES (Per Annum)
(Calculated from figures above)

Period				
1961-1971	0.86%	1.13%	1.17%	1.73%
1971-1980	0.73%	0.58%	0.94%	1.70%

Sources: Kabupaten, Kecamatan and All Bali figures from offices
of Central Bureau of Statistics; Village figures from
1980 Census returns hand tabulated at district level.

4.2.2 Village Level

The selection of the villages to be studied was based on examination of the SVRP data for birth rates for each village for the period 1974-77, and the BKKBN data from the Elco Registers for percentage of couples currently using family planning, as well as factors such as variety of socio-economic settings, access to clinics, distance from main road, etc.

The results of the examination of the SVRP data, which are not given here, was that three contiguous villages, Banjarangkan, Tusan and Bakas were selected for study. These three villages provided a wide range of birth rates (fertility levels) and a wide variety of proportions using family planning at the time of selection, although not so wide at the time of the birth rate data (Table 4.2). Of the four field workers responsible for the thirteen villages in the kecamatan (SVRP excluded two villages), one covered Banjarangkan and Tusan and a second covered Bakas, amongst other villages. The latter village was interesting in that very dramatic increases had taken place in proportions using family planning over a relatively short period, not only in the village of Bakas but also in the three other villages covered by the same fieldworker (Nyalian, Getakan and Aan).

TABLE 4.2
BIRTH RATES FROM SVRP STUDY, AND
FAMILY PLANNING PREVALENCE, FOR STUDY VILLAGES.

Village	Annual Crude Birth Rate(/1,000) 1977	Percent Couples Currently Using Family Planning			
		1976	1977	1978	1979
Banjarangkan	22.2	66.7	73.9	74.3	72.9
Tusan	30.2	61.4	58.5	63.9	66.0
Bakas	36.1	50.9	68.5	80.2	87.0

Sources: Birth rates from Klungkung office of Central Bureau of Statistics
Family Planning prevalence rates from Sistem Banjar registers.

4.3 DESCRIPTION OF THE STUDY AREA

The kecamatan of Banjarangkan is furthest west of the three kecamatan of Kabupaten Klungkung which lie on mainland Bali; the fourth kecamatan is Nusa Penida, an island off the south coast of Klungkung, formerly used as a penal colony. The kecamatan of Banjarangkan is long and narrow and extends some 15 Km. north from the coast into the hilly areas where it abuts onto Kabupaten Bangli. Like many districts in Bali it is quite narrow east to west (4 Km.) and is bordered on both east and west boundaries by substantial rivers, the Melangit to the west, and the Jinah to the east. It is also divided centrally by the river Bubuh (see Map 2).

As mentioned earlier, the regency of Klungkung is recognised as being probably the most conservative of the eight regencies in Bali. From the middle of the sixteenth century it was the political centre in Bali as the kingdom of Gelgel, until the fall of the great kingdom in the early 17th century. The royal family of Klungkung, headed at present by the Dewa Agung, is regarded very highly amongst royal families in Bali. Before the upheavals of 1965-66 Klungkung was probably the most strongly Nationalist regency in its politics, supporting the Partai Nasional Indonesia as opposed to the Communist party, the major alternative political party of the time.

The role of the royal families in relation to the commoners has undoubtedly changed since the arrival, first of the Dutch, then of the Indonesian state. However in Klungkung the traditional networks are still strong and are partly reflected in the occupation of senior government positions by members of the royal families. In the three villages studied, the village headmen, or Perbekels, were all of high caste: in Banjarangkan, an Anak Agung (Satria); in Tusan, an Ida Bagus (Brahmana); in Bakas, a Cokorda (Satria). A number of their assistants also belonged to the high castes. This is not to suggest that the royal families have simply substituted one form of power for another, since the Land Reform Act of 1960, which attempted to redistribute large landholdings, altered the relationships between the high caste and the commoners who formerly worked their lands 18.

4.3.1 The Three Villages

Apart from the fertility levels and levels of contraceptive practice, the three villages chosen differ considerably. Banjarangkan and Tusan are similar in some aspects, such as the distribution of occupations, but differ in other ways in that the inhabitants of Tusan are less well off than those of Banjarangkan, though they fare better according to most indicators, than do the inhabitants of Bakas.

-Banjarangkan Village:

Comprising two formerly separate villages, Banjarangkan and Koripan (about 1.5 kilometres apart), this village is large, having a total population of 3,400 in 1980. It is made up of five banjars containing 598 Kepala Keluarga (heads of household), and is situated on the main road from Gianyar to Klungkung in the east, no house being more than two kilometres from this main road. It is the administrative centre for the kecamatan, having a Camat's office, Police Station, a bank branch, a branch of the Department of Education and Culture, and a number of substantial shops selling consumer goods, cement, building materials , etc. Also the main banjar shows movies about once a week in the banjar hall.

-Tusan Village:

Like Banjarangkan, the second village in the study, Tusan (pop. 2,973 in 1980), is now made up of two formerly separate villages, Tusan and Sema Agung. The three banjar that make up 'down town' Tusan are virtually contiguous on their southern borders with the main western part of Banjarangkan.

-Bakas Village:

The village of Bakas lies 3 kilometres north of Tusan on the Tohpati road. It is the smallest of the three study villages having a population in 1980 of 1,744. Bakas must share irrigation water with Tusan and hence relies on growing a variety of vegetables rather than producing rice from sawah every year. There is, however, a rice slip for hulling the rice, when it can be grown.

A variety of measures reflect the differences in socio-economic status among the villages. Electricity was present in 27.2 percent of Banjarangkan houses, 7.9 percent of Tusan houses, but none of the Bakas houses. The proportions of houses having cement floors, as opposed to earth floors, were 63.4, 56.4 and 33.8 percent respectively for the above villages. Examination of consumption of preferred foods indicated that Tusan and Bakas were similarly poor compared to Banjarangkan. The proportions eating pure rice daily (not mixed with cassava) were 38.1, 15.4, and 17.7 percent respectively. The proportions eating chicken or duck regularly were 23.2, 4.1, and 1.7 percent respectively for the above villages.

4.3.2 Schools

Banjarangkan has three primary schools (SD) and a large junior second-ary school (SMP) which attracts students from many of the neighbouring villages. There is no senior secondary school, students having to travel four kilometres into the town of Klungkung. Tusan has two primary schools only, and Bakas one.

The greater presence of educational facilities in Banjarangkan is reflected in the proportions of women with some education. While 20.5 percent of women in Banjarangkan have completed primary school, the propor-tions in Tusan and Bakas are only 12.6 and 8.2 percent, respectively, and 15.4 percent overall. The proportions of men with completed primary school-ing is 43.9 percent overall (ranging from 40.2 percent in Bakas up to 47.6 percent in Banjarangkan. Proportions with no schooling are 59.0 percent for women, and 22.2 percent for men in the three villages combined.

4.3.3 Health Facilities

There is a public health clinic (Puskesmas) on the main road through Banjarangkan which is run by a full-time nurse (bidan) and assistant (mantri kesehatan). Apart from dealing with health problems, the nurse acts in a family planning capacity, mainly distributing oral contraceptive pills and inserting IUDs. A doctor visits the clinic about once a week. This clinic also provides an office for the local family planning field-worker.

There is also a clinic in Tusan though it is open less frequently, and does not have the same range of facilities as the Banjarangkan clinic. Bakas has a somewhat rundown subclinic which is rarely used.

4.3.4 Occupations

In Banjarangkan the occupations available for males are predominantly agricultural, either working their own land or sharecropping someone else's land or simply working as a cash paid farm labourer. About one quarter of all husbands in Banjarangkan (24.0%) and Tusan (25.2%) and two-fifths (39.0%) in Bakas perform some secondary occupation usually labouring.

For the women of Banjarangkan, the description of economic activity is less straightforward. Table 4.3 indicates that 57.9 percent of the women do some work which brings them an income, but only 35.2 percent are working regularly. Thus while the major occupation group is labouring (47.7%), only 33.6 percent of these women are working regularly, often on farms. The rest pick up work periodically, at harvest time in particular. After labourers, next in importance is the category of market seller or trader (27.0%), however most of these are either women who work each day at some kind of street stall selling a great variety of goods (such as cigarettes, cool drinks, fruit, headache tablets, offerings or peanuts) or they may be women who set up a stall at the market which is conducted every three days, usually in the banjar hall. On the other two days these women may follow some other occupation or they may work around the houseyard. As might be expected, the most regular type of occupation is civil servant (96.0% regular), although even in Banjarangkan only 4.2 percent of women are employed in this way.

As in Banjarangkan, the primary occupations for males in Tusan were in agriculture (36.4%) and as labourers (36.2%), followed by work in the civil service (10.1%). As in Banjarangkan, there is a wide range of minor occupations which absorb the remaining 17 percent of the men.

For the women, the primary source of employment is labouring, both regular and irregular. There are a number of women employed regularly in Tusan in the asphalt works which supplies materials for road maintenance in the surrounding area. The second major source of employment is the three day market which serves the surrounding district (including Banjarangkan). Apart from the market stalls and the regular sellers whose modest stalls line the main street, the market place becomes filled every three days with women selling fruit, vegetables, spices, fish, cooking utensils, etc.

There is also a certain amount of work for the women (and children) in the dry-land fields which are common in Tusan and Bakas. Farming, however, does not absorb as many women as it does in Bakas. These two villages currently have to share limited water from a common source and overcome this problem by alternating the supply, one village receiving all the water throughout one year, the other village receiving none at all until the following year when they swap. When no water is available for the village the residents must plant dry crops such as dry rice, sweet potato, cassava, corn, peanuts, and certain leafy vegetables in the waterless padi fields.

Situated about half a kilometre to the east of the main Tohpati road, the banjar of Sema Agung is relatively isolated and rather poor. While its subak receives water from a separate dam (Dam Sema Agung) this is insufficient to irrigate much of the adjacent land which is planted with vegetables of various kinds as described above.

Bakas is almost entirely a farming village. Three-quarters of the respondents' husbands work as farmers, even though they don't all own sawah, and a further 10.8 percent work as labourers either in construction or on someone else's farm. There are fewer alternative occupations in Bakas compared to the villages closer to the main road. There is a small number of civil servants (8.2%), mainly working in the Perbekel's office.

Bakas does not have a large market every three days as does Tusan, although there are some small street stalls selling the usual goods such as fruit,cigarettes, drinks, etc. These occupy less than one third of the local women (Table 4.3).

Although all three villages are only a few kilometres from the southern coast of Klungkung regency, virtually none of the men work as fishermen, this being restricted to those who live in the villages that actually border the coast.

TABLE 4.3
RESPONDENT'S OCCUPATION, ACCORDING TO VILLAGE.

		Village		
Occupation	Banjarangkan	Tusan	Bakas	Combined
(a) % Who do any work which brings them an income:	57.9	72.9	63.2	64.1%
(b) % Who do any REGULAR work which brings an income:	35.2	34.0	30.3	33.7%
Of those doing any work (a):				
% in farming (58.2% regular)	8.8	12.4	6.2	9.6%
% labouring (33.6% regular)	47.7	45.1	61.0	49.5%
% shop seller (94.7% regular)	3.5	3.0	0.7	2.7%
% market seller (70.9% regular)	27.0	32.0	23.3	28.1%
% Govt. employee (96.0% regular)	4.2	3.4	2.7	3.6%
% making mats/oil/ bricks/cotton etc. (81.0% regular)	6.0	0.4	2.1	3.0%
% travelling seller cakes/water/cotton (77.8% regular)	2.5	3.0	2.1	2.6%

Source: 1980 survey

4.3.5 Sawah (Wet rice land)

The main subak (irrigation society) associated with the village of Banjarangkan is Subak Delod Banjarangkan, which at 282 hectares is the largest in the kecamatan, and well supplied with water from dam (bendungan) Delod Banjarangkan. As a result of this adequate water supply, the cost of class I sawah in this subak is between Rs 100,000-150,000 (US$ 160-240) per Are (100 sqare metres). This can be compared to sawah in the neigh-

64

bouring villages of Tusan and Bakas which do not have a satisfactory water
supply and where the best _sawah_ sells for between Rs.40,000-70,000.

TABLE 4.4
LAND OWNERSHIP OF SAWAH BY RESPONDENT OR HER HUSBAND,
ACCORDING TO VILLAGE.

| | Village | | | |
Sawah Owned	Banjarangkan	Tusan	Bakas	Combined
No sawah	75.4	68.2	47.6	67.1%
1-19 Are	9.6	9.6	26.4	13.1%
20-29 Are	4.5	8.8	14.7	8.1%
30-89 Are	8.1	11.2	10.9	9.8%
90+ Are	2.4	2.2	0.4	1.9%
TOTAL	100%	100%	100%	100%

Source: 1980 survey

Data in Table 4.4 indicate that the proportion of Banjarangkan residents owning some _sawah_ is low at 24.6 percent, compared to Bakas with 52.4
percent. However, on examining the area owned by those who do own _sawah_, it
can be seen that those in Banjarangkan tend to have larger plots.

The pattern of _sawah_ rental is similar in the three villages to the
pattern of ownership except that the proportion in Bakas who were renting
(40.7%) is not as large as the proportion owning _sawah_ (52.4%). The
proportion of farmers who own _sawah_ is greatest in Bakas (58.1 percent
compared to 40.4 percent and 49.6 percent for the other two villages),
even though their plots are smaller, on average, than those in the other
villages. This pattern suggests that farmland in Banjarangkan and Tusan
are controlled more by non-farming, wealthy landlords than farmers who own
their own small plots as in Bakas.

4.3.6 Family Planning

The villages of Banjarangkan and Tusan are both served by the same
male fieldworker (MB) who lives in Banjarangkan and is also responsible for
the village of Negari in the south, between Banjarangkan and the sea.

The village of Bakas is served by a different male fieldworker
(MP) who is also responsible for the villages of Nyalian, Getakan, and Aan.
This fieldworker is a resident of Bakas and has to work largely out of his
home as the clinic in Bakas is a satellite clinic and opens only
occasionally. The Bakas clinic shares a nurse with the large clinic in
Tusan.

4.4 EVALUATION OF THE FAMILY PLANNING DATA

There are two basic sources of data concerning current usage of
family planning and new acceptors. The first is the quarterly _Laporan_

65

Sistem Banjar (System Reports) published by the BKKBN provincial office in Denpasar, and based on the reports filled out by the fieldworkers from the Elco-Registers kept at the banjar level. The second source is the 'Feed-Back' data, published by BKKBN central office in Jakarta, which is based on logistic information regarding numbers of pill cycles, IUDs, condoms, etc., that have been distributed to supply outlets throughout the province during the period concerned. Certain assumptions are made about continuation rates for the various methods, and reports on current stocks held by the clinics are supposed to be sent regularly to the regency office. The levels of current usage are estimated accordingly. These rates will be seen to vary somewhat from the current usage rates produced by BKKBN, Bali. The data from both sources are published down to the level of the kecamatan.

Initially, the two sources will be compared at province level. Then, the BKKBN data from the registers for the surveyed villages will be compared with the prevalence levels obtained by the survey.

4.4.1 Province Level Data

For purposes of comparison the data from Jakarta will be averaged for the months of July, August and September 1980 to make them directly comparable in time with the BKKBN, Bali data.

TABLE 4.5
FAMILY PLANNING PREVALENCE LEVELS FOR ALL BALI, 1980
FROM BKKBN, BALI AND JAKARTA.

| | JULY–SEPTEMBER 1980 | |
	BKKBN, BALI	BKKBN, JAKARTA
Number of Elcos	301,248	---
Number of MWRAs	---	365,307
Number of Current Users:		
Pill	34,755	14,842
IUD	152,387	154,314
Condom and		
foam tabs	26,712	6,385
Sterilization	10,742	10,894
Injection	1,252	233
TOTAL	225,848	185,668
PREVALENCE RATE		
(Current Users	74.97%	50.83%
% of ELCO/MWRA)		

(ELCO: Eligible couple aged 15-44)
(MWRA: Married women of reproductive age, 15-44)

Source: BKKBN,Bali-Quarterly Report,Triwulan III,1980.
        BKKBN,Jakarta-Monthly Statistics.

The dramatic difference of 24 percentage points in prevalence rates between the two BKKBN sources is partly due to substantial differences (40,000) in estimated numbers of pill, condom and foam users, and partly due to a difference of 64,000 in the denominator, the eligible or exposed population (Table 4.5).

The reasons for this latter difference in exposed population are unclear. In each case, they supposedly account for all currently married women aged 15 to 44, including those currently pregnant. The figure of 301,248 eligible couples used by BKKBN-Bali is equivalent to 12.9 percent of their estimated population of 2,340,187 for that period. This estimate later proved to be about 125,000 short of the actual figure as obtained by the Census in September-October 1980 (i.e., 2,469,724). On the other hand, the figure of 365,307 used by BKKBN-Jakarta, was equivalent to 15.6 percent of the estimated 1980 population, or 14.8 percent of the actual population. Both of these proportions are considerably lower than the 18 percent of the total population that used to be used as a guide to the number of eligible couples in the population (BKKBN,1974:5). The assumed growth rate of the total population of Bali from 1971 was about 1.1 percent per annum, a substantial underestimate considering the 1.8 percent p.a. growth rate in the 1961-71 period, and the 1.7 percent p.a. rate in 1971-80.

It is also worth noting the differences in pill (20,000), and condom and foam users (20,000), which are both very substantial. These differences may in fact be partly explained by the different approaches of the two BKKBN offices in estimating current use rates. In the Bali system a couple is registered as a current user as soon as they receive the first month's pill cycle, or half dozen or so condoms. The central office in Jakarta, however, estimates users on the grounds of 13 pill cycles used per year, or some number of condoms (e.g.72) used per year. This latter approach is retrospective in nature and may understate the true prevalence level a little, though not enough to explain these large differences.

Each month sources of contraceptives such as clinics fill in forms indicating the current levels of stock and how many items have been distributed or inserted during the previous month. BKKBN in Jakarta then convert such data into estimates of current users. The fact that in both sources the numbers of 'once-only' methods, i.e., IUDs and sterilisations match up, supports this explanation for why the levels differ so greatly for pills and condoms. It is also probable that pill and condom acceptors are not immediately reclassified as drop-outs if they do not obtain their resupplies at the appropriate time. Partly this is because there are several sources from which they might obtain them, and partly because the effort involved in recruiting new acceptors means that field-workers try to remotivate the couples before changing the status of the couple in the register.

4.4.2 Prevalence Rates from Present Survey

As indicated in the section of this chapter on survey area selection, the three villages of Banjarangkan, Tusan and Bakas were selected because together they formed an area which, according to BKKBN-Bali figures, was roughly representative (in terms of contraceptive practice) of the kecamatan of Banjarangkan; the kabupaten of Klungkung; and the island of Bali as a whole (Table 4.6).

TABLE 4.6

COMPARISON OF FAMILY PLANNING PREVALENCE
IN SURVEY AREA WITH PROVINCE, KABUPATEN AND KECAMATAN LEVELS, 1980.
PREVALENCE RATES
(Current users per 100 Eligible Couples)
(First quarter, 1980)

a)	Three survey villages	72.6%
b)	Kecamatan Banjarangkan	75.2%
c)	Kabupaten Banjarangkan	75.4%
d)	Province of Bali	75.9%

Source: BKKBN, Bali-Quarterly Report, Triwulan I, 1980
-Sistem Banjar Elco Registers.

Viewed separately, the three villages present a range of levels of selection. However, by the time the survey was conducted in July the figures had been altered somewhat as a result of a survey that BKKBN Bali had conducted in the month of August to check and update their figures on numbers of eligible couples. Apparently BKKBN was concerned that the National Census to be conducted in the following months (September and October) might show that there were more eligible couples than had been registered by the BKKBN fieldworkers, and possibly some couples listed as current users who had dropped out unnoticed by the fieldworkers. In fact, for these villages the data from the BKKBN survey proved to be different from that in the Elco-Register for the same year. The new data were incorporated into the registers in terms of updating the numbers of eligible couples but the data from the survey were not analysed for current user data, thus when more eligible couples were found the denominator increased while the numerator remained unchanged.

TABLE 4.7a

BKKBN 'SISTEM BANJAR' DATA, THIRD QUARTER, 1980
METHODS USED BY CURRENTLY-MARRIED WOMEN AGED 15-44,
ACCORDING TO VILLAGE.

		Village		
	Banjarangkan	Tusan	Bakas	Total
% ELCOs	71.4%	57.7%	71.9%	66.5%
Curr.Using FP				
IUD	67.0	48.6	58.6	
Pill	0.5	0	4.4	
Condom	2.4	1.1	5.9	
Tubectomy	0.5	7.2	2.5	
Other*	1.0	0.8	0.5	
Not Using	28.6%	42.3%	28.1%	33.5%
No.ELCOs	421	360	203	984
Total Popn.	3,095	2,990	1,774	7,859

* Other: Vasectomy, foam tablets, injectables.
Source: BKKBN, Bali-Sistem Banjar Elco Registers.

TABLE 4.7b
SURVEY DATA, JULY–SEPTEMBER , 1980.
METHODS USED BY CURRENTLY-MARRIED WOMEN AGED 15–44,
ACCORDING TO VILLAGE.

	Banjarangkan	Village Tusan	Bakas	Total
% ELCOs	56.4%	52.1%	36.5%	50.8%
Curr.Using FP				
IUD	52.7	41.2	33.5	
Pill	1.6	0.6	1.5	
Condom	0.2	0.3	0	
Tubectomy	1.2	8.5	1.5	
Other*	0.6	1.5	0	
Not Using	43.6%	47.9%	63.5%	49.2%
No. ELCOs	427	328	200	955
Total Popn.	3,400	2,973	1,744	8,117

*Other: vasectomy, rhythm, injectable and foam tablets.

Source: 1980 survey.

The results of the survey conducted as part of this fieldwork give the prevalence rate for the three villages combined as 50.8 percent of all the eligible couples surveyed (currently married women aged 15–44, n=955), compared to 66.5 percent of the 984 eligible couples on the BKKBN registers (Table 4.7a and b). The difference between the BKKBN register and the survey prevalence levels is greatest in the village of Bakas (+35.4%) followed by Banjarangkan (+15.0%), with Tusan (+5.6%) being in quite close agreement.

In Banjarangkan and Tusan virtually all the difference is accounted for by IUD users, only condom users in Banjarangkan show a difference greater than 2 percent. In Bakas, however, not only the IUD prevalence level was substantially overstated (+25.1%) in the BKKBN Registers, but also condom users (+5.9%) and to a lesser degree pill users (+2.9%). In fact none of the Bakas couples said that they were using condoms. This was of some interest because, according to the registers, the contraceptive prevalence rates in Bakas had risen dramatically in early 1978 entirely because of a sudden increase in condom users. A similar pattern occurred in the other three villages covered by the fieldworker for Bakas. These increases in current use had brought Bakas from near the lowest ranking village in the kecamatan in 1977, to near the highest prevalence level village in late 1979.

As the IUD is the major contributor to the differences, it is important to examine more closely the couples listed in the BKKBN Registers as IUD users to try to establish whether they had, at one time, accepted an IUD but had since stopped without notifying the fieldworker, or whether they had never used an IUD, in which case the Register figures must be quite false.

Of the couples registered as current IUD users, about 7 out of 10 were indeed using an IUD, according to the survey; a negligible number were using a different modern method. Of the remaining 3 out of the 10 not currently using any family planning, two had done so in the past but had stopped, and one had never used any family planning. This latter figure (12.0%) does not support any suggestion of substantial inflation of the BKKBN Sistem Banjar current use data. Rather it seems that many couples accept family planning for one reason or another, then later stop using without notifying the fieldworker. Alternatively, the fieldworker, having been notified of a 'dropout', may delay changing the Register.

The survey data will be examined in greater detail in Chapter 6 in regard to family planning differentials.

CHAPTER 5
FERTILITY IN THE STUDY AREA

This chapter is concerned with the pattern, timing and magnitude of the fertility decline which was believed to have occurred in the study villages.[19] These results cannot, of course, be extrapolated to all Bali as the study area could not be said to be typical of the whole island (see area characteristics in Chapter 4.[20] The role of the Family Planning Program in this apparent fertility decline will be examined in the following chapter.

This investigation of changes in the pattern and level of fertility will be performed by examining a variety of conventional measures such as age specific marital fertility rates; age specific fertility rates; total fertility rates; children ever born; parity and birth order distributions; and parity progression ratios. Various subgroups (educational, occupational, socio-economic, etc.) of the study population will also be compared in terms of their fertility.

The first step in examining any changes in fertility is to attempt to determine what proportion, if any, of the decline could be accounted for by changes in the formation and dissolution of unions in the reproductive period. A further reason for examining patterns of marriage is to enable the selection of the most appropriate pattern of proportions married for conversion of age specific marital fertility rates to age specific fertility rates and subsequently to total fertility rates. This is necessary as the respondents in the Banjarangkan survey (1980) were only ever-married women, and data were thus not collected on proportions of women never-married. An alternative source does, however, exist for the area, that being the data collected in the mid 1970s (mid-1974 to mid-1977) by the Sample Vital Registration Project conducted by the Central Bureau of Statistics (see Chapter 4). The selection of an appropriate pattern of proportions currently-married will be discussed in the next section.

5.1 MARRIAGE PATTERNS

To return to the question of change in marriage patterns during the period of operation of the Family Planning Program, the best available sources are the 1971 National Census and, more recently, the 1976 Intercensal Survey (known hereafter as SUPAS, and briefly described in Chapter 1). The Fertility-Mortality (FM) survey conducted in 1973 also collected marriage data but it is less recent than SUPAS though the sample size (n=4,300) is larger than for SUPAS (n=3,600). Data from the 1980 National Census on proportions married by five year age group are not yet available.

When the measures median and mean age at first marriage are examined there is a suggestion of a possible decline in age at first marriage. Referring to the SUPAS II data on median age at marriage (Table 5.1), Cho et al. comment that '...in the case of Bali, the median age at marriage has been high for a long time and may even have decreased slightly in recent years' (1979:15). It should be noted, however, that such a pattern of decreasing mean age at first marriage can result from the truncation effect upon the younger age groups. By definition the 20-24 age group will not contain any woman who married after reaching age 25, whereas the 25-29 age group may include women marrying up to age 30, and so on for the older age groups. This truncation effect can be overcome by comparing the median (or mean) age at first marriage of the 20-24 age group with all those in the 25-29 age group excluding those women married in the last five years; and those in the 30-34 age group excluding any married in the last ten years. The results of this recalculation can be clearly seen in both Table 5.1 (median) and Table 5.2 (mean). The unadjusted data from the 1980 Banjar-angkan survey suggest a decline in mean and median age at first marriage, whereas the recalculated figures show much less of a decline between age groups 25-29 and 20-24, and a very slight increase between groups 30-34 and 20-24.

TABLE 5.1
MEDIAN AGE AT FIRST MARRIAGE, WOMEN, BALI.

Age	1973 FMS	1976 SUPAS II	1980 Survey	1980* Survey
20-24	---	20.3	19.1	19.1
25-29	19.5	20.4	20.1	19.6
30-34	19.8	(20.7)	20.1	18.9
35-39	19.0		20.4	
40-44	19.9		20.7	

SUPAS II data are for ages 30-49, not 30-34.

1980* Survey data are recalculated by excluding all women married in the last five years from the 25-29 age group median and mean, and all women married in the last ten years from the 30-34 age group.

Sources: 1973 FMS Report, Table II.14, p.25
1976 SUPAS II, Unpublished tabulations
1980 survey is that upon which this study is based.

TABLE 5.2
MEAN AGE AT FIRST MARRIAGE, WOMEN, BALI.

AGE WFS	1976 SURVEY	1980 SURVEY	1980*
20-24	17.3	18.5	18.5
25-29	18.5	20.4	18.7
30-34	18.4	20.5	18.4
35-39	19.3	21.0	
40-44	20.2	21.7	

1980* Survey data derived as above (Table 5.1).

Sources: As for Table 5.1

72

The first conclusion to be drawn from this exercise is that the pattern in the SUPAS II data commented upon by Cho et al., may well be misleading because of the truncation effect on the younger age groups. The second conclusion is that the data for the survey area suggest a very slight delay in marriage as median age at first marriage has increased from 18.9 for the group 20-24 in 1970 (i.e., 30-34 in 1980, Table 5.1) to 19.1 for the group aged 20-24 in 1980. Over the same ten year period the mean age has increased from 18.4 to 18.5 for the age group 20-24 (Table 5.2). These changes are quite insignificant and could not be said to have any measurable impact on fertility levels.

We will now return to the selection of an appropriate pattern of proportions currently-married for conversion of the age specific marital fertility rates from the Banjarangkan survey data to age specific fertility rates and total fertility rates.

The data from the Sample Vital Registration Project (SVRP) for the district of Banjarangkan from roughly the mid- 1970s show a pattern of proportions currently-married which is consistently lower than all the other sources for the age range 20 to 40.[21] This suggests that in Banjarangkan district age at first marriage may be later than for Bali as a whole, although there is no obvious explanation for this.

If Banjarangkan district varies from all Bali in regard to patterns of marriage then the pattern of proportions married from the SVRP study would seem to be the most appropriate for converting the age specific marital fertility rates from this survey to overall fertility rates; particularly when it is remembered that the SVRP data are based on a population of 27,662 (in 1976), many more than any survey, and that considerable care was taken to ensure reliability of age data.

5.2 FERTILITY

Data from the SVRP study indicated that fertility in Banjarangkan in the mid- 1970s was quite low. Assuming that the level of fertility had been higher in the earlier times, the pattern, timing and magnitude of the decline in fertility will now be examined.

5.2.1 Age Specific Marital Fertility Rates

The data in Table 5.3a show a marked decline in the Age Specific Marital Fertility Rates (ASMFR) in groups 25-29, 30-34, and 35-39 from the early 1960s through to the late seventies, with the most important decline being between the periods 1966-70 and 1971-75 where the relative declines were 30 percent to 50 percent between 25 and 39 years of age (Table 5.3b and Figure 5-A).

This raises the question of the reliability of the rates calculated for the earlier periods, especially as the pattern of marital fertility is somewhat different from that usually seen in Bali (for the whole province). For the 1966-70 period, for example, the rate for 15-19 is lower than that for 20-24, whereas both the 1973 FM survey (for 1965-70) and the 1971 Census (for 1967-70) show the rate for the 15-19 age group being higher than any other group. In fact this latter pattern might well be the expected one where marriage is late and apparently many marriages are preceded by, and precipitated by, conception. On the other hand the ASMFR's by single years from SUPAS II show a pattern similar to the present survey (Cho et al., unpublished data). The next important aspect of the pattern of period marital fertility for 1966-70 is the very high levels in the 30-34 (387 per 1,000) and 35-39 (356 per 1,000) age groups, much higher than the values seen in the data from the 1973 FM survey (267 and 197 per 1,000 respectively, for 1964-68) and the 1971 Census (for 1967-70) for those age groups. However,it will be seen later in this chapter (section 5.2.5) that the present survey obtained considerably higher values for mean numbers of children ever-born (CEB) for women 30 years and over in 1970 than did the Census in 1971 (see Table 5.6). As CEB is a cumulative measure of fertility, the period measures (ASMFR's) for the age groups 30-34 and older, appear to have been underestimated in the 1971 Census data for Bali.

TABLE 5.3a
AGE SPECIFIC MARITAL FERTILITY RATES
(Per 1,000 Married Women)

			Age of Woman during Ref. Period				
Period	15-19	20-24	25-29	30-34	35-39	40-44	45-49
1976-80	339	376	260	157	100	57	20
(n)	(46.5)	(183.5)	(210.0)	(181.0)	(158.0)	(114.5)	(49.5)
1971-75	341	370	290	239	171	140	71
(n)	(61.5)	(171.0)	(176.0)	(155.5)	(115.5)	(50.0)	(8.5)
1966-70	321	399	416	387	356	141	n.a.
(n)	(56.0)	(139.0)	(151.0)	(111.5)	(50.0)	(8.5)	n.a.
1961-65	291	471	471	400	282	n.a.	n.a.
(n)	(44.0)	(115.5)	(107.0)	(49.5)	(8.5)	n.a.	n.a.

(These data are based on women currently married in the reference period, regardless of their marital status at the time of the 1980 survey. The 'n' values are the average values for given period.)

Source: Tables 5.3a and b from 1980 survey.

TABLE 5.3b
PERCENTAGE CHANGE IN ASMFR's BETWEEN PERIODS

Period	15-19	20-24	25-29	30-34	35-39	40-44	45-49
(1966-70) to (1971-75)	+6.2	-7.3	-30.3	-38.2	-52.0	-0.7	n.a.
(1971-75) to (1976-80)	-0.6	+1.6	-10.3	-34.3	-41.5	-59.3	-71.8
(1966-70) to (1976-80)	+5.6	-5.8	-37.5	-59.4	-71.9	-59.6	n.a.

74

FIGURE 5-A
AGE SPECIFIC MARITAL FERTILITY RATES, 1966-70 TO 1976-

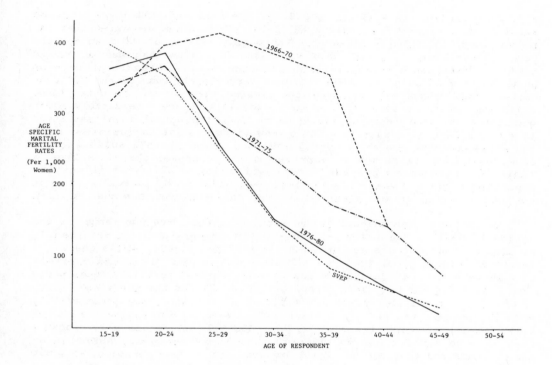

Source: 1980 Survey.

75

Another factor involved here could be data accuracy as the numbers of respondents are relatively small for the older age groups in the earlier periods. This may explain the differences in ASMFR's for these age groups between the periods 1961-65 and 1966-70 (see Table 5.3a). Finally fertility at the older ages may, in the past, simply have been higher in Banjarangkan than for Bali as a whole.

The initial reaction to the apparent dramatic decline in marital fertility between the periods 1966-70 and 1971-75 is to question whether erroneous dating of births in the past by respondents in this survey may be resulting in some exaggeration of births occurring in the period 1966-70. This could result from the bringing forward of births which in reality occurred in the early sixties, or it could result from pushing back births which occurred in the early seventies.

In regard to the first possibility, the fact that the 'ever-married total fertility rate' for women aged 15-39, the maximum age range that can be compared, is slightly higher for the period 1961-65 at 9.6 than for the period 1966-70 which is 9.4, does not support the view that such a forward shift of children's dates of birth did take place. Also the pattern of annual births through the 1960s followed very closely that of the WFS conducted four years earlier than the present survey. On the other hand, while the levels of fertility in the period 1971-75 are considerably lower than those for the preceding five-year-period, the actual level expressed as a total fertility rate (4.9 for women 15-49) is not inconsistent with the estimates for the same period obtained from the 1976 SUPAS survey, considering the later age at marriage in Banjarangkan than in Bali as a whole.[22] Also such a pattern of overestimation of age, that is mothers reporting their 5-9 year olds as 10-14 year olds, would be the reverse of the usual pattern of age misstatement for children over five(U.N.,1967:21).

Another worrying feature of the pattern is the 35-44 age range for the period 1966-70. The ASMFR for ages 35-39 (356 per 1,000) is very nearly as high as that for the age group 30-34 (387 per 1,000), while the value for the 40-44 age group (141 per 1,000) is quite low. It seems unlikely that between the periods 1966-70 and 1971-75, marital fertility rates would have fallen 52% for the 35-39 group, but only 0.7% for the 40-44 age group (Table 5.3a), particularly when fertility for the latter age group fell by some 59% between the periods 1971-75 and 1976-80. This suggests that the ASMFR (40-44) may have been higher in 1966-70. It seems more probable that for the earlier period (1966-70) the 35-39 age group ASMFR is an overestimate and that for the 40-44 age group is an underestimate. This may be a consequence of relatively small numbers in these groups, as well as possible age misstatement errors of mothers and children. That the ASMFR for the age group 35-39 is too high at 356 per 1,000 is also supported by the lower figure of 282 per 1,000 for the same age group for the period 1961-65 when overall fertility was at least as high as in 1966-70.

Finally, the problem of small numbers of respondents may well account for the fact that the ASMFR for ages 15-19 is lower than that for age group 20-24 in each of the four 5 year periods shown in Table 5.3a. Such a pattern of marital fertility is rather unusual and is particularly surprising when it is believed that a sizeable proportion of Balinese females marrying in the 15-19 age range are pregnant at the time of marriage. This situation may, however, differ somewhat in the study area owing to the high proportion of high caste families (about 27 percent compared to normal 5-10 percent). Because of the very serious problems associated with a high caste girl becoming pregnant to a boy from a lower caste, it may be that high caste parents are rather more protective of their daughters, with the result that fewer of them become pregnant before marriage. This may reduce the ASMFR for the youngest age group compared to other areas of Bali. If this is the case, we might have expected a similar pattern from the SVRP study in the Banjarangkan district, however the 15-19 ASMFR (399 per 1,000) is greater than the ASMFR for the 20-24 age group (355 per 1,000) (Gardiner, 1981:Table 4.15,p.203). It is worth noting that Cho's calculations of ASMFR's for single years for Bali from the SUPAS II data using the Own Children method, also showed a consistent pattern of a lower ASMFR for the 15-19 age group compared to the 20-24 age group (Cho, unpublished data). Finally, as the proportions married in age group 15-19 are so low the differences in ASMFR's are small.

In an attempt to circumvent the effect of these fluctuations in five year age group levels, an aggregate measure of marital fertility will be calculated, namely Coale's index 'Ig'.

The Ig values in Table 5.3c indicate a considerable decline in marital fertility during the 1970s, from a high value of 0.83 in the late 1960s to 0.49 in the period 1976-80, a decrease of 41 percent. The figures of 0.90 and 0.83 for the first and second halves of the 1960s are very high, indicating near natural fertility (= 1.0), but owing to the small (or zero) numbers of women in the older age groups for the earlier periods, where fertility might be expected to have fallen further below natural levels than for the younger women, these values might be slight overestimates.

TABLE 5.3c
COALE'S INDEX OF MARITAL FERTILITY, Ig ,FOR FIVE-YEAR PERIODS

Period	'Ig'
1961-65	0.90
1966-70	0.83
1971-75	0.61
1976-80	0.49

Source: 1980 survey

The question of the pattern of this decline in fertility, and its timing in relation to the activities of the Family Planning Program, will be discussed further in the following chapter.

5.2.2 Age Specific Fertility Rates

As the same pattern of proportions currently married, taken from the SVRP study, was used to convert age specific marital fertility rates to age specific fertility rates (see Table 5.4 and Figure 5-B), the trend in fertility over time is very similar to that seen with the ASMFR's (Table 5.3 and Figure 5-A). However because proportions married rise rapidly at the younger ages the patterns of the age specific fertility rates are somewhat different from those of marital fertility rates. For

FIGURE 5-B

AGE SPECIFIC FERTILITY RATES, 1966-1970 TO 1976-1980

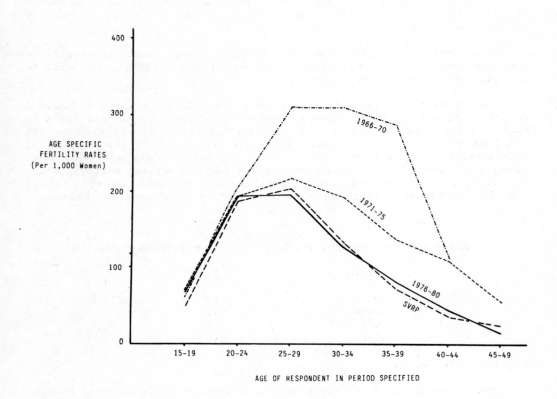

Source: 1980 Survey.

the period 1966-70 overall age specific fertility rates peak in the age
groups 25-29 and 30-34 (both 312 per 1,000). As fertility has fallen
the peak has shifted to the younger ages, to the 25-29 age group (218 per
1,000) for the period 1971-75 and to the 20-24 age group (183 per 1,000)
for the most recent period. There has been virtually no change over time in
the fertility of the youngest age groups, 15-19 and 20-24 years.

TABLE 5.4
AGE SPECIFIC FERTILITY RATES
(PER 1,000 WOMEN)

Period	15-19	20-24	25-29	30-34	35-39	40-44	45-49
1976-80	66.4	193.6	195.0	126.9	81.0	44.3	15.5
1971-75	66.8	190.6	217.5	193.1	138.5	108.9	54.9
1966-70	62.9	205.5	312.0	312.7	288.4	114.2	n.a.
1961-65	57.0	242.6	353.6	323.2	228.4	n.a.	n.a.
% Currently Married (SVRP Study)	19.6%	51.5%	75.0%	80.8%	81.0%	77.8%	77.3%

Source: ASMFR's from Table 5.8a
         SVRP% married from Table 5.2.

5.2.3 Total Fertility Rates

The age specific fertility rates examined in the previous section
indicated that a substantial fertility decline had taken place in the study
area during the 1970s. As a summary measure of age specific rates, the
total fertility rate (TFR) provides a convenient indicator of the overall
magnitude of this decline, although not of the age pattern. Table 5.5b
shows that for women aged 15-44, overall fertility fell by just under half
(45.4%) between the periods 1966-70 and 1976-80. The decline was a little
greater earlier on, falling 29.3 percent between 1966-70 and 1971-75, and
22.7 percent between 1971-75 and 1976-80.

To examine whether or not fertility had been changing during the
sixties it is necessary to examine the TFRs for women aged between 15 and
maximum 39 years.[23] The level of fertility of women in this range (see
Table 5.5a) fell only 1.8 percent (from 6.02 to 5.91) in the five years
between periods 1961-65 and 1966-70 compared to a decline of 31.8 percent
(5.91 to 4.03) between periods 1966-70 and 1971-75, and 17.9 percent (4.03
to 3.31) between periods 1971-75 and 1976-80.[24]

79

TABLE 5.5a
TOTAL FERTILITY RATES, DIFFERENT AGE RANGES,
FOUR PERIODS.

Period	15-49	15-44	15-39
1976-80	3.61	3.54	3.31
1971-75	4.85	4.58	4.03
1966-70	n.a.	6.48	5.91
1961-65	n.a.	n.a.	6.02

TABLE 5.5b
PERCENTAGE CHANGE IN TOTAL FERTILITY RATES

Period	15-49	15-44	15-39
(1961-65) to (1966-70)	n.a.	n.a.	-1.8
(1966-70) to (1971-75)	n.a.	-29.3	-31.8
(1971-75) to (1976-80)	-25.6	-22.7	-17.9
(1966-70) to (1976-80)	n.a.	-45.4	-44.0

Source: 1980 survey.

For the complete reproductive age range, 15-49 years, the total fertility rate in the most recent period (1976-80) was 3.61, somewhat higher than the figure of 3.31 from the SVRP study for the period mid-1974 to mid-1977 (Gardiner,1981:147).[25] The figure of 3.61 represents a decline of 24.7 percent in TFR over the figure of 4.85 for the period 1971-75. As already mentioned this latter figure seems not unreasonable when compared to other sources such as SUPAS I (TFR=5.1) and SUPAS II (TFR=5.3) for the same period (Cho et al.,1979:14). It should not be forgotten that the SUPAS data represent all Bali, whereas we have seen that proportions currently-married in the study area appear to be somewhat lower than for Bali as a whole, thus overall fertility might be expected also to be a little lower. In support of this view, the 'Last Birth' method, when applied by T.H.Hull to SUPAS II data, resulted in a TFR of 4.9 for all Bali in 1975 (Cho et al.,1979:14), almost half a child greater than the figure of 4.5 for the same year obtained by linear interpolation of the data in Table 5.5a. Finally, estimates from the 1980 Census give a TFR of 4.0 for the periods 1975-80 (Rele's method) and 1976-79 (Own Children method), and 3.5 for 1980 (Last Birth method) (see Dasvarma et al.,1984:4), so the above survey figures appear reasonable.

As we saw at the beginning of this chapter there had apparently been very little change in the pattern of marriage over the last ten to fifteen years in the study area, and thus it is appropriate to apply a single set of proportions currently-married to ASMFRs for each of the five-year periods under study in order to obtain ASFRs and TFRs. These data clearly indicate that very little fertility change appears to have taken place in the study area during the 1960s, whereas in the ten-year period from the late 1960s to the late 1970s fertility fell dramatically.

5.2.4 Children Ever-Born

The pattern of mean numbers of children ever born (CEB) by age of ever-married woman (Table 5.6) in the Banjarangkan survey differs somewhat from these patterns for all Bali from the main earlier sources (1971 Census; 1973 FM survey; 1976 WFS).

TABLE 5.6

MEAN CHILDREN EVER-BORN TO EVER-MARRIED WOMEN, BALI

Age	1971 Census	1973 FMS	1976 WFS	1980 Survey
15-19	0.7	0.5	0.6	0.7
20-24	1.7	1.5	1.7	1.5
25-29	3.0	2.9	2.8	2.5
30-34	4.1	4.2	4.1	3.5
35-39	4.8	4.9	4.8	4.4
40-44	5.0	5.9	5.3	5.5
45-49	4.9	6.0	5.2	7.2
50-54	---	---	---	8.2

Sources: 1971 Census, BPS, Series E,Table 26
1973 FMS, McDonald,P.F. et al.,1976:6.
1976 WFS,Vol.II,Table 3.1.6b,p.131.
1980 survey (N's as in Table 5.7).

In Figure 5-C it can be seen that the levels for the younger age groups (under 25 years) are quite similar, but between ages 25 and 40, the levels from this survey fall below those from other sources. From age forty upwards, the mean CEB rises rapidly with age to levels considerably greater than for the other sources. The dip in the age range 25 to 40 for the 1980 survey is a reflection of the fertility decline that had been taking place during the 1970s.

The high levels at the older ages (45-54 years) in Banjarangkan have been shown in Chapter 4 to reflect more complete data collection for CEB in the current survey than in the previous surveys and census. The difference of one child between the age groups 45-49 and 50-54 does not, of course, reflect additional childbearing after age 50, but rather that the fertility decline of the 1970s has resulted in lower cumulative fertility in each age group over 25 years (see Table 5.7 and Figure 5-D).[26] For example, in 1975, mean CEB for women aged 45-49 was 8.11 , but by 1980 this figure had decreased by almost one child to 7.21 for women of the same age. It is for this reason that the pattern of CEB for 1980 continues to increase after age 50.

81

FIGURE 5-C

MEAN CHILDREN EVER-BORN BY AGE, SURVEY COMPARED TO OTHER SOURCES

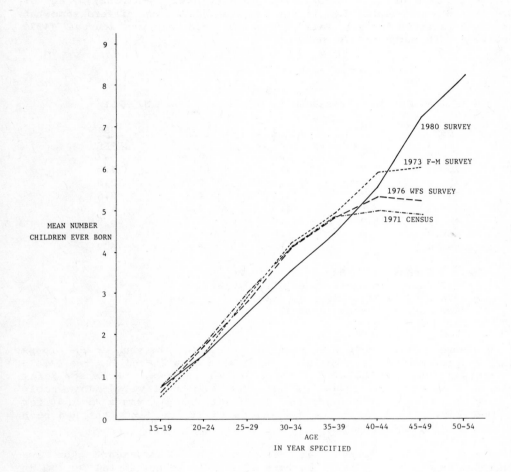

Sources: as for Table 5.6, p.81.

FIGURE 5-D

MEAN CHILDREN EVER-BORN BY AGE FOR 1970, 1975 AND 1980

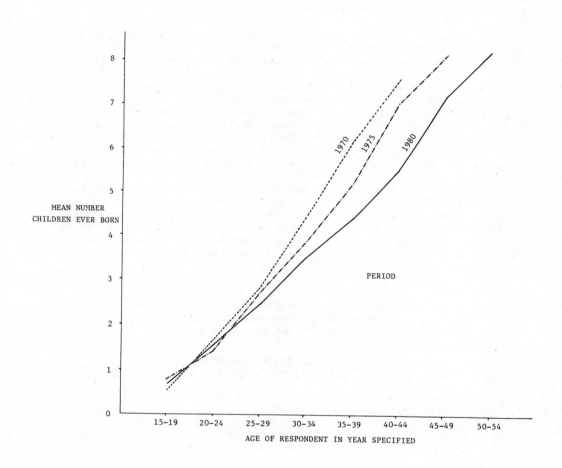

Source: 1980 Survey

That the 1980 pattern of CEB is the consequence of reductions in fertility at earlier ages is more clearly illustrated in Figure 5-E (also derived from data in Table 5.7) where four cohorts of women can be followed. These cohorts are those women whose ages at the time of the survey were (a) 35-39 years; (b) 40-44 years; (c) 45-49 years; and (d) 50-54 years.

When these cohorts are compared at any particular age group between 20 and 40 it is evident that there was negligible fertility change between 1960, 1965 and 1970. However for each age group in which years 1970 and 1975, or 1975 and 1980 can be compared (from 30 up to 54 years of age) there is an obvious and substantial decline in the increments to cumulative fertility throughout the seventies.

In the period 1965-70 the increments to total CEB averaged around 1.5 children over five years for ever-married women 20-44. Ten years later, the average increment was about half of that value over a five-year period.

The patterns in Figure 5-E illustrate dramatically the change that can be made to completed fertility by a decrease in marital fertility in each age group from 25 upwards. For women aged 40-44, mean CEB was 5.5 children in 1980 (cohort b) compared to 7.5 children ten years earlier (cohortd). The fact that since 1970 the five-yearly increment has been lower at all ages for each cohort compared to the previous cohort, supports the implications of the data on changes in total fertility rates.

It is of interest to note the difference in magnitude of fertility decline when expressed as cohort (cumulative) fertility (Table 5.7) rather than cross-sectional rates (Table 5.5a). For example, in the ten years between periods 1966-70 and 1976-80, the total fertility rate (Table 5.5b) for women 15-44 has fallen 45 percent, from 6.48 to 3.65, while the cumulative CEB up to age 44 has fallen only 27 percent, from 7.56 in 1970 to 5.52 in 1980.

TABLE 5.7
MEAN CEB TO EVER-MARRIED WOMEN,
BY AGE IN REFERENCE YEAR.

	Age of Women in Reference Year							
Period	15-19	20-24	25-29	30-34	35-39	40-44	45-49	50-54
1965	0.56	1.41	2.80	4.61	6.11	---	---	---
(n)	(57)	(132)	(154)	(87)	(18)	-	-	-
1970	0.54	1.63	2.79	4.42	6.16	7.56	---	---
(n)	(56)	(156)	(173)	(160)	(89)	(18)	-	-
1975	0.75	1.40	2.71	3.87	5.22	7.04	8.11	---
(n)	(68)	(194)	(199)	(176)	(162)	(89)	(18)	-
1980	0.69	1.54	2.47	3.51	4.41	5.52	7.21	8.22
(n)	(26)	(177)	(236)	(206)	(176)	(162)	(89)	(18)

Source: 1980 survey.

FIGURE 5-E

MEAN CHILDREN EVER-BORN BY AGE, FOR FOUR COHORTS OF WOMEN

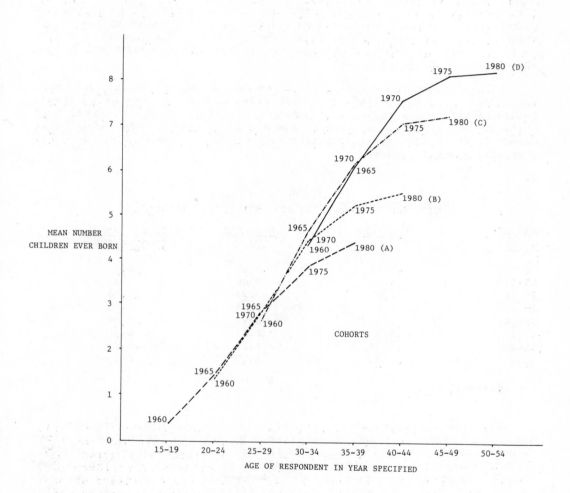

Source: 1980 Survey.

5.2.5 Child Survival

The dip in the pattern of children ever-born by age (Figure 5-F) below age 45 has been shown to be partly a function of relatively complete reporting of CEB by the older women (see Chapter 4), and partly due to the recent fertility decline (see previous section). There is however, no such dip apparent in the pattern of children still living (CSL) by age of woman (Figure 5-F). This pattern rises steadily to age 50 before flattening slightly. The explanation of the constant slope of the CSL pattern (rather than dipping as does the CEB pattern) appears to lie in the effect of the fertility decline being counteracted by a substantial decline in infant, and probably child, mortality amongst the same age groups wherein fertility has declined.

On examining proportions of children dead by age of woman (Table 5.8), the values increase, slightly erratically, to 0.18 for age group 40-44, followed by a jump to 0.27 for age group 45-49. This indicates that mortality of infants and children was almost certainly higher when women currently 45-54 were bearing their children than for the children of women currently under 45 years.

TABLE 5.8
MEAN CHILDREN EVER-BORN AND CHILDREN STILL LIVING

Age of Woman	Mean CEB	Mean CSL	Proportions Dead (CEB-CSL/CEB)
15-19	0.69	0.65	0.06
20-24	1.54	1.40	0.10
25-29	2.47	2.24	0.10
30-34	3.52	3.01	0.15
35-39	4.43	3.72	0.16
40-44	5.53	4.53	0.18
45-49	7.21	5.29	0.27
50-54	8.22	5.67	0.31

Source: 1980 survey.

That the the level of infant mortality has undergone a substantial decline in recent years is demonstrated by data in Table 5.9a obtained using the Feeney method (Feeney,1976:12) and the Brass method (Brass,1975: 50). The application of these methods to proportions of children dead (Table 5.8) indicates a drop in IMR of between 40 percent (Brass method) and 47 percent (Feeney method) over the fifteen years between the early sixties and the late seventies. The figures for age group 25-29 (both methods) are probably spuriously low (see Feeney,1976:13), otherwise the levels are similar, with the Brass method figures being higher throughout. Data extracted directly from the pregnancy histories (Table 5.9b) also support the apparent decline in infant mortality during that period, although the magnitude of decline is greater with the pregnancy history data, from IMR of 160 per 1,000 in 1961-65, to 54 per 1,000 in 1976-78, a decline of 66 percent.

FIGURE 5-F
MEAN NUMBER CHILDREN EVER-BORN AND CHILDREN STILL LIVING.

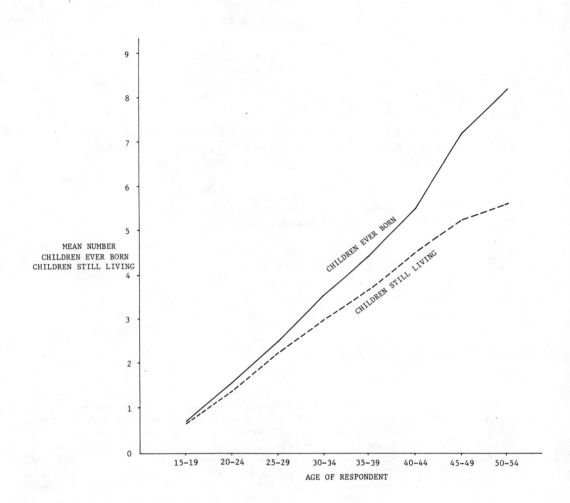

Source: 1980 Survey.

TABLE 5.9a

ESTIMATES OF INFANT MORTALITY AT DIFFERENT TIMES
(Feeney and Brass Methods)

Age of Woman	(Feeney Method)			(Brass Method) Using West Model Tables
	IMR	Years Prior to Survey		
20-24	66.6	3.6	(1976.4)	74.6
25-29	60.2	5.8	(1974.2)	72.6
30-34	87.2	8.2	(1971.8)	96.6
35-39	90.9	10.9	(1969.0)	97.0
40-44	92.4	14.2	(1965.8)	123.8
45-49	124.8	17.6	(1962.4)	144.0

The mean age at childbearing used for the Feeney method was
25.3 years, calculated as described by Feeney (1976:13).

TABLE 5.9b

ESTIMATES OF INFANT MORTALITY RATES
FROM PREGNANCY HISTORIES

Period	IMR (Per 1,000 Livebirths)	N (Livebirths)
1961-65	160	704
1965-70	104	1,005
1971-75	104	958
1976-78	54	607

Source: 1980 survey for Table 5.9a, b and c.

The data used in the three estimates of infant mortality are not controlled for age of woman and thus the absolute values for the earlier
periods may be distorted somewhat. However the expected effect would be
to understate mortality in the earlier periods. The births occurring at
those times would have been, on average, of lower birth order, and the
mothers would have been younger, than was the case in the more recent
periods. Generally, mortality of infants and children tends to be lower
for lower birth order children and younger mothers, down to age twenty or
so (Puffer and Serrano,1973:123). The value of Infant Mortality Rates
(IMR) of 160 per 1,000 for the period 1961-65 is rather higher than those
obtained by the other methods, but as the Feeney method estimates were
arrived at assuming constant mean age at childbearing, based on that for
women currently aged 15-34, the values for older women, and hence an
earlier time, may be underestimates.[27] This is supported by data from the
1971 Census which give an IMR of 132 per 1,000 for the period 1960-70 (Cho
et al.,1980:20).

A decline in mortality has undoubtedly occurred since 1960, and data
from the 1973 FM survey suggest that child mortality had been declining

since the late 1940s (McDonald, et al.,1976:69). The decline in IMR between the early seventies and the late seventies may be also partly a consequence of the fertility decline whereby the proportion of higher order births has decreased considerably (see next section).

5.2.6 Rates of Pregnancy Loss

The data on pregnancy losses were collected in the survey primarily to achieve more complete reporting of live births. It was not expected that the reporting of pregnancy losses would be complete, particularly in respect of spontaneous or induced abortions, the latter being illegal.

TABLE 5.9c
RATES OF PREGNANCY LOSS PER 1,000 PREGNANCIES

Period	Stillbirths	Spontaneous Abortions	Induced Abortions	Total	
1970-80	24.2 (46.4%)	24.7 (47.3%)	3.3 (6.4%)	52.2 (100%)	(n=2218 pregs.)
Pre-1970	28.7 (59.6%)	19.0 (39.4%)	0.5 (1.1%)	48.2 (100%)	(n=2043 pregs.)

The rate of pregnancy loss was relatively low at 52 per 1,000 live births for the period 1970-80, although slightly higher than the rate of 48 per 1,000 reported pre- 1970 (Table 5.9c). Comparable data from the 1973 FM survey are 66 per 1,000 live births for 1964-67, and 69 per 1,000 for 1971-73, although that survey cautioned that the reporting was probably incomplete (McDonald et al.,1976:70).

The proportion of pregnancies lost as induced abortions, 6.2 percent in the 1970s, was the same as for the FM survey for 1969-72, and about 70 percent of the absolute level, as a rate per thousand live births, of that in the FM survey. It seems unlikely that the incidence of induced abortions has declined since the 1960s as there are a number of doctors performing them, usually by vacuum aspiration, both privately and in certain hospitals (see Astawa,1980:63). As this procedure is commonly termed 'menstrual regulation' a number of women are almost certainly unaware that they are undergoing an induced abortion but rather believe that a late period is being induced. Overall there is no indication that any substantial changes have occurred during the 1970s in the two 'gestation variables' of Davis and Blake: foetal mortality due to (a) involuntary causes (spontaneous abortion or stillbirth), or (b) voluntary causes (induced abortion).

5.2.7 Parity Distribution

The report of the 1973 FM survey points out that while mean parity levels are a useful summary measure, they conceal the frequency distribution upon which they are based, as the same mean value can derive from different frequency distributions (McDonald et al., 1976:7).

89

A comparison of the parity distributions at different times using the 1971 Census, the 1973 FM survey, and the 1980 Banjarangkan survey is shown in Table 5.10. In the 1980 survey the distribution of parities is narrower than for other sources for both age groups 35-39 and age group 40-44, that is, the majority of women are in the parity group 4 to 6 in 1980 with relatively few women in the extreme parity groups of 0 and 10+. The means however, do not vary greatly from one source to another. [28]

TABLE 5.10
PERCENT DISTRIBUTION OF EVER-MARRIED WOMEN BY PARITY

	0	1-3	4-6	7-9	10+	MEAN
WOMEN 35-39						
1980 Survey	2.8	23.9	60.8	11.4	1.1	4.4
1973 FM Survey	5.2	25.1	40.8	25.8	3.1	4.9
1971 Census	11.7	24.1	32.8	25.8	5.7	4.8
WOMEN 40-44						
1980 Survey	1.2	14.2	54.3	29.0	1.2	5.5
1973 FM Survey	4.8	17.2	33.8	31.8	12.4	5.9
1971 Census	12.8	25.1	26.2	25.7	10.1	5.0

Source: as for Table 5.6.

The exceedingly low proportions in parity zero in the 1980 survey are considerably lower than expected from knowledge of proportions of couples sufferingprimarysterility in most populations. According to the FM survey, in other countries of the region for which data are available, the proportion childless is generally between 6 and 9 percent.

There are however, several reasons which might account for relatively low proportions of zero parity women in Bali. Firstly such importance is attached to becoming a parent[29] (see Chapters 2 and 7) that many couples do not marry officially until they are certain that they can produce a child, '...often the (marriage) ceremony is not celebrated until the girl has shown by her pregnancy that she is not barren but fully able to bear children' (Belo,1970:5). Thus by implication, a number of sterile females will never marry, resulting in a reduced proportion of ever-married women being sterile (zero parity). The second possibility is that married women are not at risk of becoming pregnant only by their husbands. There is only anecdotal evidence gathered during fieldwork to support the view that if a couple is having difficulty conceiving occasionally another male of proven fertility may be called upon to try to help solve the problem. Such an 'assistance scheme' might be expected to reduce the proportion of zero parity couples substantially.

These hypotheses do not, however, explain the variation in proportions of parity zero women among sources within Bali. There is some reason to believe that very careful questioning of respondents may reveal that a woman who initially claims never to have given birth may have, at some time, had a child which has since died.[30] A conscientious interviewer would find this relatively easy in Bali, as the respondent's name, and that of her husband, would normally have changed when she first became a parent, and it would not have reverted even if the single child subsequently died.[31] We cannot know how many of the 54 women stating their parity as zero have, in fact, had a child in the past. The interviewers were also careful to ensure that the women included only children to whom they had given birth, not adopted children. This concept of biological motherhood is quite familiar to the Balinese who describe an adopted child as <u>anak ngidih</u> (asked-for-person).

A final possibility is that over time the proportions of women childless may genuinely have been decreasing. With the construction of readily accessible health clinics and the increasingly widespread use of powerful antibiotics it might be expected that sterility due, for example, to chronic bacterial infection of the fallopian tubes, may have declined since 1971.

To return to the higher parity groups, it is apparent that the fertility decline taking place during the seventies has resulted from the avoidance of the very high birth order births (7+) which were not uncommon in the 1960s, producing a concentration of women in the parity group 4 - 6. There is no indication that women are limiting their births to 1, 2 or 3 children (proportions in parity 0-3 have fallen between 1971 and 1980) (Table 5.10), although as parity is a measure of cumulative fertility some time will be expected to elapse before behavioural changes are reflected in parity distributions.

5.3 DIFFERENTIAL FERTILITY

The first part of this chapter has been concerned with using a variety of measures to examine the overall pattern of fertility change in the study villages. It is now clear that a very substantial decline in fertility has taken place since the late sixties and that this decline has occurred largely through decreased marital fertility, especially at the older reproductive ages.

This part of the chapter is concerned with examining various subgroups of the village populations in the hope that the presence or absence of differentials in the fertility of these different educational, occupational and socio-economic subgroups may throw further light on the process of fertility decline.

Also fertility trends in some variables, such as woman's education, will be examined where the data permit estimation of past levels. This is important because comparisons based only on cumulative measures of fertility (e.g, children ever born) may not be satisfactory when one is trying to relate changes in fertility to cross-sectional events such as socio-economic change or the Family Planning Program. As mentioned in section 5.2.5, while the total fertility rate fell 45 percent between the periods 1966-70 and 1976-80, the cumulative mean CEB fell only 27 percent, reflecting the delay in fertility change being registered by the cumulative measure.

5.3.1 Respondent's Education

This variable is now seen as being of key importance in determining the timing of a couple's decision to limit their family size '...there now appears to be increasing recognition of the possibility that education itself may be of fundamental significance (in fertility transition).' (Caldwell,J.C.,1980:227). This naturally holds implications for the propensity of women to accept family planning. The general pattern is that the higher the level of education of the woman the more likely she is to practise family planning, and the lower will be her fertility.

Before examining the data on fertility according to respondent's education (Table 5.11a) it is necessary to point out the bias resulting from education having become more widespread in recent times. It tends largely to be the younger women who have had access to modern education, while the majority of the older women fall into the 'no school' category.[32] This age difference in the educational categories accounts for some of the fertility differential and its effect must therefore be negated by standardising for age. Also because the numbers of women in the higher educational categories are small, these will be combined to form a new category 'completed primary and above', comprising 15 percent of the total.

TABLE 5.11a

MEAN NUMBER OF CHILDREN EVER-BORN
BY AGE AND EDUCATION OF RESPONDENT

Education	15-19	20-24	25-29	30-34	35-39	40-44	45-49	MEAN CEB
No School	0.78	1.74	2.69	3.56	4.36	5.61	7.26	=3.82
	(9)	(74)	(110)	(120)	(115)	(131)	(66)	(625)
Some Primary	0.44	1.52	2.49	3.85	4.52	5.50	7.40	=3.81
	(9)	(69)	(78)	(48)	(31)	(16)	(20)	(271)
Complete Prim+Above	0.88	1.15	1.96	2.85	4.05	4.93	5.00	=3.02
	(8)	(34)	(48)	(38)	(30)	(15)	(3)	(166)
All Levels	0.69	1.54	2.47	3.52	4.43	5.53	7.21	

Note: Completed Primary, n=91; Junior Secondary, n=39;
       Senior Secondary, n=30; University/Academy, n=6.

After control for age (Table 5.11a), there is virtually no difference in the fertility of the lower educational groups, whereas the highest educational category (comprising one-sixth of all the women) averages 0.7-0.8 children ever born fewer than the other groups.   The pattern is virtually identical if differentials are standardised by duration of marriage.   The fact that there is no difference in the mean CEB for the educational categories of 'No Schooling' and 'Some Primary', including 85 percent of the respondents, is somewhat unexpected considering the view that 'In countries in the early stages of fertility transition ...the most marked fertility differentials appear to be educational ones' (Caldwell, 1980: 227).[33]

As will be seen the modest difference (0.7-0.8 CEB) between the 'completed primary and above' group and the others proved to be the widest differential within any of the variables examined, except for a couple of small occupational groups. These data suggest that among the majority of the women in the study area female education has not been of great importance in affecting fertility behaviour, particularly as some 59 percent of the women had no schooling in 1980, although high school education appears to have been of considerable importance in causing women to limit their childbearing.

TABLE 5.11b
ACTUAL AND EXPECTED BIRTHS AND INDEX
BY RESPONDENT'S EDUCATION, FOR DIFFERENT PERIODS.

	Respondent's Education		
	(1) No School	(2) Some Primary	(3) Completed Primary and Above
ACTUAL BIRTHS			
1966-70	762	187	97
1971-75	644	235	117
1976-80	478	270	134
EXPECTED BIRTHS			
1966-70	553	152	81
1971-75	636	231	133
1976-80	665	333	200
INDEX (ACTUAL/EXPECTED)			
A)1966-70	1.38	1.23	1.20
B)1971-75	1.01	1.02	0.88
C)1976-80	0.72	0.81	0.67
% CHANGE A)-C)	-47.8%	-34.1%	-44.1%

Source: 1980 survey.

A factor which urges caution in the interpretation of these differentials is that they are based on cumulated fertility from previous years, rather than on current fertility. Thus trends within subgroups may be dampened by long-term fertility levels. An alternative approach is to examine cross-sectional fertility amongst the educational subgroups for certain periods of time. This could take the form of age-specific marital fertility rates for five year periods, however in this case the numbers of women in the earlier periods (e.g.1966-70) would be too small to provide reliable ASMFR's. Instead a method of indirect standardisation is preferable. A standard schedule of ASMFR's (in this case 1971-75 for the whole study population, see Table 5.3a) can be applied to the women in each five year age group and educational subgroup for the particular period, to produce an expected number of births. An index can then be made of actual over expected births.

For the various education levels of the respondents, the indices are presented in Table 5.11b, indicating that in the period 1966-70, cross-sectional fertility of the 'No School' subgroup was somewhat higher at 1.38 than that of the groups with 'Some Primary' education (1.23), or 'Completed Primary and above'(1.20). This is not as wide a differential as suggested by the cumulative fertility levels in the 1973 FM survey where after standardisation for age the 'No School' category had a mean CEB of 4.4 compared to 3.8 for the 'Some Primary' group and 3.0 for the 'Completed Primary and above' group (McDonald,et al.,1976:5). However between 1966-70 and 1976-80 the indices (for the 'No School' group) fell some 48 percent for the 'No School' subgroup, 44 percent for the 'Completed Primary and above' subgroup, but only 34 percent for the 'Some Primary' subgroup. So, while fertility has fallen within each educational subgroup between the late 1960s and late 1970s, the levels of the subgroups relative to each other have remained much the same. Thus it appears that the educational differentials were of similar magnitude before the fertility decline, as at present.

When fertility is examined according to respondent's husband's education (standardized either by age of respondent as husband's age was not collected, or by marriage duration) the differences in mean number of children ever-born are even smaller than the differentials according to respondent's education. (For details see Streatfield,1982,Chapter 5.3.2).

5.3.2 Economic Score

The decision to measure economic status by the possession of certain items in the household rather than by estimating income was discussed in Chapter 4.[34] It should be noted that the concept of ownership of household items differs in Bali from that in some other places. The Balinese tend to live in a houseyard or compound comprising many buildings occupied by several families related patrilineally and sharing many of the facilities and goods in the compound (see Geertz and Geertz,1975:49). However there does exist the notion of personal ownership in that an individual may own and sell certain items such as chickens or pigs, whereas other 'household items', such as lamps or buckets may be considered communal property and thus be less reliable guides to economic status.

After standardisation by age[35] the fertility differentials are reduced to one third of a child among the different groups (mean CEB=3.5-3.9)[36] and after standardisation by duration of marriage (mean CEB = 3.5-3.9) the differential covers a range of half a child. The pattern bears little resemblance to the positive relationship between economic status and fertility as observed in Java by Hull and Hull (1976). Although overall the higher economic score groups combined tend to have fractionally higher mean CEB than the lower two economic groups, there could not be said to be any real fertility differential by economic score.

5.3.3 Land Ownership

Among couples where the husband's primary occupation was farming about half (N=227) the couples own some sawah, while the remainder work land belonging to another, in some cases the husband's father.[37] It might be expected that for a farming couple, ownership of sawah would be of considerable significance in determining aspirations for childbearing and that this would be reflected in the level of fertility. However there proved to be no difference in mean CEB between those farmers who own sawah (mean CEB=4.3) and those who do not (mean CEB=4.3), although both groups have somewhat higher fertility levels than the overall average of 3.7 CEB.

Part of the explanation for the absence of any substantial fertility differential according to land ownership may be related to the fact that even those farmers who do own land tend to own relatively little. Of the 227 farmers owning some sawah, about two-thirds (64.5%) own less than 30 ares (0.3 hectares), generally considered to be the minimum area necessary to support a family with three or four children.[38]

5.3.4 Respondent's Occupation

It has been noted that after marriage Balinese women often continue to work outside the house in a wide variety of occupations including heavy manual labouring. This can be an important contribution to total household income, and also reflects a degree of economic independence amongst women in Bali. The disrupting effect of frequent childbearing on women's capacity to perform income-earning work has been put forward as one possible factor underlying the Balinese fertility decline.

The respondents were asked if they did any work for which they received an income, in cash or in kind (e.g. a share of rice harvested). About two-thirds (n=691) of the women said that they did do some such work, and of these 374 (54%) said it was regular work, while 317 (46%) said the work was irregular (for less than half the weeks of the year). Overall the working women (n=691) had a mean CEB of 3.6, virtually the same as those who did not do work (mean CEB=3.8) which brought them an income.

After standardisation of CEB by either age or duration of marriage there remain some substantial differences among occupational categories. Both civil servants (n=25) and workers in cottage industries (making cloth, coconut oil, shirts, etc.) have a low mean CEB of 2.8-3.1, while the labourers (n=345), farmers (n=67), and street sellers (n=18) (for example, women who carry water from the spring or river to sell in the town) have mean CEB of 3.6-3.9. Initially this may not appear to be a very substantial difference but in the context of almost negligible fertility differentials, a difference in mean CEB of 0.8-1.1 is worth noting, although the numbers in some occupational groups are very small, and may be atypical. It should not be surprising that the lowest fertility group, the civil servants, also have the highest educational levels, and were seen earlier in this chapter to be younger and of lower than average fertility.[39] Except for street sellers, it tends to be the occupational groups with the higher proportions in regular work (civil servants, cottage industry, and shop sellers) who have the lower levels of fertility.

The data suggest that, overall, there are differences in fertility, though not very large ones, between the different occupational groups. This effect is not simply restricted to those occupations where the women tend to have higher educational levels, which has also been associated with lower fertility.

5.3.5 Caste

It is generally held that between five and ten percent of the population of Bali belong to the 'gentry', those persons whom the Balinese refer to as triwangsa, the 'three (upper) castes' (Geertz and Geertz, 1975:6), comprising all those of Brahmana, Satria, and Wesia status, as opposed to the Sudra or commoners, who make up the rest of the Balinese population. However in the three survey villages the overall proportion of high caste people was 27.2 percent (see Chapter 4 for village characteristics), the proportion varying between 4 percent in Bakas and 60 percent in Tusan.[40]

After standardising for age, the values of mean CEB were insignificant at mean 3.8 for commoners and 3.7 for grouped caste members. There is some variation amongst the caste groups in mean CEB, although numbers were quite small for Brahmana (mean CEB=4.1,n=51) and the Wesia group (mean CEB=4.6, n=10).

5.4 CONCLUSION

There can be no doubt that during the 1970s a substantial fall in fertility took place in the study villages. During the ten-year period from the late sixties to the late seventies, the total fertility rate fell from about 6.5 to 3.6 children ever-born, whereas during the 1960s fertility had remained almost unchanged. The timing of this fertility decline coincided quite closely with the introduction of the Family Planning Program in Bali.

Although the data on marriage patterns are not conclusive it appears that virtually all the fertility decline has occurred due to decreased fertility within marriage. This decline has been particularly marked amongst the older women between 30 and 49, while amongst women 15 to 24 fertility has changed very little. This pattern is consistent with the expected effects of a Family Planning Program which emphasizes birth limitation rather than birth spacing. The magnitude of the fertility decline between the late sixties and the early seventies (some 30 percent decrease in TFR) is remarkable considering the short period that the Family Planning Program had been in operation. This point will be examined more closely in the following chapter.

The changes in fertility during the 1970s do not appear to have resulted from changes in the factors governing the formation and dissolution of unions in the reproductive period, nor from involuntary changes in factors affecting exposure to conception (i.e., from increased involuntary infecundity). The data are not highly reliable, although apparently not from changes in the factors affecting gestation and successful parturition (foetal mortality from involuntary or voluntary causes). The voluntary factors affecting exposure to conception (use or non-use of contraception, etc.,) will be examined in the following chapter.

It is important, and somewhat surprising, that for the variables examined: education of both husband and wife; occupation; economic status; land ownership; and caste; very few substantial fertility differentials emerged.

Although the data on fertility in the past suggest that while the differentials for variable subgroups may have changed relative to each other, the magnitude of the differences was not very much greater then than at present. This suggests that whatever forces were at work to reduce fertility operated across all sections of the community simultaneously, and to a similar extent.

CHAPTER 6
FAMILY PLANNING IN THE STUDY AREA
AND ITS EFFECT ON FERTILITY

This chapter is concerned with family planning practice in the three villages of the study area. The questions to be answered are: how many couples are using family planning; what methods are being used; who is using them (i.e., which subgroups); and what are the reasons for accepting family planning? For those users of family planning, what are their experiences with the methods; what is the effect on their fertility; and where do they obtain the contraceptive services? For those who have stopped using family planning, what are the reasons?[41]

6.1 PATTERNS OF USE OF CONTRACEPTION

6.1.1 Village

The patterns of current use of family planning[42] varied somewhat among the three villages, and more widely among the banjars within the villages. However, overall just under half (48.9%) of the ever-married women aged 15 to 49 said that they were currently using family planning at the time of the survey (Table 6.1).

TABLE 6.1
CURRENT FAMILY PLANNING USE
ALL EVER-MARRIED WOMEN 15-49 YEARS
BY METHOD AND VILLAGE.

Method	Banjarangkan	Tusan	Bakas	Total	Users only
IUD	49.9	40.4	34.4	43.4	(88.7)
Tubectomy	1.0	8.0	1.3	3.5	(7.1)
Pill	1.5	0.6	1.3	1.1	(2.3)
Vasectomy	0.2	0.8	0	0.4	(0.8)
Condom	0.2	0.3	0	0.2	(0.4)
Rhythm	0.2	0.3	0	0.2	(0.4)
Vag.Tablet	0	0.3	0	0.1	(0.2)
Injectable	0.2	0	0	0.1	(0.2)
Total% Using	53.2%	50.7%	37.0%	48.9%	(100%)
Total % Not Using	46.8%	49.3%	63.0%	51.1%	
N	(481)	(361)	(227)	(1,069)	(530)

Source: 1980 survey.

When all women thought to be not exposed to risk were excluded the prevalence rate for non-pregnant, currently-married women aged 15 to 44 years was 56.5 percent for the three villages combined. The data presented in this chapter will normally not be restricted in this way but will cover all ever-married women aged 15 to 49 years.

The villages of Banjarangkan and Tusan had prevalence rates of family planning use of around 50 percent (Table 6.1), while the smallest village, Bakas, had a prevalence rate of only 37.0 percent.[43] Amongst the three villages there was some use of each of the eight modern methods available, although in no village were all eight methods being used simultaneously, and the vast majority of users had an IUD. The lower prevalence rate in Bakas, compared to the other two villages, is interesting because it is not only lower for the IUD (34.4 percent of eligible women) but because there is no use of the five 'less popular' methods. Bakas differs from the other two villages in being relatively isolated although it is only about 3.5 kilometres north of Tusan. It is also poorer, it has no school, and there are few jobs outside farming. The population density is also lower, at 7.3 per sq.kilometre, than for the villages of Tusan (11.2 per sq.km.) and Banjarangkan (12.8 per sq.km.). The 'satellite' health clinic is small and rather dilapidated compared to the clinics in Banjarangkan and Tusan. It does not have a resident nurse, although it is visited each week by a nurse from one of the neighbouring villages, and indeed all the current IUD users in Bakas (n=79) said that they had obtained their IUD at the Bakas clinic. Nevertheless, there is some suggestion that availability of clinic services may explain some of the difference in contraceptive use rates between Bakas and the other two villages. The importance of available services in explaining differential family planning practice is suggested by Freedman et al.,(1981:14) in their analysis of the situation in Java-Bali.

As can be seen in Table 6.1, the IUD is the method used by almost all current users (88.7%), and together with tubectomy (7.1%), leaves less than 5 percent for the remaining six modern methods. The only significant variations among the three villages were the greater use of tubectomy in Tusan, although this was not a function of different age structures (tubectomy acceptors normally being older than other acceptors on average); and the considerably lower prevalence of contraceptive use in the village of Bakas. This may be partly explained by the different fieldworker (MP) responsible for Bakas, being less 'successful' than the fieldworker (MB) who covers both Banjarangkan and Tusan, or it may also be due to differences in the circumstances of the inhabitants of Bakas which makes them less inclined to accept family planning.

If we concentrate here on the IUD as the primary method of family planning, the argument that availability of services is a major distinguishing factor among couples in the three villages loses some of its explanatory power. The data in Table 6.2 show that while there are substantial differences between current use of the IUD in Bakas as opposed to the other two villages, the differences in ever-use are not nearly so great. This implies that the lower Bakas prevalence rates are as much a result of a greater proportion of IUD users dropping out of the program, as they are of lower acceptance rates.

TABLE 6.2

EVER-USE OF FAMILY PLANNING, CURRENTLY-MARRIED WOMEN 15-49,
BY METHOD AND VILLAGE.

Method	Banjarangkan	Tusan	Bakas	Total
IUD	64.3	62.0	55.1	61.6%
Tubectomy	1.0	8.0	1.3	3.5%
Pill	6.0	3.0	5.7	5.0%
Vasectomy	0.2	1.1	0	0.5%
Condom	2.1	1.7	1.8	1.9%
Rhythm	1.0	1.4	0	0.9%
Vag.Tablet	1.2	0.6	0.4	0.8%
Injectable	0.4	0	0	0.2%
Total % Ever Used	66.4%	66.8%	59.0%	65.0%
Total % Current Users	53.2%	50.7%	37.0%	51.1%
Difference	13.2%	16.1%	22.0%	13.9%
n	(481)	(361)	(227)	(1069)

Source: 1980 survey.

6.1.2 Age of Respondent

The pattern of family planning use indicates a rapid rise in prevalence of current contraceptive use from the 15-19 year age group (15.4%) up
to the late twenties (49.6%), then the level rises to a peak of around 60
percent of women in the late thirties (Table 6.3). This is followed by a
decline to a level of about 42 percent for women 45-49; and one-third of
the 18 women aged 50-54.

The levelling off in the late twenties and early thirties is matched
by an increase in the difference between proportions ever using and
proportions currently using, this difference reflecting proportions dropping out (see Table 6.3). This is indicative of the pattern that women
initially accept family planning after their first, or more commonly, their
second child, then after a period of spacing they stop using that
method (drop-out) in order to have another child (see next Chapter 6.1.3,
on parity).

With the low levels of fertility current at the time of the survey,
many of the women would have completed their childbearing by their
late thirties or early forties, hence it is in these ages that the rate of
contraceptive use was highest. Following the first period with a high
drop-out rate (parity two), the second period was, as might be expected,
the late forties when many women considered themselves too old to produce
more children, and indeed many would have been post-menopausal.[44]

6.1.3 Parity of Respondent

The pattern of acceptance of family planning suggested by the age
related prevalence is indeed supported by the proportions of women, by
parity, currently using family planning (see Table 6.4). The prevalence

rate rises rapidly to 56.6 percent for parity two women then drops to 48.9 percent for parity three women, rising again thereafter to levels above 60 percent for parities 4,5 and 6 before dropping back to below half of the women with parity 7+ (13.1 percent of total women).

TABLE 6.3
RATES OF CURRENT-USE AND EVER-USE OF FAMILY PLANNING,
BY AGE OF WOMAN.

Age	% Current Users	% Ever Users	Absolute Difference
15-19	15.4	26.9	11.5
20-24	36.7	45.2	8.5
25-29	49.6	67.4	17.8
30-34	52.9	71.6	18.7
35-39	59.7	73.9	14.2
40-44	54.3	71.0	16.7
45-49	41.6	65.2	23.6
50-54	33.3	55.6	22.3
TOTAL	48.7%	64.8%	16.1%
n	(530)	(705)	(1,088)

Source: 1980 survey.

This suggests a tendency for women to accept family planning after their second child[45] then having delayed the third pregnancy to stop using contraception until after their third and possibly fourth pregnancies. However the data (lengths of closed birth intervals) do not support the expected difference between lengths of the second and third intervals.

TABLE 6.4
CURRENT-USE AND EVER-USE OF FAMILY PLANNING,
BY PARITY

Parity	% Currently Using F.P.	% Ever Using F.P.	n
0	0	1.9	54
1	20.8	32.8	125
2	56.6	68.8	221
3	48.9	71.1	190
4	62.1	80.0	145
5	60.0	73.2	112
6	66.3	82.6	92
7+	46.3	68.5	149
TOTAL	48.7%	64.8%	1,088

Source: 1980 survey.

This pattern of acceptance is very much a consequence of the emphasis by the program on starting women off with the IUD because of its high theoretical use-effectiveness, high continuation rate, low cost, and the fact that only one visit to the clinic is required (Astawa et al., 1975:95). The women will normally only be given the choice of an alternative method if the IUD proves to be too troublesome for them.

TABLE 6.5
CURRENT-USE OF FAMILY PLANNING METHODS
BY NUMBER OF PERIODS OF FAMILY PLANNING USE

Number of Periods

Method	1	2	3+
IUD	95.6	71.1	47.1
Pill	1.6	4.3	5.9
Tubectomy	2.5	17.8	41.2
Vasectomy	0.3	1.7	5.9
Other *	0	5.4	0
Total	100%	100%	100%
n	393(74.4%)	118(22.3%)	17(3.2%) (100%=528)

Other : * includes condom,vaginal tablets,rhythm and injectable.

Source: 1980 survey.

Consistent with starting acceptors with the IUD but permitting a change of method if problems arise, is the pattern of method currently used according to total number of periods of ever-use of any family planning methods (see Table 6.5). This pattern shows a halving of the proportions using the IUD as acceptors move from first period of use to third or more period of use. As proportions using the IUD decline, users change primarily to tubectomy, vasectomy and the pill. Amongst those users in their third or greater period of use (n=17 only), approximately equal proportions are using the IUD and sterilisation.

6.1.4 Annual Prevalence Rates of Family Planning Use

The annual prevalence rates were calculated from the pregnancy and family planning histories for women who were currently-married during the reference year. Before the beginning of the National Family Planning Program in 1969-70, fewer than 5 percent of married women were using family planning (see Table 6.6); however the prevalence rate increased dramatically during the early 1970s to a level of 38.6 percent by 1975 in the study villages. After 1975 the level of current users continued to rise steadily but less steeply, to the level for currently married women aged 15-49 in 1980 of 50.1 percent.

The high levels of current use in the early 1970s are consistent with the substantial decline in fertility observed in the study villages (see Chapter 5.2). The estimated crude birth rate for the period 1971-75 was 29.7 per 1,000, a level which was roughly consistent with a mean prevalence rate of current contraceptive practice of 31.0 percent of married women. This agrees with the so-called '30-30' rule (Berelson,1974:34).   The levels of current use were also somewhat higher than the reported levels for all Bali for the same years.

TABLE 6.6
ANNUAL PREVALENCE RATES OF FAMILY PLANNING USE
FOR CURRENTLY-MARRIED WOMEN   15-49

Year	% Currently Using F.P.	Mean N
1965	0.1%	413.0
1966	0.3%	451.6
1967	0.7%	490.2
1968	1.9%	528.8
1969	4.4%	567.4
1970	9.4%	606.0
1971	17.0%	655.6
1972	26.7%	705.2
1973	33.4%	754.8
1974	35.9%	804.4
1975	38.6%	854.0
1976	40.7%	889.8
1977	42.3%	925.6
1978	45.2%	961.4
1979	47.9%	997.2
1980	50.1%	1,033.0
1966-70	3.7%	
1971-75	31.0%	
1976-80	48.1%	

Source: 1980 survey.

     The prevalence levels from the survey data are obtained retrospective-ly so the age distribution is distorted somewhat, although the proportion in the high family planning use age range of 25-44 was similar in 1971-75 (67.4%) to that in 1976-80 (70.2%).   For the period 1976-80 the mean level of current use was 48.1 percent of married women, a little lower than might be expected considering that the crude birth rate for that period was estimated at 21.7 per 1,000.

6.1.5 Occupations of Respondent and Husband

     The data show some variation in proportions of women using family planning among several occupational categories, although the variant categ-ories tend to be quite small in terms of numbers of women. For example, among those women who work as saleswomen in a shop of some kind (other than a market or roadside stall) only 36.8 percent were currently using family planning at the time of the survey, while of those working in a

103

skilled job as a civil servant, some 68.0 percewnt were currently using family planning (Table 6.7a). The proportions using family planning among occupational categories are signicantly different at the 95 percent level only for shopsellers and civil servants.

This difference in levels of usage is not just a function of different age distributions as the mean age of the shopseller group is 35.1 years compared to 34.3 years for all working women. On the other hand the mean age for the civil servant group is only 31.9 years, as might be expected from the previous chapter where it was seen that this occupational group (including teachers and nurses) had higher than average education which had only become generally available relatively recently, thus only for younger women. This group also had the lowest fertility even after standardisation for age or duration of marriage. Apart from the obvious difficulties that would arise from repeated pregnancies for women in the civil service, it will be seen in Chapter 7 that this group of civil servants have high educational aspirations for their children, many with the hope that these children will later also enter the civil service. Civil servants are also encouraged by the government to accept family planning, not only through means such as a rice allowance for the first three children only, but in some cases, obtaining a civil service position has been conditional on acceptance of family planning.

TABLE 6.7a
CURRENT-USE OF FAMILY PLANNING METHODS
BY RESPONDENT'S OCCUPATION

	Respondent's Occupation						
	Farmer	Shop-Seller	Market Seller	Labour-er	Civil Servt.	Cottage Indust.	Street Seller
Total % Using FP	55.2%	36.8%	51.0%	48.7%	68.0%	57.1%	55.6%
n	67	19	196	345	25	21	18 (=691)

TABLE 6.7b
CURRENT-USE OF FAMILY PLANNING METHODS
BY OCCUPATION OF RESPONDENT'S HUSBAND

	Occupation of Respondent's Husband							
	Farmer	Civil Srvt.	Pte Employee	Entre Preneur	Street Seller	Lab-ourer	Other	Not-Work
Total % Using FP	46.2	68.2	27.3	57.1	47.4	46.4	44.1	69.2
n	461	132	22	14	19	321	102	13 (=1,084)

Source for Tables 6.7a & b: 1980 survey.

In regard to the group of shopsellers (n=19), apart from the problem of small numbers, it is not clear why so few were currently practising family planning (36.8%), although there does tend to be more capacity to absorb the labour of one's children when self-employed in a shop than in many other occupations. The shops in which these women work are generally rather small although crammed with an extraordinary array of goods[46], and if they sell prepared food, as many do, it is common to see the shopkeeper's children helping out. Data on ideal family size (presented in Chapter 7) support the view that women working in shops believe they can benefit from larger families in that the mean ideal family size for these women, at the time of marriage, was given as 4.2 compared to only 3.4 for the total survey population (see Chapter 7.3).

Apart from these two occupational categories, accounting for only 6.3 percent of all working women between them, the proportions currently using family planning range from 48.7 percent for labourers to 57.1 percent for women working in cottage industry. The average for all working women is 50.8 percent, compared to 45.1 percent of non-working women. The lower prevalence rate for non-working women may be partly a consequence of their being younger (mean age = 31.6 years) than working women (mean age = 34.3 years), also they are more likely to be currently pregnant (11.7 percent of non-working women compared to only 6.5 percent of working women).

The pattern of family planning use for the different occupational groups of respondents' husbands is similar to that for occupational groups of working respondents themselves, with over two-thirds of those working as Government employees (civil servants) currently using family planning while only a little more than a quarter of 'own-account' workers or employees in private industry or business were using family planning, (Table 6.7b). It should be noted that 13 of the 22 private employees (Pegawai Swasta) category had two or fewer children (they had the lowest mean CEB at 2.6), and thus they may not be as unusual a group as at first appears; that is, they may accept family planning after the third child as do many others. Only the groups of civil servants and private employees had levels of family planning use significantly higher and lower (at the 95 percent level) respectively, than the other occupational categories such as farmers, labourers, etc.

More important in terms of numbers is the category of civil servants (n=132) of whom 68.2 percent were currently using family planning consistent with higher levels of education, and with the pattern observed amongst female civil servants. While there is no reason per se that male civil servants would jeopardize their jobs by their wives having many children, it turns out that the wives of 50 percent of these civil servants have regular jobs, compared to an overall average of 33.8 percent of wives in regular employment. Thus it is their wife's job which would be jeopardised by frequent pregnancies [47].

6.1.6 Education of Respondent

The level of education achieved by the woman appears to have very little effect on the likelihood that she will be using family planning.

When the women are grouped into those with no formal schooling, those with some primary schooling, and those who have completed primary or above, the prevalence rates of family planning use range from 48.2 percnt for those with no schooling to only 52.4 percent for the highest educational group (see Table 6.8). This is a surprisingly small range considering the differences in mean CEB for the different educational categories seen in the previous chapter (Table 5.11a) where the two lower educational groups had mean CEBs of 3.8 while the highest educational group had a mean CEB of only 3.0-3.1, after standardisation for age.

TABLE 6.8
PERCENT CURRENTLY USING FAMILY PLANNING
BY RESPONDENT'S EDUCATION
(Standardised for Respondent's Age).

Education	% Currently Using	n
No School	48.2%	642
Some Primary Completed	50.5%	272
Primary & above	52.4%	166
		(1,080)

Source: 1980 survey.

6.1.7 Respondent's Husband's Education

This variable shows greater variation in proportions currently using family planning (see Table 6.9) as only 39.7 percent of the couples where husband is in the 'No Schooling' category were currently using family planning, compared to around 50 percent of those couples where the husband had some schooling.

TABLE 6.9
PERCENT CURRENTLY USING FAMILY PLANNING
BY EDUCATION OF RESPONDENT'S HUSBAND
(Standardised for Respondent's Age)

Education	% Currently Using	n
No School	39.7%	242
Some Primary Completed	48.5%	360
Primary & above	53.2%	479
		(1,081)

Source: 1980 survey.

There is very little variation within the individual higher educational groups except for the small University/Academy group where two-thirds of the 21 were using family planning. This pattern suggests that husband's education may be more important than many other factors, including wife's education where, although there is a larger proportion of women with no schooling (59.4%) than of men (22.4%), the difference in proportions using family planning is striking considering the normally small differentials observed. It is not surprising that over 90 percent of the 'No-School' category (for husbands) are either farmers or labourers, both groups having slightly lower than average prevalence rates of contraceptive practice (see Table 6.7b).

6.1.8 Economic Status (Household Possessions)

As with husband's education there is a direct relationship
between prevalence of contraceptive practice and economic status as
indicated by the household possessions score (see Table 6.10).

TABLE 6.10
PERCENT CURRENTLY USING FAMILY PLANNING
BY ECONOMIC SCORE

Economic Score	% Currently Using	n
0- 19	39.7%	277
20-199	47.5%	305
200-299	49.3%	304
300-899	63.0%	100
900+	60.8%	102
		(1,088)

Source: 1980 survey.

Just under 40 percent of the very poorest group, comprising one
quarter of the population and having a score of less than 20, were
currently practising family planning compared to about half of the
middle group (scores 20-199, and 200-299), while 61.9 percent of the
wealthiest groups (scores 300-899, and 900+) were using family planning.
It should not be surprising to find that civil servants are strongly
represented among the wealthier economic groups. Where the husband is a
civil servant, 51.5 percent of the couples fall into the 300+ economic
score category, while if the wife is a civil servant 68.0 percent of the
couples fall into this category, compared to 18.5 percent of total couples
falling into the 300+ category. Of course, as we saw in Table 6.7, a very
high proportion of civil servants were currently using family planning.
Conversely, farmers and labourers are somewhat over-represented in the
poorest categories (scores: 0-19) of which they make up 83.3 percent
compared to 72.1 percent of the total population. These two occupational
categories have lower than average rates of family planning use at 46.2
percent and 46.4 percent, respectively (Table 6.7).

6.1.9 Desire for more Children

Emphasis at the beginning of the Family Planning Program in the early
1970s was mainly on preventing unwanted extra pregnancies (see Chapter 3),
but as prevalence rates have increased there has been greater emphasis on
encouraging women to space births, as will be seen in section 6.3 on
patterns of first acceptance.

Thus at the time of this survey in 1980, 32.5 percent of those 351
women wanting to have more children were currently using family planning[48]
compared to 56.4 percent of the 737 women who did not want more children,
or were uncertain (see Table 6.11).

TABLE 6.11

PERCENT CURRENTLY USING FAMILY PLANNING, BY EXTRA CHILDREN DESIRED

Extra Number Desired	Percentage Currently Using	n
0	58.9%	621
Uncertain	53.8%	116
1	42.6%	169
2	26.4%	125
3	19.0%	42
4+	6.7%	15
(1+)	(32.5%)	

Source: 1980 survey   (1,088)

As might be expected when family planning is being used for spacing births, the fewer extra births desired by the couple, the more likely they were to be using family planning. In fact, for those wanting only one extra child the proportion using family planning (42.6%) was not greatly less than the proportion (58.9%) of those not wanting more children.

6.2 FAMILY PLANNING AND FERTILITY

6.2.1 Children Ever-Born

As is often observed the level of achieved fertility of couples currently using family planning (mean CEB=4.1) is higher than the level for couples who are not using family planning (mean CEB=3.4). This pattern persists when controlled for age (Table 6.12), and even when parity zero women, who are not eligible for family planning, are excluded from the analysis. The explanation of this paradoxical situation is that family planning acceptors are not typical of the population. As Brass points out:

> For example, women aged, say, 35 years enter a programme with, in general, a higher parity, greater fertility in the past five years and shorter interval to the last birth than the average for married women of the same age in the population. Part of the difference is due to sterility, part to risk exposure and fecundity and part to chance (Brass,1978:167).

The consequence for these 'high fertility' couples then, is that their achieved fertility is reduced below the level of their potential fertility by using family planning, while remaining higher than the level of achieved fertility of the 'low fertility' couples who do not use family planning. Consequently, fertility at community level can decline while this fertility differential persists.

The fertility decline during the 1970s in the study villages has certainly coincided with a rapid rise in contraceptive use but it still

remains to demonstrate a causal link between the practice of family planning and the decrease in fertility levels described in Chapter 5. This
will be attempted in the following subsections.

TABLE 6.12

MEAN CHILDREN EVER-BORN BY AGE OF RESPONDENT
BY CURRENT FAMILY PLANNING STATUS

				Age of Respondent				
Current Status	15-19	20-24	25-29	30-34	35-39	40-44	45-49	50-54
Using FP	1.25	1.94	2.75	3.69	4.68	5.81	7.38	8.83
(n=530)	(4)	(65)	(117)	(108)	(105)	(88)	(37)	(6)
Not Using	0.59	1.31	2.20	3.31	4.07	5.19	7.10	7.92
(n=558)	(22)	(112)	(119)	(96)	(71)	(74)	(52)	(12)
(All women)								
Not Using	1.08	1.69	2.30	3.50	4.38	5.33	7.10	7.92
(n=504)	(12)	(87)	(112)	(91)	(66)	(72)	(52)	(12)
(Women with 1+ children)								

Source: 1980 survey.

6.2.2 Closed Birth Intervals

As only one of the 1,088 respondents stated that she had used any
form of family planning in the initial interval between marriage and the
first live birth (in her case, the pill), this interval was ignored for
purposes of comparing lengths of birth intervals for family planning users
with those for non-users.

Also excluded were intervals between pregnancies that did not end
in a live birth, but rather in a stillbirth or abortion, spontaneous or
induced. Such intervals composed 6.9 percent (n=146) of total closed
intervals (n=2108). That is, this analysis of closed birth intervals is
concerned only with intervals which start and finish with a live birth, and
are not interrupted by any other pregnancy, regardless of outcome.

Regarding the use of family planning, the interval was allocated to
the 'family planning user' category if any form of modern contraception was
practised for any length of time during the given interval. It was
considered unnecessary to devise a system to weight the various possible
methods used as in 91 percent of the closed live-birth intervals where
contraception was used, the method was the IUD, the remainder being taken
up by the pill which is of similar use effectiveness over the short term,
as is the case for most closed intervals. Naturally sterilisation could
not be used in a closed interval.

Finally, time was controlled by limiting the comparison to the
period during which contraception has been available, the ten years before
the survey during which time the Family Planning Program has been in
operation. Also, the data on date of birth are considered to be quite
accurate for the last five years, however before that (1975) the accuracy
and completeness of birth recording almost certainly declines progressively

the further back one goes.

The data indicate an extension of the mean closed live-birth interval (26.9 months) by 14.4 months, or 53.6 percent , to 41.3 months when some method of family planning was used in the interval. This assumes that the former (26.9 months) would have been the overall mean if family planning had not been available. It cannot be argued validly here that the group not using family planning were a selected lower fecundity (or infecund) group, because these are closed intervals, thus all the women were fecund in the interval.

In terms of overall impact on fertility however, it should be noted that family planning as used in only 18.7 percent of all the closed live birth- live-birth intervals during this period of ten years (for spacing births). The consequence of this is that for all closed live-birth intervals the mean length is 29.6 months, an increase of 10.0 percent over the mean length of 26.9 months for closed livebirth intervals where family planning was not used. The effect of spacing has only been to increase mean interval length by ten percent. The prevalence of contraceptive use is considerably higher however, for the open intervals, those between the most recent live birth and the time of the survey, uninterrupted by any other pregnancy.

6.2.3 Open Birth Intervals

The extension of the open live-birth interval when family planning has been used, was considerably more dramatic than for the closed intervals The mean open interval length of 54.4 months when family planning has been used, is some two years longer (an increase of 77.8 percent) than the mean length of 30.6 months where family planning has not been used.

This is a very significant increase, not only because of the magnitude of the extension of the mean open interval length, but because the open intervals in which family planning has been used account for nearly two-thirds (63.4%) of all the open intervals, in comparison to only 18.7 percent for the closed intervals. The effect of this is that the mean length of all open livebirth intervals is 52.8 percent greater (at 46.6 months) than the mean open interval for non-users of family planning (30.6 months). This is clearly an effect of much greater magnitude than that which occurred within the closed live-birth intervals.

6.2.4 Parity Progression

This is a measure of the proportion of women who move from a particular parity level on to the next higher parity level within a given period of time after the occurrence of the earlier birth. It can be used to compare the tempo of fertility for the same population over different times, or different populations at the same time, or, as in this case, different subgroups of the same (study) population over the same time period.

For this particular analysis, the time period is limited to the ten years prior to the survey, as was the birth interval analysis. It takes as a useful cut-off point for the time frame, three years, which is greater than the mean lengths of both open and closed birth intervals for the group not using family planning, but is less than the mean lengths of both open and closed intervals for the group which did use family planning following the initial birth.

The data in Table 6.13 demonstrate very clearly the effect on the tempo of childbearing, of the use of family planning, with the consequent lowering of parity progression. The implication of the very low percentages moving on to higher parities within three years for the group using family planning, is that many of these women will never have another child but that they are, in fact, using family planning to limit their childbearing.

TABLE 6.13
PROPORTIONS OF WOMEN MOVING FROM PARITY 'X' TO PARITY 'X+1'
WITHIN THREE YEARS, BY FAMILY PLANNING STATUS IN INTERVAL, 1970-77.

Parity From To	F.P. Used	n	F.P. Not Used	n
1 - 2	50.0%	(68)	85.9%	(319)
2 - 3	34.6%	(104)	86.3%	(205)
3 - 4	21.3%	(89)	78.3%	(143)
4 - 5	12.5%	(88)	79.4%	(102)
5 - 6	8.6%	(56)	71.6%	(74)
6+ - 7+	4.8%	(109)	70.6%	(153)
Total Parities 'X' TO 'X+1':	21.4%	(514)	80.9%	(996)

Source: 1980 survey.

The view that many of the 'family planning user' category will probably never go on to a further birth is supported by the rapid decline in proportions moving on to higher parity as one looks at the values for the higher birth orders in that (the Family Planning user) group (Table 6.13). These proportions decline much faster than might be expected simply from the slight lengthening of mean birth interval length (mainly for open intervals) that occurs as birth order increases, and clearly these proportions decline much faster than do those for the 'non-user of family planning' group.

6.2.5 Births Averted

In Chapter 5 we saw that a substantial decline in fertility had taken place during the 1970s in the study villages. In the previous section of the present chapter, the data on lengths of open and closed birth intervals, according to whether or not family planning had been practised, indicated that the practice of family planning certainly contributed to the fertility decline. However it is not intuitively obvious what proportion of the decline can be accounted for by use of family planning compared to other factors. For this reason the numbers of births averted by family planning use will be estimated, for the periods 1971-75 and 1976-80.

Many of the existing techniques for evaluating the impact of family planning use on fertility are designed for use with program statistics, comprising mainly numbers of acceptors according to method used and a number of acceptor characteristics such as age and parity. Sets of theoretical method-continuation rates, either standard schedules or from surveys of the acceptors, are then applied to the numbers of acceptors to estimate prevalence of contraceptive use at particular points in time, allowing for method failure, users dropping out, etc.

The data gathered in the pregnancy and family planning history in the present survey are of a somewhat different nature. For each pregnancy interval (open or closed), data on family planning practice were recorded, including date of starting use, date of stopping use (if applicable) and reason for stopping, as well as method(s) used in the interval.

The significance of this is that it negates the need to use method-continuation rates borrowed from another source which may not be appropriate for the study population. Also, as method failure is one of the reasons for stopping use , any segment of family planning use can be legitimately considered totally effective in terms of protection against pregnancy. All methods used can therefore be considered as equally effective (i.e.,100%) while they are being used [49] thus there is no need to separate methods for analysis. In this analysis all segments of family planning use, whether an initial segment or otherwise, are treated together; 63.3 percent of current use segments were of initial use.

Finally, this survey covered all ever-married women 15-54 years in the study villages and hence is not limited only to users of Program contraception. Thus one of the shortcomings of births averted analysis based on program acceptor statistics is avoided and in this case the estimates of births averted will cover users of contraception from all sources, although there appeared to be very little resort to private sources by women in these villages.

6.2.5.1 Methodology

The method selected for this analysis is the Component Projection Approach derived from the methodology originally proposed by Lee and Isbister (1966:737-58). In this case, the version used is the 'model for desk calculators' described in Chapter 4 of U.N. Manual IX (U.N.,1979:63-75).

The method is designed to estimate the births averted in a given calendar year through the use of birth regulation methods provided by a Family Planning Program (in this case, all sources). The logic is that:

...if 't' is the year for which births averted are estimated and since there is an interval of about nine months between conception and birth, it follows that births prevented in year 't' result from the practice of family planning that took place approximately between 1 April of the year 't-1' and 1 April of year 't'. The number of births averted of couples or women in age group 'i' is thus obtained as the product:

$$\text{'}Q_{i,t} \cdot g_i\text{'}$$

where $\text{'}Q_{i,t}\text{'}$ = number of women in the ith age group in year 't' who were practising totally effective contraception during the period from 1 April of year 't-1' to 1 April of year 't'; $\text{'}g_i\text{'}$ = potential fertility estimate of the number of women $\text{'}Q_{i,t}\text{'}$ in age group 'i'; 'i' = successive age groups of women of reproductive ages 15-19, 20-24,25-29, etc. (U.N.,1979:63).

There are therefore two major steps, the estimation of $Q_{i,t}$ and g_i.

The computation of $Q_{i,t}$ involves the following assumptions:

(a) Acceptance occurs at a constant rate throughout each year of the program, so that acceptors who do not discontinue use will be in the program for an average of six months during the year of acceptance (the survey data did not include exact month of accepting or stopping use);

(b) The number of users as of 1 October of year 't-1', mid-point between 1 April of year 't-1' and 1 April of year 't', is assumed to represent the average number of users of that period.

Thus the number of users was estimated as of 1 July of year 't-1' and 1 July of year 't', then linear interpolation was used to obtain the estimated number of users as of 1 October of year 't-1', this being the value of $\text{'}Q_{i,t}\text{'}$ to be used in estimating births averted in year 't'.

Computation of $\text{'}g_i\text{'}$.

The selection of appropriate potential age-specific fertility rates raises a number of problems. There has been a variety used in the past, from the age-specific marital fertility rates of the population as a whole, to the acceptors' own fertility during the period prior to entering the program, to the approach of Lee and Isbister (1966:737-58) who used the marital fertility of the general population increased by 20 percent to account for the acceptors' higher fecundity. The assumption in the past has been that acceptors are more likely to have a higher potential fertility than do married women in general, since the chances are that the latter include some sterile women and some subfecund women, and women whose husbands are temporarily absent etc. It has also been contended that the higher fertility of acceptors might not have remained so had they not started using family planning. That is, many acceptors may have entered a period of relatively low fertility, without family planning use, following the initial period of above average fertility, a phenomenon described as 'regression to the mean' by Brass (personal communication).

When these factors are taken into consideration, it does not seem reasonable to elevate the ASMFRs by 20 percent. Instead the fertility schedules that are preferred are those for the general population but for fecund women only , for the period 1966-70, before the Family Planning Program commenced operations.50 This assumption (Assumption A), that acceptors are all fecund, has been made by Nortman in her more sophisticated version of the Component Projection Method suitable for computer analysis, CONVERSE (U.N.Manual IX:57), and seems reasonable in this case as couples are not eligible to become acceptors until they have demonstrated their fertility with at least one child.   Thus this analysis includes only parous women, although such women may of course, experience secondary sterility after bearing a child. By way of comparison, the births averted calculations will be repeated using another set of assumptions (B) where the women using family planning are not assumed to include only fecund women but to have the characteristics of all married women in the population.   Thus, the ASMFRs will not be increased by the reciprocal of the estimated proportions sterile in each age group.

For the period 1966-70 the age-specific marital fertility rates (see Table 5.3a) have been adjusted upwards by the inverse of the proportions fecund (one minus the proportion sterile), from Nortman's article (cited in U.N. Manual IX:53, from Henry,1961:81-92) and are presented in Table 6.14a.

The 1966-70 schedule of fecund marital fertility was then applied to the mean number of users of family planning by five year age groups on 1 October 1970, 1971, 1972, 1973 and 1974 to produce estimated numbers of births averted in years 1971 to 1975. The reasoning is that conceptions resulting in live births between 1 January and 31 December of year 't', occur between 1 April of year 't-1', and 31 March of year 't'. Thus protection due to family planning use can be taken as the average number of family planning users between 1 April of year 't-1', and 1 April of year 't', the mid-point being 1 October of year 't-1'.   It is also necessary to eliminate the segment of ineffective contraceptive protection at the beginning of use caused by overlap with post-partum amenorrhoea. As mean length of breastfeeding was 20 months, usually with supplementation starting early, the mean length of post-partum amenorrhoea might be expected to be about 9 months.   No data were collected on post-partum amenorrhoea in this survey. The mean time at which family planning was accepted after the most recent birth was 3.6 months, so it was concluded that a period of 6 months overlap of contraceptive use with post-partum amenorrhoea would be a reasonable estimate. Thus the first 6 months of contraceptive use was eliminated from each interval of use in these calculations. The total of 340 births averted represents 34.0 percent of the 999 births which actually did occur in that five-year period, 1971-75 (the 291 births averted according to assumption B represent 29.1 percent of actual births) (see Table 6.14b).

TABLE 6.14
ANNUAL BIRTHS AVERTED DUE TO FAMILY PLANNING USE

(a) Age Specific Marital Fertility Rates for Fecund Women, 1966-70.

Age Group	1966-70
15 - 19	0.328
20 - 24	0.418
25 - 29	0.452
30 - 34	0.445
35 - 39	0.392
40 - 44	0.367
45 - 49	0.067

(b) Births Averted for Periods 1971-75 and 1976-80*.

Period	Births Averted.	
	Assumption A	Assumption B
1971-75	340	291
1976-80*	716	590

Assumption A: ASFRs assume only fecund women protected by FP.
Assumption B:ASMFRs assume women protected by FP may or may not be fecund
      - therefore fertility rates not adjusted for sterility.

(Six months was subtracted from each woman's period of contraceptive use
 for the overlap of post-partum amenorrhoea and contraceptive use.)
 (1980: * Estimated for Full Year 1980)

(c) Total Fertility Rates, Women 15-49
    (i) Actual, (ii) If Births not Averted

Period	(i) Actual	(ii) If Births Not Averted.	
		Ass. A	Ass. B
1966-70	(6.8)		
1971-75	4.85	6.8	6.4
1976-80*	3.61	6.9	6.2

(1980: * Estimated for Full Year 1980)
(1966-70 TFR is estimated for women aged 15-49 using ASFR(45-49) from
 1971-75, as no ASFR available for women 45-49 in 1966-70.)

(d) Total Fertility Rates, Women 15-44.
    (i) Actual (ii) If Births not Averted

Period	(i) Actual	(ii) If Births Not Averted	
		Ass. A	Ass. B
1966-70	6.48		
1971-75	4.58	6.5	6.1
1976-80*	3.56	6.8	6.1

(1980: * Estimated for Full Year 1980)

When the 1966-70 schedule of fecund marital fertility was applied to
the numbers of users on 1 October 1975 to 1979, the total number of births
averted was estimated at 715.5 for the period 1976-80. This represents
74.8 percent of the 956 births which actually occurred (assuming a full
year of births in 1980) in the period 1976-80.

It must be noted that simply adding births averted per calendar year
to   actual births per calendar year does not necessarily give an accurate
indication of the number of births that would have occurred had there been
no family planning (program or otherwise) available.   Other factors may
well have come into operation.

115

However, to put the magnitude of the effect of the births averted into perspective, these births have been added to the actual births and hypothetical total fertility rates for the periods 1971-75 and 1976-80 have been derived. For women aged 15-44 (Table 6.14d), the hypothetical TFR, had no births been averted by family planning, would have been 6.5 in 1971-75, some 42 percent higher than the actual TFR of 4.58. For the period 1976-80, the hypothetical TFR would have been 6.8, higher by 90 percent than the actual TFR of 3.61. The pattern and magnitude of changes is similar for women aged 15 - 49 (Table 6.14c). These calculations cannot, of course, account for changes that may have occurred in fertility due to factors other than family planning, although the question of changes in patterns of marriage was examined early in Chapter 5 and found to be virtually negligible. Thus it appears that the use of family planning has resulted in very substantial numbers of births being averted during the period of operation of the National Program in the study area.

6.3 DECISION TO ACCEPT FAMILY PLANNING

A series of questions were asked of the 705 women who had ever used family planning to elucidate their reasons for initial acceptance, and to examine the role of social pressure at the local (village or banjar) level in the decision-making process.

In response to the question 507: 'Can you recall any reasons or information given by the government as to why people should accept family planning?' The 680 responses were grouped as follows (see Table 6.15). Of the 70 percent who could recall any Government information, the answers tended to be strongly on personal aspects, e.g., 'limit or space your children for the future prosperity of your family', but only rarely 'limit your children to ensure that Indonesia's population does not grow too large'. In fact the 21 responses related to population pressure or problems were all obtained by one particular interviewer who, in informal discussion, showed great interest in the population situation of his country, which suggests prompting of respondents.

Also the responses to 'limit' or 'space' children do not really answer the question and probably conceal other motivations, although it will be argued later (Chapter 8) that a sizeable number of couples would not have made a purely personal decision to accept family planning, but would have followed the guidance of village (or banjar) authorities on the grounds that such behaviour was considered beneficial to the community.

What is striking about the data in Table 6.15 is how few replies there were which mentioned health of children (n=16) or of mother and child (n=18), although this may have been the reason implicit in a number of the 'limiting' or 'spacing' responses, had the interviewers probed more deeply.

It is also the case that much of the propaganda, in the form of posters to be seen in village clinics and banjar halls, emphasises that spacing or limiting childbearing can make life easier for women, but there is also some emphasis on the economic benefits of small families. However only two respondents replied that they recalled information suggesting that acceptance of family planning would leave the mother freer to work although economic reasons were of much greater importance in the personal reasons of

116

the couples for accepting family planning (see Table 6.16), comprising 20.8 percent of the replies.

TABLE 6.15
REASONS GIVEN BY GOVERNMENT FOR ACCEPTANCE OF FAMILY PLANNING.
(As recalled by respondents)

Number	%	Reason
174	25.6	LIMIT CHILDBEARING
146	21.5	SPACING CHILDREN
88	12.9	PROSPERITY OF CHILDREN/FAMILY
21	3.1	POPULATION PRESSURE/DENSITY
18	2.6	HEALTH OF FAMILY/MOTHER/MOTHER +CHILDREN
16	2.4	HEALTH OF CHILDREN ONLY
11	1.6	FOLLOW GOVT. PROGRAM
8	1.2	FORCED/MUSTFOLLOW F.P.PROGRAM
3	0.4	ADVISED CAN CHANGE/STOP LATER
2	0.3	MOTHER FREER TO WORK
2	0.3	ENSURE CHILDREN'S EDUCATION
191	28.1	FORGOTTEN/NEVER HEARD ANY INFORMATION
680	100%	

Source: 1980 survey.

TABLE 6.16
PERSONAL REASONS GIVEN BY RESPONDENTS FOR
FIRST CHOOSING TO ACCEPT FAMILY PLANNING.

Number	%	Reason
302	43.0%	Limiting Births
171	24.3%	Spacing Births
146	20.8%	Economic Reasons
52	7.4%	Government Pressure
4	0.6%	Following Others/As Example
13	1.8%	Forget/Don't Know
688	100%	

Source: 1980 survey.

In reply to the question on reasons why the respondent and her husband first decided to accept family planning, two-thirds were related to limiting and spacing births (n=473). A further 20.8 percent were for economic reasons, and 7.4 percent were said to be primarily due to government pressure (at the local level). The economic reasons ranged from their current situation being too poor to support more children to concern that their future economic well-being would be threatened by too many children.

The government pressure replies ranged from simply wishing to follow the government program or contribute to its success, to being forced

117

(dipaksa) by local officials (including the Family Planning Program field-worker, the kelian dinas, or the village policeman) sometimes with threats of a fine and, in one case, with the threat of expulsion from the village. These incidents of blatant pressure were, however, few in number. This is not to say that there was very little external pressure put on couples to accept family planning, but rather that if there was it was not seen as coming directly from the government. This will be followed up in Chapter 8.

6.3.1 Decision-Making Process

We have seen some of the reasons that respondents gave for their initial acceptance of family planning, and this section will examine more closely the decision making process: who was involved in the decision, and what external pressures if any, were brought to bear on the respondent. The possibilities are that before the introduction of the National Family Planning Program, Balinese couples wanted fewer children than they were having but either found existing methods of birth control to be unsatisfactory or not readily available. Alternatively, these couples may previously have wanted large families but since the 1960s circumstances changed such that high fertility in the 1970s had become less desirable. Finally, the rapid and widespread acceptance of family planning during the 1970s may have been motivated largely by an awareness of Indonesia's population problems and the desire to participate in the government's program to alleviate the situation.

TABLE 6.17
OTHER PEOPLE INVOLVED IN DECISION
TO ACCEPT FAMILY PLANNING.

Percent	Person
68.8%	Husband
8.3%	F.P.Fieldworker
7.4%	Respondent alone
3.9%	Kelian Dinas
3.4%	Nurse/Doctor/Healthworker
2.9%	Village Policeman
2.1%	Neichbours/Friends
1.7%	Family (Not Husband)
1.1%	Perbekel (Village Head)
0.3%	Balian (Trad.Healer)
100%	(N=712)

Source: 1980 survey.

When women who had at some time accepted use of family planning were asked who else had been involved in the decision, the vast majority indicated that only the husband had been involved (68.8%) (see Table 6.17). The other main individuals involved were the family planning fieldworkers (8.3%), kelian dinas (3.9%), nurse/doctor/health-worker (3.4%). There were several other categories all smaller than 3 percent, with friends, neighbours or other members of the family (other than the husband) being virtually negligible, surprisingly. The very high proportion of respondents indicating that only the husband had been involved in the decision must be viewed with caution as it does not necessarily mean that no external forces were operating on the couple via the husband. Unfortunately the respondent's husband was generally not present at the interview for further enquiries to be made. In the final chapter a case will be made that there were very powerful influences bearing on the husbands to encourage them and their wives to accept family planning and limit their childbearing.

The question of the extent of social pressure being applied by other women (neighbours, family, etc.,) is also of interest considering the widespread interest in the family planning status of members of the community which was apparent, particularly during the early days of the program. It was quite striking how ready Balinese women were to discuss their reproductive behaviour and/or problems. This made the interviewers' job much easier than it might otherwise have been, considering that privacy was impossible in many of the interviews as groups of small boys and girls followed the interviewers into each household and listened attentively to the details of the respondent's reproductive history.

It is important, however, to distinguish between interest in the behaviour of others, and attempting to influence their behaviour. One of the difficulties for some Western researchers in Bali is coming to terms with the different concept of privacy. The Balinese do not readily doubt the right of another to ask personal questions, but they are adept at avoiding direct answers to such questions if they don't wish to reply. On the other hand, a characteristic of immanent cultures such as that found in Bali, is a reluctance to try to alter the behaviour of others, or to express direct criticism, provided that such behaviour is not infringing social custom. This attitude is reflected in the responses to a question where respondents were asked for their opinion of a hypothetical couple in the same banjar, who already had 5 or 6 children but decided not to use family planning (Table 6.18).

TABLE 6.18
RESPONSES TO HYPOTHETICAL COUPLE REFUSING FAMILY PLANNING

Percent	Response
64.2%	Would not do or say anything/Doesn't Matter
11.1%	Suggest they use F.P.
9.1%	Bad/Better if they use F.P.
7.4%	If they can manage, doesn't matter
4.3%	If poor, must use F.P.
3.9%	'Poor them'/Would worry for them
100%	(N=584)

Source: 1980 survey.

Of the 584 replies, only 11 percent said that they would 'do' anything, usually to suggest that the couple should use family planning. The remainder varied from expressing disapproval, e.g. that such a situation was not good (9.1%), to pity for the mother or children (3.9%), to the majority stating that they would simply keep silent, that it is not their

119

business (64.2%). The overall feeling expressed by the women was that if the couple could care for the children in a satisfactory manner then the situation was no cause for concern. Had the hypothetical couple been given 8 or 9 children the replies might have been different.

It appears then that in the majority of cases, the decision to accept family planning was made by the couple themselves, without significant influence from informal sources such as neighbours, other family members, etc. This does not, however, exclude influences from more formal sources within the community, such as the banjar council. Indeed, it will later be argued that this institution has been of great importance in encouraging community members to accept family planning.

6.4   EXPERIENCES OF CONTRACEPTIVE PRACTICE

As described earlier in this chapter while 705 women (or couples) had ever used some form of modern contraception only 530 were currently using contraception at the time of the survey. However because some women have used family planning several times, the total number of periods of use of contraception is 878, comprising the 530 continuing periods of use by current users ('open') and a further 348 periods of past use which have stopped for one reason or another ('closed').

Naturally the more that contraception is used for spacing the greater will be the proportion of periods of family planning use which have been terminated. However the following table (6.19) indicates that only in one-third of cases where family planning use was terminated was the reason that the couple wanted another child. The remaining two-thirds stopped because of side-effects (41.8%); involuntary expulsion of an IUD (16.2%); method failure (6.4%); while 'having no further need' accounted for only 1.5 percent.

Within the major category, Side-Effects, the actual problem was described only as unspecified pain in many cases, although considering the distribution of methods used this would very often be the IUD, and consequently the pain would probably be stomach pain or cramps even though this was only specified by nine women. A more detailed examination of side-effects of use of the IUD follows.

There also appear in the list of side-effects, several, such as dizziness, poor vision, chest problems, hepatitis, for which there is no immediately obvious connection to contraceptive practice. It is possible that anaemia resulting from heavier menstrual periods may account for dizziness, but it is also possible that certain other conditions, either pre-existing, or developing during the period of contraceptive use, may be viewed by the woman as a direct consequence of contraceptive practice when in fact the condition occurred independently.

TABLE 6.19
REASONS FOR STOPPING FAMILY PLANNING USE (ALL METHODS)

Percent	n	Reason
41.8%	137	Side effects experienced*
33.8%	111	Wanted another child
16.2%	53	IUD Fell out/expelled
6.4%	21	Method failed/Pregnant
1.55%	5	No further need (Widow; Menopause)
0.3%	1	Forced to accept initially
100%	328	

*Side Effects Include: Unspecified pain (26.5%); Loss of body weight (3.0 %); Stomach pain (2.7%); Breakthrough bleeding (2.7%); Dizziness (1.5%); Poor vision (0.9 %); Nausea (0.9%); Heavier menstruation (0.6%); Chest problems (0.6%); Tiredness (0.6%); Vomiting (0.6%); Hepatitis (0.3%); Dissatisfied (0.3%); Fear that IUD would enter insides (0.3%); (100% = 137).

Source: 1980 survey.

6.4.1 Experience of Side-Effects of IUD Use

Of the 705 couples who had ever-used any modern family planning method some 95 percent (n=669) had used the IUD, and of those 470 were currently using an IUD. A sub-section of the survey questionnaire was aimed specifically at these women, regardless of whether or not they were continuing to use an IUD.

In answer to the question: 'Some women who use the Loop/IUD experience some problems. Have you ever experienced any problems while using the IUD?', some 360 (53.8%) of the women answered that they had experienced problems. These women were then asked whether they had ever experienced any of the specific problems listed, and also about any other problems not listed. The women mentioned, on average, three problems of varying degrees of severity and importance.

The problems experienced by those 360 women are listed in Table 6.20. One half experienced longer menstrual periods while using the IUD, and over 60 percent experienced heavier menstrual bleeding. Stomach pain and increased tiredness were each felt by 44 percent of the women, and about half (49.4%) experienced loss of body weight.

The consequences of the high incidence of heavier and longer menstrual periods, and the occurrence of breakthrough bleeding for some of the women are of both spiritual and corporeal nature. Entry to all temples is forbidden to menstruating women, nor can they be involved in the making of offerings, an almost daily duty in Bali, particularly in rural areas. Indeed in the past, women were obliged to wear a black sarong during menstruation to ensure that no mistakes would be made in regard to temple attendance. Although it is less common these days, in traditional households a husband would sleep in a separate room, sometimes a separate house, from his menstruating wife. During this time however, a Balinese woman may normally still prepare and cook food, unlike a Moslem woman.

121

TABLE 6.20
EXPERIENCE OF SIDE EFFECTS OF IUD USE

QUESTION: 'What were these problems that you experienced (felt), and did it/they occur regularly each month, or just occasionally?'

Problem	Regularly	Irregularly	Total	(% of 360)
Menstruation longer	99	83	182	(50.6%)
Menstruation heavier	159	63	222	(61.7%)
Breakthrough bleeding	55	31	86	(23.9%)
Stomach pain/Cramps	104	55	159	(44.2%)
Increased Tiredness	107	52	159	(44.2%)
Body weight decreased	178 (49.4%)			
Body weight increased	36 (10.0%)			

OTHER PROBLEMS:

White vaginal discharge	21	(5.8%)
Dizzy or Asthma	13	(5.8%)
Sick	13	(3.6%)
Vision disturbed	13	(3.6%)
Heart rate increased	4	(1.1%)
Itchiness/Odour	2	(0.6%)
Fever	1	(0.3%)
Blood pressure dropped	1	(0.3%)

Source: 1980 survey.

When questioned about the loss of body weight, the nurse at the clinic where most of the IUDs had been inserted said that she had seen women lose about three to five kilograms[51] and she believed that the women who experienced such weight losses were those who had been pressured, by either the village head, Banjar head, mobile medical teams which travel the rural areas, or someone else, into accepting the IUD against their wishes. She believed that this view (of a psychosomatic element) was supported by the example of a woman who came to the clinic asking to have the loop removed because she was losing weight, whereupon the nurse pretended to remove it and the woman's weight proceeded to increase! Also mentioned in 36 cases was weight gain although this does not tend to be viewed so much as a problem in moderate cases, as the 'ideal' body morphology tends to be slightly heavier than average.

6.4.2 Response to Side Effects

This raises the question of how the women responded to the experience of side-effects of IUD use. Over half of the women stopped (n=264) using the IUD, but of those who did not stop, nearly half (48.1%) did nothing, just putting up with the problems, while 42 percent went back to the clinic (doctor or nurse) where often they were given an injection.[52] Only 7 women said that they used traditional medicine to treat the problem, while 12 used one of the locally available analgesics (e.g., Bodrex).

The other response to the problems associated with IUD use was to stop using it. Of the 264 women who stopped, about half (46.6%) stopped because of side effects such as excessive menstrual bleeding; nausea;

122

stomach and chest pain; dizziness and affected vision. One quarter (25.0%) stopped to have another child; for one-fifth the loop fell out; 14 became pregnant accidentally, and 7 no longer needed protection, because of either menopause, widowhood, divorce or husband vasectomised.

When those who said that they had stopped using the loop were asked who had removed it, only 3 of the 250 women said that they had done so themselves. Of the remainder, 191 (76.4%) said that the doctor or nurse had removed it; 53 (21.2%) said it had spontaneously been expelled, many noting that this had occurred while they were washing or bathing in the river - coincidence or cold water?; one had the IUD removed by a Dukun (traditional healer), and two were uncertain whether it had in fact fallen out.

In determining the role of side-effects on the decision to stop using the IUD it is not surprising to find that the more different side-effects were experienced, the more likely a woman was to stop using. Of those women experiencing only one or two side-effects, 41.2 percent stopped, while of those with three side-effects 51.0 percent (n=51) stopped, and of those with four or more side-effects 68.6 percent (n=137) stopped.

To return to the 48 percent who experienced side-effects but did not stop using the IUD, there is some anecdotal evidence from fieldwork to suggest that Balinese women are capable of regarding physical discomfort as 'mind over matter' and thereby ignoring the problem. Also Jane Belo states that:

> ...there is an undercurrent of superstition in the Balinese mind that to 'give up' will cause weakness and increased vulnerability to the dangers of illness. For illness is conceived as imposed from the outside by malevolent forces, which lurk everywhere, ready to rush into the body of anyone whose strength and purity (both physical and spiritual) are for the time below the normal, outbalanced by the share of weakness and impurity which form a part of every human being. (Belo,1970:89)

This is not to say that Balinese women regard side-effects of IUD use in the same way as an illness, but it throws some light on their response to discomfort or pain.

When the nurse responsible for inserting IUDs at one of the village clinics was asked about the usual practice regarding the informing of clients about possible side-effects of IUD use, she replied that if the women were forewarned of all the possible side-effects they would be too afraid to have an IUD inserted! So her policy was only to advise the women to return if they had any problems, although as indicated only about 15 percent recalled having received even this information.

When considering the question of what could be done to reduce the incidence of side-effects, and increase continuation rates, it is necessary to consider the nature of the IUDs themselves, the insertion process, and their suitability for Balinese women.

The IUDs used by the Family Planning Program in Bali have generally been the well-known Lippes Loop available in the study villages in sizes B, C, and D (the smallest, A, is unavailable), although there has been limited use of the copper clad Multi-Load 250 device which is much more expensive. The selection of the appropriate size IUD is purely on the parity of the woman; nulliparous women are ineligible. Size B is for parity one women, size C for parities 2 or 3, and size D for parities 4 or more. Apparently a woman complaining of stomach pains or excessive bleeding would not normally have her IUD replaced with a smaller or more flexible one, even though it is conceivable that this would reduce the problem[53]. Considering that more than half of the women who had ever used IUDs had experienced problems, the vast majority of which were related to menstrual bleeding, stomach pain, etc., it seems that there may be alternative strategies which could be tested to try to reduce the incidence of side-effects.

This raises the point of the process of IUD insertion. In the clinics in the study villages (and probably elsewhere), the Lippes Loops are kept (nonsterile) in bulk in large bottles according to size.[54] When required, the plastic inserter and the IUD are placed for five minutes in a sterilising solution of dilute iodine in water, while the metal sound and other instruments are boiled in Lysol and water. At first sight this appeared to be possibly inadequate sterilisation for the loop and the inserter, but the low incidence of vaginal discharge (keputihan), characteristic of bacterial infection (only 21 or 3.0 percent of the 691 ever-users of a loop), suggests that infection may not be an important problem, particularly when compared to the incidence of other side-effects.

6.5 CONCLUSION

The data in this chapter have shown a remarkable consistency in the levels of current family planning use among all population groups. This is the same pattern as seen for the analysis of Java-Bali, 1976, by Freedman et al.(1981:4), although the levels in the present survey are somewhat higher than in 1976.

There are few substantial family planning use differentials, apart from economic score and husband's education; also some occupational categories are analytically interesting, but not important in terms of overall impact on fertility. Finally, there is a marked geographic differential whereby the isolated village of Bakas has a considerably lower prevalence rate than the other two villages, as well as being poorer and lacking in facilities such as a school and good health clinic.

While some observers have suggested that several forces may be operating separately on different sections of the population in Indonesia:

..the increases in contraceptive use among the (highest standard of living) group are attributable to modernization, while sheer Malthusian pressures coupled with access to new influences - including the information and services of the family planning program - may have worked together to increase contraceptive use among the poor (Freedman,et al.,1981:4), the patterns of use, and the limited range of methods used, suggest that family planning acceptance is being heavily influenced by social forces outside the individual couples concerned. This will be followed up in Chapter 8.

The influence of family planning use on fertility has been demonstrated as operating primarily through limiting of births, as indicated by the extension of the open livebirth intervals, and the consequent decrease in high order parity progression ratios. Also the births averted analysis supports the view that the use of family planning has been responsible for most of the substantial fertility decline in the study villages. The question of why family planning has received such widespread acceptance still remains, and will be examined in the following chapters.

CHAPTER 7
VALUE OF, AND ASPIRATIONS FOR CHILDREN

In the preceding chapters it was seen that fertility in the study area has declined dramatically in recent years (Chapter 5), and that the use of modern, program contraception has become widespread (Chapter 6), and yet there have been few changes in the social and economic sphere (Chapters 1 and 2) which can throw light on this remarkably rapid uptake of modern contraception. Can it be that in a predominantly rural agricultural society, children have long been of relatively low value in terms of the assistance that they provide their parents, or of such a cost to their parents that many parents have chosen to limit their childbearing as soon as acceptable contraceptive methods became readily available: that there was a latent demand for contraception before 1970? Or has Balinese society undergone recent changes which have altered the value of, and costs of children? It is difficult to obtain definitive answers to these questions and this study has only gone a short way to providing clues.

In recent years the study of how parents make their childbearing decisions has broadened from economic and sociological theories to include applications of social-psychological theories.[55] One such model was that of Hoffman (1972), and Hoffman and Hoffman (1973), which has been used as a framework in the cross-cultural study of value of children sponsored by the East-West Population Institute and described by Fawcett (1974) and Arnold (1975).

One of the features that a model such as this shares with the micro-economic models is the emphasis on the micro-unit of decision-making. According to both these approaches, the fertility decisions of parents are made by their weighing up the benefits or values deriving from having children against the costs incurred in rearing those children. The 'value of children' studies such as that conducted by the East-West Population Institute tended to gather mainly attitudinal and descriptive information, but there have also been a number of studies which have concentrated on trying to obtain precise estimates of type and duration of work performed by children (see White,1976; Hull,1975; Cain,1977).

While the present study was not in this mould in terms of collecting precise data on hours spent by children on different tasks, nevertheless it is hoped that by utilising the information that was collected, combined with knowledge of tasks which Balinese children perform, it will be possible to draw some conclusions on the value of children in Bali.

7.1 ROLES OF CHILDREN

As described in Chapter 5, the capacity to bear children is considered of such importance in Balinese society that a number of marriages are not performed until the girl has become pregnant. The explanation of the importance of parenthood, and therein the first of the 'returns' from childbearing, is involved and complex and requires a temporary diversion at this stage to explain how the individual Balinese passes through many stages in life and in death, some of which are marked by ceremonies, while others such as parenthood and grandparenthood are marked by a change of name.

7.1.1 Social Value of Parenthood

The conjugal couple is usually considered to be an essential unit for most social purposes in Bali as stated by Geertze and Geertze: 'membership in any temple congregation, in the hamlet organisation, in an irrigation society, all require the joint participation of a man and a woman, preferably a husband and wife' (1975:90). In such hamlets, it seems that a young man can, and indeed must, join the hamlet council at his marriage and remain a member as long as he is capable of carrying out the demands deriving from such membership, or until he is replaced by a married son.[56]

While marriage and subsequent membership of the banjar council bring an elevation in social standing to a couple, it is the custom of teknonymy, wherein the parents take the name of the first born child, which illustrates the stress placed on fertility in the conferring of social status. As Geertz points out, one of the effects of teknonymy is:

> ...to identify the husband and wife pair, rather as the bride's taking on of her husband's surname does in our society; except that here it is not the act of marriage which brings about the identification but of procreation. Symbolically, the link between husband and wife is expressed in terms of their common relation to their children, grandchildren...(1966:24).

It is the most recent addition to the line of descent which is the focus in Bali. What matters is 'not who one's ancestor is, or was, ...but who one's descendent is, whom one is ancestor to' (Geertz and Geertz,1975: 90). Thus the importance of parenthood:

> ...a man who has never had a child remains all his life a child terminologically. When all of his age-mates have become 'father of-' and 'grandfather of-', he retains his childhood name, and the shame of this is often very deeply felt.

So it is not the quantitative aspect of reproductive capacity that is considered critical, it is the number of generations which stem from a person that bestows status. Elevation of status occurs in 'quantum leaps' with no gradation between generations. For example, a couple with four children has the same status as a couple with eight children (other things being equal), and both couples are lower in status than a couple with only a single child who in turn has a single child. This situation is unlike so many traditional communities, particularly in Africa where status increases in proportion to the number of children a man has. In Bali, however, the wellbeing and stability of the community is paramount: 'What counts is reproductive continuity, the preservation of the community's ability to perpetuate itself just as it is' (Geertz,1966:25).

7.1.2 Activities of Children

For some time after birth a Balinese child is viewed as a small god, also often the reincarnation of one or more ancestors, an individual who, while independent in terms of rights, is not responsible for its actions and requires a certain lenient guidance from the parents. However, by the age of two or three years, the children live in a 'children's republic', according to Covarrubias (1937:132), and are permitted considerable freedom

127

to spend time with their age-mates, outside the home.

A change which follows the end of the early independent stage is that the child is expected to assist its parents in a number of ways, particularly if a female (see Table 7.1). Young girls can frequently be seen caring for their younger siblings, freeing the mother to work. The girls also assist by learning at an early age to make the daily offerings to the gods and spirits. This requires the collection of coconut fronds, banana leaves and flowers to be cut and woven into a variety of shapes. On certain days of the Balinese calendar, rice must be moulded into shapes and cooked in small packets, later to be distributed to the appropriate temple or shrine. While it is possible to purchase some of these offerings in street stalls (warungs) usually one or more female members of the household must spend a considerable amount of time in their preparation.

Although the groups of youngsters seen wandering through the villages are composed mainly of boys, giving the distinct impression that they are not required to do any work, in fact, four and five year old boys can be seen performing specific tasks such as washing water buffalo, minding ducks in the field, scaring birds from the ripening rice, etc.

Apart from the latter duty, young children tend not to be included in the variety of tasks associated with rice production, although traditionally they could follow the harvesting teams and gather up and keep any dropped rice heads or grains. When they grow older and stronger, boys are often expected to help with ploughing, and girls with weeding and hulling the gabah (rice), but the most important steps such as planting and harvesting tend to be carried out by teams (seka, see Chapter 2) of adults from the same banjar. For religious reasons rice planting is carried out only by men, unlike in Java, but harvesting can be carried out by women or men. With changes occurring in rice production, some of the traditional jobs for children are being lost. Most of the gabah will be husked in a cooperative owned/built slip or mill with diesel-powered, rubber-rollered hullers. The new high yielding varieties of rice are not attractive to birds, thus 'scarecrows' are required now only in the occasional plots of traditional 'padi Bali'. There is even a limited trend towards roving harvesting teams operating on a cash basis (see Chapter 2, and Astika, 1978:47).

In the study villages, Tusan and Bakas, when water was unavailable for wet rice production (alternate years), the land was used to grow corn, cassava, sweet potato and various leafy vegetables, thus there was a frequent demand for children to scour the family plot to gather such produce.

Thus the role of young children in agriculture appears to be less important in Bali than in some other agricultural societies such as Java where White's detailed research led him to conclude that Javanese children 'most probably have a net positive economic value to their parents in these villages' (White,1976:311-27). The same conclusion was reached in a similar household study in Nepal (Nag, Peet and White,1977:138), and also the study by Cain in Bangladesh (Cain,1977:224)

While the present study was not of the same type as those mentioned above, the overall impression, particularly in light of recent developments in agriculture, is that children's participation in agricultural activities was very limited. This conclusion was also reached by Hull from his research in Java (Hull,1975:251-60). Although this is not to say, as Mueller has, that 'children have negative economic value in peasant agriculture' (1975:70), rather that their value is marginal.

With a system of inheritance (waris) whereby farm land is, in principle, divided equally amongst all the sons and any unmarried daughters it is not surprising that average sawah plot size has declined dramatically in recent generations and that present day farmers are very concerned about the further fragmentation of their land, as indicated by the desire of the majority of farmers that their children prepare for non-farming occupations (see Chapter 7.2 regarding aspirations for children's jobs). In practice it seems that when plot size is subdivided to a certain size, it is accepted that the farm would no longer be viable if divided further so one of the sons would take responsibility for the whole farm and arrange to buy out the other brothers over time. Indeed, the children of farmers in the study villages frequently expressed despair that they would ever be able to afford to buy farmland of their own. With monthly salaries, even for civil servants, ranging from Rs.15,000 to 30,000, it would clearly be an onerous task to save sufficient money to purchase the generally accepted minimum of 30 Ares necessary to support a family with three or four children. The cost of this land in desa Banjarangkan would be Rs.3 to 4 million. In the less well irrigated areas where unit cost is lower, e.g., Tusan and Bakas, more land would be required for the same output.

As a consequence of this situation young people in the study villages, if they had limited education, were aiming at finding work as labourers in the roof-tile factories, quarries, farms, on road repair gangs, etc., or if more adventurous, in the tourist industry or business in the capital, Denpasar; and if they have sufficient education many hope to enter the civil service.

An important reason for parents to encourage their children to enter the cash economy is the frequent need for cash, not only for the educational expenses of the younger siblings in the household, but for the ceremonies involved along the path to adulthood. As will be described in the following section (7.2) on costs of childbearing and rearing, each major milestone in a child's life must be commemorated with an appropriate ceremony. The costs of the priest, food for guests, and entertainment, can be very considerable, and 98 percent of respondents expected their sons to assist in this when they were earning; 73 percent expected daughters to contribute (Table 7.1).

Another major factor, which has contributed to the growing dependence on cash in everyday life, has been the shift from traditional rice varieties to the new high yielding types of rice. The traditional varieties could be stored for years on the stalk (as gabah) in the family rice barn (lumbung), and a portion removed when required, only to be husked to be ready for cooking (Mears,1981:141). As long as sufficient rice was stored, there was no need to purchase rice in the market. The new varieties, however, do not store well but rather deteriorate markedly within a year of harvesting. Thus the normal practice now is to sell most of one's rice crop in the market immediately after it is harvested, then later purchase (using cash) different rice in the market. A common pattern is that when the time comes to purchase more rice, the money obtained from the previous harvest has been spent. Thus it is useful, at such times, if the parents can call upon a working son or unmarried daughter for financial assistance.

It is largely for such cash requirements that 80 percent of parents expect their sons to send remittances home once they start paid work. That only 41 percent expect the same of a daughter reflects the different attitude to daughters who, upon finishing school and starting work, are seen to be preparing to leave their immediate family.   On marrying, the daughter will become responsible to, and the responsibility of, her husband's family.   In theory a daughter, once married, cuts all ties with her parents, no longer worshipping the ancestors of her parents but rather those of her husband and his family.   In practice she will often maintain contact and, as reflected in parental expectations of help in old age, will often contribute to the support of her parents, though she is under no formal obligation to do so.

TABLE 7.1

EXPECTATIONS OF HELP FROM SONS AND DAUGHTERS

(i) SONS ONLY

Type of Assistance	Percentage Responding			n
	Yes	No	Don't Know	
Help Around House	85.5	13.5	1.0	1048
Help in Farming	82.2	14.5	3.3	1025
Care for Siblings	65.3	28.8	5.9	1030
Help Parents Work	85.8	8.0	6.2	1045
-When receiving income:				
Give Money for Ceremonies	97.5	1.2	1.2	1050
Remit Part Income Home	80.2	12.2	7.6	1050
Help Parents in Old Age	98.0	0.9	1.1	1051

(ii) DAUGHTERS ONLY

Type of Assistance	Percentage Responding			n
	Yes	No	Don't Know	
Help around House	94.3	4.0	1.6	1040
Help in Farming	47.5	46.9	5.7	1020
Care for Siblings	89.9	4.9	5.2	1017
Help Parents Work	89.6	3.9	6.6	1037
-When receiving income:				
Give Money for Ceremonies	73.1	22.8	7.1	1043
Remit part Income Home	41.1	42.3	16.4	1043
Help Parents in Old Age	59.3	23.9	17.6	1038

(Source: 1980 survey for all tables in this chapter)

Probably the most obvious and important factor behind the growing demand for cash has been the expansion of the range of goods and services competing for the financial resources of the family. The influx of consumer goods which are both desirable and within reach of an average poor household, for example, domestic items like torches, kerosene lamps, radios, cooking utensils, plastic buckets for water or agricultural implements such as sickles, steel plough blades, hoes, etc., is relatively recent. As described in Chapter 2, Bali remained isolated from the outside world rather longer than many other areas of Indonesia, partly because the Balinese were not seafarers, and partly because of the unwelcoming nature of the island's coastline.

As everywhere, parents in Bali are concerned that they will be secure and cared for in old age. With the custom of having several households[57] within a family houseyard or compound (see Chapter 2), it is most uncommon for a couple to be living alone in old age, or indeed at any time in their lives.

When a man's son becomes a parent, the son may take responsibility for the family agricultural land even though he and his brothers do not inherit it until the father dies. Also the responsibility for the wellbeing of the parents rests with all the sons, even though very often only one married son will remain living in the same houseyard as the father, the others having to move out on marrying.

The last major duty for which children are called upon to assist their parents is the funeral and cremation of the latter. To the Balinese Hindu, the cremation ritual must be carried out to release the spirit from its earthly body, and allow it to join the pool of deified ancestors to which all spirits aspire. The cremation is traditionally an expensive, and often spectacular affair requiring the efforts not only of all family members, but also of the members of the <u>banjar</u> to which the deceased belonged. In past times, the body was normally interred after the funeral, sometimes for many years while the family saved to pay for an appropriate cremation; however, the present government has been trying to encourage cremation as soon as possible after death. For this, and other reasons, the extravagant cremations seen in the past are much less frequent these days. Nevertheless, it is still a substantial expense for most families, since, as with most ceremonies in Bali, the cost is not uniform but should be proportional to one's wealth, or more specifically, one's wealth and status.

To summarise this section, the roles performed by Balinese children are quite similar to those of Javanese children with the exception of certain practices associated with wet rice production. In Bali certain aspects of rice growing, such as planting, are only performed by men; others, such as harvesting, only by groups of adults. The remaining tasks provide a limited capacity to absorb child labour depending on the size of agricultural plot, and the nature of the crop grown. The increased availability of education, and a growing concern that agriculture will not continue to be a reliable source of work, has resulted in parents turning to other avenues to ensure their children's wellbeing, and in turn, their own. This increasing emphasis on preparing children for occupations which require a number of years of schooling will be examined further in Chapter 7.2.

7.2   COSTS OF CHILDREARING

There are a number of aspects to the examination of significant costs of childrearing, and the changes over time. These include changes in the actual costs of types of, say, food, which may have always had to be bought rather than grown or made; there are changes in the system of payment where formerly a credit or barter system may have been the practice, now cash is required; and there is an expansion in the variety of goods or services considered desirable, transistor radios being an example of the former, education of the latter.

A generation or more ago, the major costs of childbearing and rearing for the typical Balinese family would have been ceremonies and food. The family would have had a wide network of relatives upon whom they could call in times of need, for example, to assist with labour, goods or money for a major family ceremony; or in normal times by a reciprocal arrangement whereby children could eat, from time to time, in a cousin's or uncle's house. As Hull says about Bali:

> ...the child's natural parents bear only a portion of the costs - and reap only a portion of the rewards of childbearing, the rest being 'externalized to the other household members, the child himself, and the larger community'(1978:4).

Recent work on this support network, however, suggests that it is shrinking. The degree of kin distance of a relative to whom one can turn and reasonably expect help, is decreasing. Conversely, one's former obligations to, say, first and second cousins might now apply only as far as first cousins (Cole,1980, personal communication,1980). Certain other supports have also weakened in recent times.

There are no longer the big ceremonies conducted in the past, by the royal families, which served to redistribute special foods (e.g., turtle satay) to the general populace. These ceremonies provided a regular, if not frequent, source of a variety of nutritious foods for the poor who, otherwise, might not have been able to obtain them.

At the same time as the support network is declining in importance, the cost of food is rising. In real terms the cost of rice, though subsidised, has increased about five times since 1972 while wages have not risen nearly as much as that. And now a much greater proportion of rice consumed has to be purchased in the market rather than stored as homegrown produce (see Chapter 7.1).

7.2.1   Life Cycle Ceremonies

The cost of ceremonies has also risen markedly in recent years, partly because of increased food prices, but also because of the astronomical increase in gold prices during the 1970s. While in theory silver can be substituted, gold is believed to possess magical protective properties which make it far more desirable for the amulets, bracelets, etc., so vital a part of many of the early life cycle ceremonies (Covarrubias,1937:129). Because of the nature of the costs of childrearing, there are few 'economies of scale' within a family, the cost being largely for the guests' food, for musicians or <u>wayang kulit</u> (shadow play), etc., which cannot be held over for the next child, although certain pieces of jewellery can be handed down.

To give an indication of the expenditure involved in childhood ceremonies, and the seriousness with which they are taken, data are presented for estimated expenditure by couples on the most recent first oton ceremony. This ceremony is conducted promptly, though on an auspicious day, when the child is 210 days old (6 Bali months). The ceremony is taken most seriously because it is at this point in the child's life, when it has survived the hazardous early months, it is introduced to its ancestors. It is considered vital that the ancestors be aware of the child's existence as it is they who oversee and protect the child on its journey through life.

In Table 7.2 what is surprising is that the mean expenditures for the very poor (economic score,0-19), poor (20-199) and medium (200-299) groups, constituting over 80 percent of the families, are almost identical, being a little less than the overall mean of Rs.36,000 (A$50). Also the distributions as reflected in proportions of couples in each group spending Rs.10,000 or less, and spending more than Rs.50,000, indicate a minimum necessary expenditure on bracelets and anklets for the child, and for the entertainment and food which usually includes luxuries which the hosts and many of the guests would not normally eat, other than at such ceremonies.

TABLE 7.2

EXPENDITURE ON FIRST OTONAN, ACCORDING TO ECONOMIC SCORE

| OTON Cost | Economic Score | | | | | |
	0-19	20-199	200-299	300-899	900+	Total
UP TO 10,000	23.5	22.1	21.1	16.0	10.3	20.5
10,001-15,000	16.3	12.9	11.9	16.0	4.1	13.0
15,001-25,000	23.5	28.4	27.0	24.5	29.9	26.5
25,001-50,000	23.5	27.3	25.9	28.7	32.0	26.5
50,001-100,000	11.7	6.3	11.9	9.6	12.4	10.2
Over 100,000	1.5	3.0	2.0	5.3	11.3	3.3
	100 %	100 %	100 %	100 %	100 %	100 %
Mean (Rs.)	31,300	33,200	33,900	42,700	63,200	36,600
Numbers	(264)	(271)	(293)	(94)	(97)	(1019)

As mentioned earlier in this chapter, ceremonies and food were the two most significant expenses in childrearing in the past. To these has been added education (see Table 7.3) which is becoming increasingly widespread.

The less obvious, but still possibly significant expense, is the lost 'opportunity' cost where, by going to school, the child is not directly assisting the parents or indirectly freeing the mother to work outside the home, or working away from the family and remitting income.

133

TABLE 7.3
MAJOR EXPENSES IN CHILDREARING

	Percentage
Ceremonies	35.0
Food	28.7
Education	22.3
Daily Living	4.7
Health	2.1
Other	4.7
Not Applicable	2.5
Total	100% (N=1088)

(N.B.: This is the category stated as greatest expense, although about one third of mothers mentioned more than one category.)

7.2.2 Educational Aspirations

The data in Table 7.4 show that 88 percent of respondents indicated that all their children would get some schooling, only 9 percent saying that they would be selective about which children attended school.   Of those respondents who were selective, 7 out of 10 said that it would be only the boys who would receive some education.

TABLE 7.4
RESPONSES TO QUESTION REGARDING WHICH CHILDREN
ARE EXPECTED TO RECEIVE SOME SCHOOLING

Response	Percentage
All children	88.0
Some children only	9.2
Not applicable	2.9
Total	100% (N=1088)

While there is relatively little selectivity according to sex in terms of which children will receive some education, the survey data showed a slight preference for sons to receive education beyond primary school (Table 7.5).   While the proportion of respondents expecting their children to complete primary school is around 90 percent for both sons and daughters, the proportion expecting their children to complete senior high (secondary) school was 41 percent for sons and 33 percent for daughters.

In regard to the effect of parents' education on hopes for children's education, for the higher levels of intended education for sons, e.g., senior secondary school, the proportion rises steadily from 18.9 percent for fathers with no education, to 49.0 percent for fathers who have completed primary school, to 85.9 percent for fathers who have senior secondary education themselves (Table 7.5).

134

For daughters' intended education, the pattern is similar, although the levels are a little lower. The proportion of parents intending to send their daughters to senior secondary school rises from 13.7 percent for fathers with no education, to 37.7 percent for fathers with completed primary schooling, to 83.3 percent for fathers with senior secondary (Table 7.5).

TABLE 7.5
ASPIRATIONS FOR CHILDRENS' EDUCATION (Cumulated Percent)
ACCORDING TO EDUCATION OF RESPONDENT'S HUSBAND

Husband's Education	Expected Level Achieved			
	Primary School		Senior Secondary	
	Sons	Daughters	Sons	Daughters
No Education	96.5	86.4	18.9	13.7
Some Primary	91.7	86.7	31.4	23.7
Complete Primary	90.8	89.6	49.0	37.7
Junior Secondary	90.3	89.9	64.0	53.2
Senior Secondary	92.9	92.4	85.9	83.3
University	90.0	95.0	90.0	90.0
Total	92.5%	88.2%	41.2%	33.2%

As higher education tends, in Indonesia, to be associated with higher status and higher income, it would be expected that those parents with the highest education levels would also score highly in economic status and thus be more able to support their children through school. This proved to be the pattern (Streatfield, 1982:405) with the parents from the wealthiest group (economic score of 900+) making up 41 percent of the parents expecting their children to obtain tertiary education while they comprise only 9.4 percent of total respondents. Although the wealthier families had higher aspirations for education of their children than the poorer families, even the poorest families (economic score of 0-19) had quite high hopes for their children. Of this group about two-thirds (64.4 percent) expected their sons and about half (55.3 percent) expected their daughters to go on beyond primary school.

It is possible, of course, that parents' intentions do not match actuality in regard to their children's education. While data were not gathered on achieved or current levels of education of the respondents' children, the data gathered on parents' aspirations for their children's education and subsequent occupation suggest that considerable emphasis is now being placed on education as a path to a secure job which it may be hoped will ultimately benefit the parents.

7.2.3 Occupation Aspirations for Children

The aspirations of parents for their children's education leads natur-ally to the question: what are the parents' aspirations for jobs for their children on completing their education?[58] The data in Tables 7.6a and 7.6b indicate a remarkable concentration of occupational aspirations into the category of civil servant. While only 12.5 percent of the children's

135

fathers, and 2.3 percent of mothers, fall into this category themselves virtually two-thirds (64.6 percent) hope that their sons will become civil servants, and half (51.1 percent) want the same for their daughters.

TABLE 7.6a

PARENTS' ASPIRATIONS FOR OCCUPATION OF SONS,
ACCORDING TO RESPONDENT'S HUSBAND'S OCCUPATION

Husband's Occupation	Farmer	Civil Servant	Profess- ional	Other	Whatever	Total	n
Farmer	18.0	65.0	1.2	4.4	11.4	100%	(428)
Civil Svt.	3.2	71.4	10.3	1.6	13.5	100%	(126)
Entrepreneur	4.8	85.7	4.8	4.8	0	100%	(21)
Other	7.7	70.8	3.1	10.8	7.7	100%	(65)
Labourer	23.5	57.5	0	4.8	14.3	100%	(294)
Unemployed	23.1	46.2	0	15.4	15.4	100%	(13)
Total	16.4	64.6	2.1	4.9	12.1	100%	(1010)

Job Aspired to for Sons

TABLE 7.6b

PARENTS' ASPIRATIONS FOR OCCUPATION OF DAUGHTERS,
ACCORDING TO RESPONDENT'S HUSBAND'S OCCUPATION

Husband's Occupation	Farmer	Civil Servant	Profess- ional	Other	Whatever	Total	n
Farmer	16.7	49.8	0.2	22.3	11.0	100%	(420)
Civil Svt.	4.8	71.0	5.6	6.4	12.1	100%	(124)
Entrepreneur	9.1	77.3	0	13.6	0	100%	(22)
Other	15.0	61.7	1.7	11.7	5.0	100%	(60)
Labourer	24.0	38.7	0	21.9	15.3	100%	(300)
Unemployed	16.7	41.7	0	25.0	16.7	100%	(12)
Total	16.9	51.1	0.9	19.3	11.8	100%	(999)

Job Aspired to for Daughters

The father's current occupation had little bearing on this variable except for those who were labourers (or the 13 unemployed) where just under a quarter hoped that their children would become farmers, compared to one sixth overall. It is striking that of the largest category of current occupation, farmers (n=428 or 42 percent), the occupational aspirations were so markedly toward the civil service for their sons (65 percent) and daughters (50 percent).

The patterns of occupation aspired to for both sons and daughters according to respondents' husband's education and economic score are as expected. The higher the level of education or the higher the economic score the more likely the parents are to expect their children to become civil servants or professionals (see Streatfield, 1982:412-14).

It is interesting that many writers point to the fact that education raises children's aspirations even if there is little possibility of such aspirations ever being realised, e.g.:

It is true that many rural youth who have gone beyond primary school are reluctant to work in agriculture and that many of them leave the villages in search of urban employment (Sinaga, 1978:111).

Such a statement implies that it is the educated youth who aspires to an occupation outside agriculture, possibly to the regret of his farming parents, whereas the data presented above suggest that the parents are very much involved in encouraging such aspirations.

7.3 DESIRE FOR ADDITIONAL CHILDREN

There has been considerable disagreement about the real meaning and validity of questions regarding ideal family size in different societies, the argument usually centring around the belief in many societies that the number of children one has is up to god, fate, destiny (Ware,1974). Also the answers of many women are influenced by the number of children that they already have. Data on desires for additional children are more reliable and take into account the present situation of the women. Analysis of data on desire for additional children, while controlling for various demographic characteristics of women, can indicate which women are most likely to try to prevent future births and will therefore be most amenable to family planning (see Chapter 6.1).

The data in Table 7.7 show an implied ideal family size calculated by adding mean number of additional children wanted to the mean number of children still living (CSL). However, unlike the World Fertility Survey, the present survey did not ask whether the last child was wanted, thus this calculation assumes that all the children still living were desired. The mean ideal family size was 3.7 (mean of 3.1 plus mean extra children wanted of 0.6). The mean ideal family size obtained by the FM survey in Bali, 1973 was also 3.7 children (FM Report,1974:29). Taking the above limitation into account, one could assume that the desired number of children at the time of the survey was around 3.5, although it is notable that some 43 percent claim a desired family size of less than three children (i.e., those with CSL of 0, 1 or 2).

The effect of age on desire for additional children is as expected. The older the woman the more likely she is 'not' to want any additional children. The proportions wanting no additional children increased from 8.7 percent for women aged 15-19 years to 32.6 percent (20-29 years), to 72.0 percent (30-39 years) to 95.4 percent of those aged 40-44 years (Streatfield,1982:417). This pattern largely holds even when controlled for the number of living children.

This does not necessarily mean that older women have a lower 'ideal family size' but is more probably due to the concern to have no more children once becoming a grandparent. The belief that grandmothers should not become mothers is very much in keeping with the Balinese view that individuals, ideally, are reincarnated through a series of lives on the way to the next, and hopefully last, life on earth.

137

TABLE 7.7
NUMBER OF CHILDREN STILL LIVING
PLUS ADDITIONAL CHILDREN WANTED[*]

(a) CSL	(b) Addtl.Children Wanted(mean)	(a + b) Current IFS	n
0	2.2	2.2	61
1	1.6	2.6	150
2	0.7	2.7	257
3	0.3	3.3	233
4	0.14	4.1	140
5	0.03	5.0	120
6	0.01	6.0	79
7+	0		48
Means			Total
3.1	0.6	3.7	1,088

(Current IFS: * If extra children wanted equals zero, it is
assumed that R wanted all previous children.
No way to determine otherwise).

When the sex of desired additional children according to the sex
pattern of living children is examined (Table 7.8) the desire for a balance
of both male and female children becomes obvious, although underlying that
is a somewhat more marked desire to restore the balance if it is deficient
in males.

TABLE 7.8
SEX BALANCE OF DESIRED ADDITIONAL CHILDREN
BY COUPLES WITH 0 TO 3 LIVING CHILDREN,
ACCORDING TO SEX BALANCE OF
CHILDREN STILL LIVING

Children Still Living		Sex Balance of Desired Additional Children(%)					
Male	Female	Male	Female	Either	Both	Total	n
0	0	2.0	0	52.0	46.0	100%	(50)
1	0	4.5	36.4	39.4	19.7	100%	(66)
0	1	53.4	0	24.1	22.4	100%	(58)
1	1	19.4	0	69.4	11.3	100%	(62)
2	0	2.9	80.0	14.2	2.9	100%	(35)
0	2	86.7	3.3	6.6	3.3	100%	(30)
2	1	0	62.5	37.5	0	100%	(16)
1	2	80.0	0	15.0	5.0	100%	(20)

For couples with no CSL, virtually all want either or both sons and daughters, only 2 percent specifying boys only. Where there is an existing imbalance, for example, one son and no daughters, 36 percent want a daughter specifically, while if they have no son and one daughter, 53 percent want a son specifically. The specificity is stronger where the couple have two children of the same sex. On the other hand where the couple's children comprise son and daughter, the percentage not specifying the sex of the additional child desired (i.e., replying 'either') jumps to 69 percent. Once a couple has two children of the same sex, plus one of the other sex, none of the couples want a third child of the same sex.

These results support the data presented above (Chapter 7.1.2) on roles of Balinese children. There it was suggested that becoming parents was of great importance to married couples, but this was not directly proportional to the total number of children produced, only the first child being the source of increased prestige. It was also described how there are a number of activities wherein sons and daughters have sex-specific contributions to make. These are of both a secular kind, as in agriculture and descent for sons, and a religious kind, as in daughters making the frequent household offerings for the gods.

7.4 CONCLUSION

At the beginning of the chapter the question was asked 'was there a longstanding latent demand for family planning before the Family Planning Program came into being around 1970 or has Balinese society undergone social and economic changes during the decade of the seventies which have raised the costs and lowered the value of children?'

The answer is that there have clearly been certain social and economic changes over the decade which have changed the value of children and these have occurred in a context where there probably was some pre-existing latent demand for satisfactory means of controlling fertility.

Before 1970 marital fertility in Bali was relatively high but the social network was such that this level of fertility could be absorbed without too much difficulty. Costs of childrearing were relatively low and diffused through a strongly supportive network of kin and fellow banjar members. On the other hand, apart from the initial elevation of a married couple to the socially functional level of parents, repeated childbearing does not appear to have been particularly advantageous. The high levels of fertility pre-1970 were more by default than due to high demand. Available methods of fertility control were inconvenient, not always effective, and often unsafe.

The severe problems of land shortage have changed the orientation of what is basically an agricultural society towards what will become a 'service' society. The concern over agriculture as a viable occupation for the next generation has coincided with a dramatic increase in emphasis on education. This is partly government development strategy and partly an almost desperate attempt by parents to ensure secure employment for their chidren. At this time secure employment very largely means a civil service job. The hope for employment of children in the civil service is remarkably widespread and crosses all economic strata in the society. What this requires is a large investment in just a few children. That this process is taking place is reflected in the rapid rise in school attendance in Bali and in parents' high aspirations for their children's education and, later, occupation.

While there were, in the past, a number of activities carried out primarily by children, there are none which can be carried out only by children. A number of the former roles of small children have even become redundant with the changes in agriculture and the decline in the average size of agricultural landholdings.

There is no suggestion that childbearing is being replaced altogether by the rising demand for consumer goods and services. Rather that the important functions of childbearing, both social and economic, can be fulfilled with just a few children. The data on desired family size indicated that a balance of at least one child of each sex with another of either sex was considered ideal. This pattern results from the fact that, on the one hand, both sons and daughters have sex-specific roles to play, while there are also sex-specific costs such as the subdivision of family agricultural land amongst all sons and the loss of the daughter from the household at marriage. This situation requires that a couple have some children but may disadvantage them if they have many. Also, the recent decline in infant mortality means that the desired number of surviving children can be attained with fewer births than in the past.

CHAPTER 8
CONCLUSION
THE BALINESE SETTING AND FAMILY PLANNING
'A Climate Favourable to a Take-Off'

It is useful at this stage to briefly recapitulate the major findings. These fall into three areas: fertility levels and trends; family planning levels and the effect on fertility levels; social or economic factors underlying the uptake of family planning and the subsequent fertility decline.

In Chapter 5 it was seen that in the study villages there had been a substantial fertility decline during the 1970s. During the 1960s the total fertility rate (TFR) was high and constant. After 1970 the TFR fell from about 6.5 to 3.6. The timing of the decline coincided with the introduction of the National Family Planning Program. The decline was not due to changes in marriage but to marital fertility falling some 45 percent over a decade. The marital fertility decline was concentrated in the older, over 30 age group, which is consistent with the pattern of family planning acceptance primarily by older, higher parity women. There was very little change in fertility levels among women aged less than 25 years.

The most important aspect of the fertility differentials was the marked lack of variation. With the possible exception of woman's education, there were no important differentials among economic or social variables. Although women with primary education had somewhat lower fertility than their less educated sisters the difference averaged less than one child ever-born. This differential was maintained in the group of female civil servants. This small, low fertility group was composed largely of well educated women who are exposed to certain incentives, in addition to local social pressure, to limit their childbearing.

The pattern of family planning use was that of rapid and widespread rise in acceptance (see Chapter 6). This was primarily use of the IUD obtained from the National Family Planning Program. There was very little use of privately obtained modern contraceptives, or traditional contraception or abortion, either before or during the operation of the program. While the prevalence level had reached about half of eligible couples at the time of the survey, there were remarkably few social or economic differentials in use. This pattern is consistent with the absence of fertility differentials. Births averted analysis indicated that the substantial overall fertility decline was almost entirely due to the use of program contraception, mainly to limit higher parity births rather than for spacing.

In Chapter 7, the role of children in Balinese society was examined. It was seen that there is a great incentive for a married couple to bear a child, and the social functioning of the couple is strongly dependent on this. Thereafter, however, the benefits of childbearing are not directly related to the number of children borne.

While agriculture still absorbs the majority of the working population, the distribution of land is such that the labour of numerous children

is no longer a necessity.   The growing concern over the future of agriculture, as well as a high regard for knowledge and the power that attends it,
has precipitated a universal demand for education.   Underlying this demand
is the hope that at least one child will succeed in finding secure, permanent employment, preferably in the civil service.   This far sightedness is
not only to ensure support in the parents' old age but, possibly more
importantly, because a contented afterlife requires the children to be in a
position to perform satisfactorily the appropriate ceremonies and offerings.

It has been shown that family planning was readily accepted and used
by the Balinese. The key question that remains to be answered concerns the
prevalence levels. Why was there such a rapid rise in prevalence levels in
Bali compared to other provinces?

To explain why this traditional, agricultural society apparently
willingly underwent a dramatic social change in fertility behaviour, three
categories of important factors will be presented.   The first category
includes aspects of the circumstances or setting in Bali at the time the
National Family Planning Program was introduced.   The second category
includes certain characteristics of the social structure which facilitated
the rapid spread of the concept of fertility limitation and ensured widespread conformity in the acceptance, and continued practice of family
planning.   The third category is that of aspects of the Family Planning
Program itself and the way it was implemented by the provincial BKKBN
office in Bali.   These factors will now be elucidated.

8.1 SETTING FACTORS

8.1.1 Land

The most important physical aspect of the setting at the time the
Family Planning Program began was that of land availability.   In Chapter 2
it was seen that between 1950 and 1970 the area of sawah (wet rice land)
had remained virtually unchanged at around 100,000 hectares, while the
population had increased by 40 percent.   Indeed, the area of sawah had
increased only slightly since 1930, although increases in productivity were
occurring due to the change to high yielding rice varieties, and to some
improvements in irrigation.   Thus, the situation in 1973 was that 37.7
percent of agricultural households did not own or rent any sawah.   For
those who did have access to some sawah, the average size of holding was
0.43 hectares which is approaching the minimum size of average quality
sawah which will support a household of five or six members.

The hopes of the Balinese peasants that the political system would
bring about increased access to farm land were probably not high.   The
Land Reform Act of 1960 had brought about some redistribution of land, but
the law was relatively easily circumvented (Parker: personal communication)
and the benefits were often shortlived. The depth of concern about the land
situation during the 1960s was reflected in the wide appeal of the platform
of the Indonesian Communist Party (PKI) who promised genuine land reform.
After the attempted coup of late 1965 the PKI was smashed and thereafter
there can have remained little optimism for substantial progress in the
availability of farmland through political action, even if there was
support for the New Order government of President Suharto.   Indeed such

pessimism has proved well-founded.   In 1973 the proportion of agricultural households owning no agricultural land whatever was already markedly higher in Bali (8.4%) than in the nation as a whole (3.2%), and the situation has since deteriorated.   By 1980 the proportion of agricultural households owning no agricultural land had risen to 23.4 percent in Bali compared to 14.9 percent for Indonesia as a whole (BPS,1980 Seri L7, Table 8; BPS,1973 Vol.1:208,Table 7.   Ironically, it appears that because Bali is so well endowed with well-irrigated, fertile rice land there is relatively little low-priced, marginal land which a poor peasant can purchase and eke out a living, if not a prosperous living.

Another factor which underlies this high proportion of landless agricultural households is the system of land inheritance.   In many areas the traditional system is that of equal portions of land inherited by all siblings, except married daughters.   As Wittfogel discusses at some length in 'Oriental Despotism' (1978:78), such arrangements must inevitably lead to fragmentation of landholdings (and reduction in average size) as has already occurred in Bali.   However, in practice, there seems to be an accepted minimum viable area of agricultural land which should not be subdivided.   When household sawah is reduced to around one-third of a hectare of good quality land the pattern appears to be for one son to take responsibility for working the entire plot.   He will gradually buy out the other siblings who would normally move out of the parental household upon marriage.   Many of the household plots of sawah are now sufficiently small that they can be managed by a single couple, particularly with the assistance of fellow banjar or subak members at planting or harvesting times. Thus a proportion of the children of farming families can no longer rely on receiving an allocation of land through natural inheritance.   If they wish to farm they must either rent or buy (or both) agricultural land, but for many the price is too high.   The alternatives are to try to obtain cheaper land often far from one's village of origin, or to transmigrate to another island.

There is a marked reluctance by the Balinese to move away from their village of origin, particularly to another island.   The nature of the bonds linking individuals to their community has been described in some detail by Lansing.   He discussed how 'the Balinese are "tied" (kaiket) from birth to a bewildering variety of obligations, duties, organisations, temples, places, people and things' (1974:1).   It is these links, or rather the groups to which one is tied, that provide the reference points for defining oneself.   In other words, kaiket emphasises a sense of the self as a social being.   It also emphasises the place of the self in hierarchies which are not exclusively social but merge into the realms of the divine (Lansing, 1974:27).

There are also more earthly reasons for such reluctance to move out of one's banjar.   On acceptance into another banjar one may expect many kinds of support but this may well not extend, for example, to financial support in times of need, support which would normally be expected from fellow banjar members who are also kin.

These factors which explain the reluctance to leave the village of origin are also relevant in explaining the resistance to transmigration. In addition there has traditionally been a fear of leaving the spiritual protection of the ancestors and gods who reside only in Bali.   By taking leave of these protecting spirits one places oneself in spiritual danger (see Chapter 2.1).

If agriculture no longer appeared to offer a viable livelihood locally for the children of many rural Balinese, and they 'viewed migration as an alternative only if all others failed' (Davis,1976:170), then it might be expected that parents would wish to prepare their children for non-agricultural occupations.   The survey results presented in Chapter 7 confirm this.   Of the households where farming was the primary occupation (42 percent of all households) fewer than one in five wanted their sons and only half wanted their daughters to become farmers, whereas two-thirds wanted their sons, and half wanted their daughters to become civil servants (Table 7.6a and b).   The proportions were about the same for the entire group of respondents.[59]   There was a marked desire to have one's children enter a non-agricultural occupation which, although requiring a substantial level of education, offered job security together with a variety of other benefits.   In the survey area the ideal job stereotype was in the civil service, though work in the tourist areas in hotels and shops was also considered desirable.

8.1.2 Education

Clearly, the growth areas of the workforce are those requiring at least some education (with a few exceptions, such as craftsmen). The results presented in Section 7.2.2 reflect quite clearly the virtually universal desire for education of children, this is regardless of the level of the parents' education or economic status.   In some cases it seems probable that financial constraints will prevent attainment of these aspirations.   Nevertheless these aspirations, attainable or otherwise, are powerful influences on fertility behaviour.

In regard to the investment in education, parents in some societies invest heavily in the education of only one of their children, for example the eldest son or the youngest son.   In Bali children are considered to have equal rights to whatever support their parents can provide.   This absence of preferential treatment is reflected in the data in Table 7.4. Under such a system education costs, naturally, are virtually directly proportional to the number of children, and the choice in many cases will be between many poorly educated children or few well-educated children.

8.1.3 Other Factors

The above mentioned 'setting factors' of limited and increasingly expensive agricultural land, and the consequent increased demand for education and jobs in the modern sectors of the economy are considered vital in predisposing the Balinese to reduce their fertility.   There are also a number of aspects of the setting which may be expected to inhibit the desire to reduce fertility.   These aspects, however, will be shown as motivations only to bear some children, rather than for high fertility.

8.1.3.1 Social Value of Children

As discussed in Chapter 2.4 the parenting of the first child is, in many banjar, a prerequisite for active participation and voting rights in community affairs.   The arrival of the first child bestows the important

144

status of adulthood upon the parents and is marked by a change from child-hood name to 'father-of-x' or 'mother-of-x'. The arrival of additional children brings about no further change or elevation in this form of status.

8.1.3.2 Economic Value of Children

In most societies lacking a centralised social security system there is concern about financial support in old age. Indeed, this is often put forward as a major obstacle to fertility decline when mortality levels are still relatively high. For the majority of Balinese parents too, such old age security is a vital concern. But, unlike many societies where aged parents usually rely on those married sons who remain in the parental household, in Bali the system is more flexible. There, a couple with no living sons can arrange for a daughter to remain, after marriage, in their household. The incoming son-in-law takes on the support obligations which would normally lie with a natural son. This pattern of sentana marriage means that a couple giving birth to only two children, even two daughters, can be reasonably sure that there will be one male residing in their household during their old age. For such a couple, even if both children should fail to survive to marriageable age there remains the acceptable fall-back of adopting a relative's child. Apart from support by immediate family members in old age, there is generally an assurance of support in times of need from a wider network, both of relatives and other banjar members.

A more immediate economic function of children in farming households is assistance with agricultural tasks. The data presented in Chapter 7.1 indicated that the landholdings of the majority of agricultural households are now so small that maintenance jobs (weeding, etc.) can be performed by the parents and one or two children. The labour-intensive tasks of planting and harvesting are normally performed by teams composed of other banjar or seka members (see Chapter 2.1). The data in Chapter 7 also showed that many of those owning the larger plots of agricultural land are not, in fact, farmers and thus do not require the labour of their children in the process of generating income from their land. It was also clear that even those genuine farmers with large landholdings generally had no intention of their children working that land themselves. Very often these wealthy farmers would have sharecroppers or other labourers working their lands. It appears then that the economic function of children as labourers in many agricultural families is now quite limited.

This view does not necessarily conflict with the results from various 'value-of children' studies, such as White's work in Java (1975:136) where children have been observed performing economically useful tasks from an early age. It is argued here that numerous children are not essential to the performance of these tasks, although if children are present they would be expected to assist their parents.

8.1.3.3 Political Climate

As described elsewhere (Streatfield,1982:441-5), the decade of the 1960s, and to a lesser extent the two previous decades, was a particularly turbulent period in Indonesian history. The Sukarno era ended in chaos in 1966; in Bali the schools were closed because teachers had not been paid

145

and there were few books. The health clinics were out of medicines, and the few factories were either closed or barely functioning for want of raw materials and spare parts. Hopes for significant redistribution of land through political action had faded. The Suharto government had demonstrated an ability to restore function to an ineffective administration and had offered some hope for an improvement in the well being of the society through discipline and communal effort. The implementation of a Family Planning Program, one of the new government's many initiatives, was viewed as one aspect of the attempt to improve the lot of the citizens of Indonesia.

8.1.3.4 Latent Demand for Fertility Control

It appears that scarcity of agricultural land is not a phenomenon limited to the decade of the 1970s. Why then did fertility not decline until that time? One reason could be that no satisfactory means of fertility control were available. The proportion of respondents admitting to ever having used traditional methods (including abortion and abstinence) was less than 2 percent for any method. Either those methods which could possibly have been used were considered unsafe or unsuitable for other reasons, or there was not considered to be a sufficient need for fertility limitation. The argument here stresses both these factors. The methods that could have been used were considered unsatisfactory in a situation where a couple with many children were not particularly disadvantaged in comparison to a couple with few children. The strong social support network spread the burden of high fertility. The system of land distribution, with a heavy concentration in the hands of high caste landlords, actually may have provided greater certainty of employment and security to the landlord's subjects than the arrangement after the implementation of the 1960 Land Reform Act.

It is thus arguable that before 1970 concern about the problems of land shortage were beginning to emerge but that the appropriate response had not yet become apparent. The use of artificial means of limiting fertility on a wide scale was not yet contemplated. Fertility limitation, in the words of Coale, had not entered 'the calculus of conscious choice' (1973:65). But, for the reasons described herein, when the New Order government introduced the National Family Planning Program in 1970, the population found the concept acceptable and appropriate to the problems confronting their island.

8.2 SOCIAL STRUCTURE FACTORS

The most striking feature of the patterns of fertility and family planning use in the study area is the virtual absence of social or economic differentials (see Chapter 5.3). While fertility had undergone a decline of almost 50 percent during the preceding ten years, the average level in the late 1970s (TFR of 3.5) was still high enough for considerable variation to be possible among the different subgroups within the society. The widest fertility differential was between women with less than completed primary education and those with completed primary or above. Even there the difference in mean number of children ever born was less than one child.

146

With regard to differentials in family planning use, apart from the expected variations according to age and parity, the only marked variation from the average prevalence was the group of civil servants who had a markedly higher prevalence rate (68 percent for both sexes), and small groups of shop saleswomen and male employees in private enterprise who had markedly lower prevalence rates. Even the largest of these outlying groups, the male civil servants, accounts for only one in eight of the study population, the vast majority of whom had rates of current use quite close to the average.

8.2.1 Conformity

The pattern of few substantial fertility differentials overall is quite consistent with the oft-noted high degree of conformity amongst Balinese. It is worthwhile examining this characteristic in more detail as it plays an important role in the explanation of the rapidity of the increase in family planning use.

The observation that there is no latitude for non-conformity within the village community has been made by Belo in 'The Balinese Temper' (1970b:85) and Swellengrebel in 'Nonconformity in the Balinese Family' (1969:202). Swellengrebel has gone further in suggesting that solidarity and cooperation among community members is essential for the performance of those group duties which ensure the well-being of the community. This is consistent with the view of Lekkerkerker (1919) and Covarrubias (1937:262) who earlier emphasised that the communities as a whole must perform regular ceremonies to earn the protection of the gods and ancestors. It is only by constant attention to these benevolent supernatural forces that the spiritual health of the village can be maintained in the face of the omnipresent forces of evil.

It is important to emphasise that Balinese Hinduism not only requires the performance of regular offerings and ceremonies, but also strongly influences individuals' behaviour. In fact, behaviour in many aspects of life is strictly regulated and nonconformity is not tolerated. Failure by an individual to observe traditional etiquette associated with caste, or to fulfil other social obligations, is considered threatening to the well-being of the community and may invoke severe sanctions (see Chapter 2.1). The severity of the sanction is not because other persons have to take over the responsibilities of the offender but because the presence of the offender threatens the spiritual safety and harmony of the community. Thus it can be said that the well-being of the community is dependent on the fulfilment of obligations, social and religious, by all members of the community. Conversely, the wellbeing of the individual is seen as being dependant on the state of the community. The Geertzes sum up this conformist attitude as follows: 'it is better, the Balinese say, to be wrong with the many than right by yourself' (1975:115).

It might be anticipated that this reluctance to be 'right by yourself' would result in weak, indecisive leadership. But the system of consensus decision-making has the important feature of avoiding placing full responsibility for the consequences of a decision on the shoulders of one person. Rather the responsibility for success or failure is diffused equally over the entire group. This permits the decisive action so characteristic of the Balinese even though the individual members of the group may, in other

aspects of daily life, prefer to avoid taking decisions which expose them
to heavy responsibility.

The point of the preceding discussion is that the behaviour of
individual Balinese must be in accordance with the traditional scheme which
operates to ensure the maintenance of order in the community, what Bateson
called the 'steady state' (1978:91). While the Balinese see events as
being caused by friendly or unfriendly spirits, constructive or destructive
gods, they could not be said to be fatalistic or apathetic. Rather, they
go to considerable lengths to discover the appropriate means to try to keep
the gods happy, and to appease those who are displeased. In times of
difficulty or uncertainty advice will be sought, discussed at the village
or banjar council level and, if accepted, acted upon with total commitment
by community members. Covarrubias described the village as a 'closely
unified organism in which the communal policy is harmony and cooperation'
(1937:15), the important point here being that the process of decision-
making is primarily at the level of the community, not at the level of the
individual couple. This includes decisions about fertility.

Such a mechanism permits quite rapid adaptation to new circumstances
(contrary to what might be expected in a traditional society), and allows
for acceptance of innovative ideas or programs whilst the society continues
to function in a traditional way.[60] This is with the proviso that the
innovations do not conflict with traditional values and endanger the
community.

The purpose of this discussion has been to convey the point that the
primary traditional social unit in Bali, the banjar, was and is the basic
decision-making body for most community, and many domestic matters. The
religious basis of banjar obligations, and the potential sanctions which
ensure fulfilment of those obligations remain strong.

8.2.2. Independence of Banjar Decisions

A question now arises as to whether the Balinese accepted family
planning because the government was able to instruct the banjar councils,
through the administrative hierarchy, to ensure that as many village
inhabitants as possible would participate in the program. Or, was it that
many communities decided for themselves (within the banjar council) that it
was to their benefit that their inhabitants should act to reduce their
fertility?

To address the first possibility, the government hierarchy has been
described earlier (Chapter 2.3), but the relevant point here is that the
village headman (the Perbekel) is a full-time, government paid administrative official who necessarily must pass on instructions from government
to the lower level (banjar) officials. The banjar leaders (Kelian Dinas),
however, are in a situation of conflict of interests. In receipt of a
moderate salary from the government, they are required to pass instructions
and information about government programs on to banjar members. On the
other hand, they are elected by the banjar council to act as headmen and
are expected to put the well-being of the banjar community above any other
consideration. As Hobart states:

The assembly (Banjar) remains, in many senses, an autonomous
decision making council independent of the government,
political parties and local factions and these rights are
jealously guarded (1975:84).

It is also important to keep in mind that the function of the Kelian
Dinas is to ensure that council meetings are run in the correct manner, and
that council decisions are implemented.   He is basically an administrator
rather than a leader wielding power over the community.   So the Kelian
Dinas would normally not be in a position to automatically implement
government instructions - he must first persuade the banjar council that
such action would be to the advantage of the community.   If this interpretation is correct then the implication is that the decision of whether
or not to accept family planning is made at the level of the banjar
council.

An example of the independence of the banjar is an incident in Celuk
village, a silver and goldsmith village on the tourist route some 10 kilometres northeast of Denpasar.   A couple of years ago the banjar members
and leaders assembled to hear a plea from the provincial Governor that the
'green belt' along the tourist route should be preserved.   The Governor
requested that no further shops be built along this main route to the
eastern and northeastern attractions.   Whilst apparently acquiescing to
the Governor's request the banjar members remained unmoved in their
decision and persisted with the building of shops along the main road
because of the economic benefit derived by the banjar as a whole, and by
the individual members.

While emphasis has been placed on the independence of the banjar
councils in their decision-making, a qualification must be added.   The
traditional system of consensus decision-making relied, and still relies on
the persuasive abilities of orators.   It was not uncommon for members of
the high caste ruling families to have their views expressed through an
orator whom they patronised.   This avoided the conflict resulting from
being superior in caste but equal as a member of the banjar council (see
Hobart,1975:62ff).   The ruling families also had other indirect ways of
influencing the behaviour of their subjects.

So, although the ruling families with their monopoly on education and
the sources of knowledge and historical information did not exert a direct
influence on the decision-making process they often played an important
advisory role.   In recent decades this situation has changed.   During the
Dutch rule and since Independence the established ruling families lost much
of the basis of their traditional power.   Without large land estates and
no longer holding the right to tax citizens, the former ruling families
have adapted to the changing circumstances by utilising their strong family
networks and superior education to dominate the important areas of central
Government administration in the province.   In the study area the village
headmen (desa), the district head (kecamatan), the regency head (kabupaten)
and the provincial Governor were all members of high caste families, as
were many of their assistants.   This is not an uncommon pattern throughout
Bali even though members of the high castes comprise less than ten percent
of the total population.

Dutch colonisation was only quite recent in Bali (1906-08) compared to

149

Java (17th century).   So the traditional position of leadership ascribed
to the ruling families, though weakened, remains much stronger in Bali than
in Java.   As a result there is an overlap, a blurring of the distinction
between traditional power and modern Government power, as the present day
bureaucrats frequently embody both types.   While the Balinese commoners
may, in theory, decide independently about such personal matters as family
planning use, it is likely that Government advice transmitted to the banjar
level via the modern bureaucratic infrastructure will carry additional
influence because it is seen as deriving from the traditional
advisors/leaders of the Balinese community.

Another related aspect of the blurring of the distinction between
traditional and modern authority is the process of 'dinasisation' of banjar
leaders.   This is a process whereby the central Government has extended
its infrastructure to the banjar level by incorporating the traditional
banjar leaders.   By paying a part-time salary to these locally elected
officials[61] the Government ensures that they convey information and
instructions about Government plans and programs.   Many banjar have
overcome this loss of independence of the leaders by distinguishing the
position of Kelian Dinas (official or Government headman of the banjar)
from the position of Kelian Adat (traditional headman of the banjar) both
of whom attend all banjar meetings (sangkep).

Nevertheless, the central Government has effectively penetrated and,
to a degree, incorporated the system of traditional authority in Bali.
The Balinese are taught from birth that there are four authorities who must
always be obeyed: God (or the gods); one's parents; one's school
teacher; and the Government.   To not obey risks one being labelled a
renegade (murtad) who will be cursed or damned (kualat). In the past, the
'Government' was the Raja (King) and his representatives.   Now the
situation is less clear as the limits to modern government authority are
blurred by the association with traditional authorities functioning as
modern bureaucrats.   The consequence is a powerful incentive to follow
central government instruction provided, as emphasised earlier, to do so is
not viewed as detrimental to the local community.

In explaining the speed of implementation of Government programs in
Bali, the importance of the tendency to 'conform' could presumably be
tested by comparing areas where the banjar is not an important social unit,
with other areas where it is still important.   It is known that the banjar
is no longer important in parts of north Bali due to a longer Dutch
presence there.   In some banjar, council meetings take place as infrequently as once a year.   Unfortunately the data to test this hypothesis
are unavailable at this time.

An alternative approach is to compare family planning prevalence
within villages where the banjar system is still strong, with villages in
the same area where the banjar system does not operate for a different
reason to that above, the difference being that the former villages are
occupied by Hindus, the latter by Muslims.   If the family planning prevalence recorded by the Sistem Banjar of BKKBN Bali in the kecamatan of
Negara, Kabupaten Jembrana, west Bali, is examined for three villages
composed almost entirely of Muslims (99.7% of the total population of 1,856
persons), the average prevalence was 35.9 percent of eligible couples

currently using family planning.   This can be compared to three neighbouring villages with similar access to facilities where 99.8 percent of
the population of 9,146 are Hindu.   There the prevalence of current use is
reported as an average of 80.2 percent.[62]   While religion may be a con-
founding factor in this comparison, the magnitude of the difference in
prevalence rates is consistent with the hypothesis that the continuing
strength of the banjar as the basic social unit among Balinese Hindus
almost certainly plays a vital role in the explanation of the rapid and
widespread acceptance of program family planning in Bali.[63]

8.3 PROGRAM FACTORS

As mentioned above, the importance of the Bali case lies in the
rapidity with which program family planning use spread through the
province.   The most important program factors will be discussed below.
It is relevant that the provincial offices of the BKKBN program were given
considerable latitude in how they organised and presented the program in
their own province.   In Bali the program was presented in many ways as a
Balinese program rather than a national program.

8.3.1 IUD

One of the key reasons which has often been noted but not always
sufficiently emphasised was the decision by the provincial office of BKKBN
to rely almost totally on the IUD as the method to be given.   The
advantages of the IUD compared to pills are both personal and
administrative.   The user need do no more than make one visit to a clinic
for insertion of the IUD.   The pill, of course, must be taken daily and in
the correct sequence, a practice which is not always easy for women with
little education and possibly little instruction on pill use.
Administratively, the IUD was markedly preferable to the pill because,
apart from training nurses how to insert the devices, little additional
infrastructure was required to support continued use.   This is
particularly important for a new family planning program as difficulties in
maintaining reliable re-supply routes to pill users can result in quite
low continuation rates with obvious consequences for the overall prevalence
rate.

These factors are reflected in the marked differences in the twelve-
month continuation rates for the IUD and the pill.   Results from the 1976-
77 Quarterly Acceptor Survey gave rates for Java-Bali of 89.8 percent for
IUD users compared to 64.2 percent for pill users (BKKBN,1982:105).   Similar rates were recently obtained from the 1982 BKKBN Modular Survey for
Bali.   The twelve-month continuation rates were 83.5 percent for IUD users
and 63.8 percent for pill users (Wirawan,1983: personal communication).
There were few objections to male doctors inserting the IUDs as Bali has
long had a tradition of birth attendants being male (see cover).   This is
in contrast to the more inhibited attitude of Muslim women in the other
islands (see Hull, 1978:6).

8.3.2 Banjar Leaders

The second important program factor was that the provincial BKKBN gave
responsibility to the banjar leaders for attaining targets of numbers of

new acceptors and prevalence levels.[64]   The BKKBN avoided circumventing the banjar leaders or superimposing a strict format on them.   Such action may well have alienated the banjar leaders and without their support it is unlikely that the program would have succeeded as it did.   The BKKBN also included a positive incentive for the banjar leaders based on the Balinese penchant for inter-community competitions.   Monthly prevalence levels are reported back to each banjar and the leader of the most 'successful' banjar in terms of new acceptors or prevalence levels receives a reward, possibly a certificate of commendation, possibly a trip to Jakarta.

The decision to give freedom to individual banjar leaders to motivate high levels of family planning acceptance has sometimes resulted in leaders using traditional banjar council decisions to support the Family Planning Program.   These sanctions may take the form of mild threats of a fine, as noted in one of the study villages (see Chapter 6.4), or more serious threats such as expulsion from the village, or refusal of permission for deceased relatives to be cremated in the village graveyard (Affandi, 1983: personal communication).   This is not to imply that the program relied on widespread, overt pressure to ensure success in Bali, only that the support of the banjar leaders, with the authority of their position, was a key factor in that success.

8.3.3   Other Program Factors

There are a number of other important factors, not all of which were unique to Bali.   The favourable distribution of clinics and fieldworkers in Bali (see Hull et al., 1977:14) certainly must have facilitated the entry of Balinese couples into the Family Planning Program.   Though still predominantly rural, Bali has an excellent road network and internal transportation system, so that the inconvenience involved in visiting a clinic, or a fieldworker visiting the homes of eligible couples, is generally not too daunting.

Potential religious objections to family planning use were anticipated by the provincial BKKBN authorities who went to some lengths to induce discussion by the Hindu authorities and to disseminate the subsequent conclusions that the practice of contraception did not contravene the tenets of the Bali-Hindu religion (see Chapter 3.2).

Another aspect of the Family Planning Program that should be con-sidered, though not limited to Bali, is the unambiguous commitment made by the New Order Government from the very beginning of the program.   From the President down visible government figures repeatedly exhorted the popula-tion to participate in the program for the good of the nation.   The message was not only carried by the mass media but also, more subtly, through the education system to influence the young while their norms are still being formulated.   The following passage from a Jakarta issued fourth-class school lesson (for 11 year olds) on the 'Rights and Responsi-bilities of Pupils' illustrates this approach:

We live in a family. A family usually consists of father, mother, and children. A good family consists of father, mother, and three children.   A family like that is called a happy family.   As the size of a family increases, the costs of daily living increase.

It is possible that this passage has since been rewitten stressing a two-child family.

8.4 SUMMARY

The title of this work stresses the point that Balinese society appears to have undergone a dramatic social change in the form of a rapid fertility decline. This is in spite of remaining largely traditional in terms of social arrangements for living, for family relationships, for community cooperation, economic distribution and social control. In the above discussion of the setting factors, the social structure factors, and the program factors underlying the uptake of family planning in Bali, aspects of the traditional nature of the society have come to the fore.

Among the setting factors, concern about shortage of agricultural land, combined with a strong desire to remain in the natal village, are at the root of the awareness of the need to reduce fertility. The usual concerns about old age security in a society where mortality is still relatively high are diffused by reliance on the strong, traditional support network of relatives and banjar members and the pattern of sentana marriage (adopting a son-in-law). Among the social factors, the linking of the arms of the central Government with the community-level administration (banjar) with its remarkable capacity to ensure conformity to its decisions, is probably the single most important factor in the Balinese family planning story. Finally, among the program factors, the decision to give considerable responsibility to the traditional banjar leaders was also important in ensuring the success of the program.

To place the lesson of the Family Planning Program in Bali in a broader context, there are a number of aspects of this case which are sufficiently specific to Bali to mean that it cannot be assumed that any poor rural society would respond equally rapidly to the introduction of a similarly well organised Family Planning Program. In the Foreword to Agricultural Involution Clifford Geertz states that:

> There seems to be in the history of each country an 'optimal moment' for launching development, a short period of time when sociological, political, and economic factors coalesce to provide a climate unusually favourable for a take-off into economic growth (1963:ix).

The success of the Family Planning Program in Bali is very much a result of its introduction at just such an 'optimal moment' in Balinese history. As described above, by the late 1960s, the economic, political and social circumstances were such that the climate was 'unusually favourable' for ready acceptance of the concept of fertility limitation. Both as an attempt to alleviate some of the existing problems besetting the island at the time, and to minimise problems, particularly of land shortage, for future generations.

While the above argument suggests that Bali is a special case, there is no doubt that it provides an important exception to the demographic transition theories which place great emphasis on the attainment of a 'threshold' of economic development before a major fertility decline can occur.

NOTES

1   See Chapter 5 (5.2.5) for discussion of the reliability of this method.

2   Raffles makes no mention of where he obtained the figure of 215,000 males whose teeth had been filed. But on the grounds that tooth-filing immediately precedes puberty, and age at marriage is early, he assumes that most of those whose teeth have been filed have 'entered into family connections'. Assuming four persons to a family, this gives a population of over 800,000 for all Bali. This is almost certainly an over estimate.

3   In fact the growth rate from official census data was only 1.6 percent per annum from 1930 to 1971, (see Table 1.1b).

    For a discussion of the shortcomings and possible errors in the estimates derived from census and survey data see Streatfield, 1982 (Section 1.4.1.).

4   It should be noted that this is not the same suggestion as that of Astawa, who emphasised the benefits to the nuclear family rather than to the community.

5   <u>Kahyangan-Tiga</u> means literally 'the three great temples'.

6   Balinese has in common with Javanese its use of the so-called 'vocabularies of courtesy'. The Balinese determines his choice of words according to the social relation between the person he is speaking to or speaking about and himself. One employs the ordinary, common language when speaking with intimates, equals, or inferiors; polite terms must be used as soon as one begins to speak to one's superiors or to strangers; and 'deferential' terms are obligatory in all cases when one is so bold as to speak of parts of the body or the acts, possessions, or qualities of important people. The Balinese sum up the last two vocabularies under the term <u>alus</u> (fine or noble) (Swellengrebel, 1960:8).

7   See Rimbawan Dayuh (1982).

8   This situation has probably been altered somewhat by the Land Reform Act of 1960 which reduced the land holdings of many of the princes, traditionally the main group practising polygyny.

9   This is somewhat different from the popular legend of the creation of Kala, to whom Siva gave birth alone by producing a single drop of semen, rather like the 'homunculus' idea held by early biologists. However it was necessary for the sperm to be repeatedly hit by the arrows of the gods before it became alive.

10 Nearly 7 and 18 percent respectively of the island's total
    cultivated area.

11 This elasticity measures the percent increase in average
    yield for each percentage increase in total area irrigated.

12 It should be noted that these figures may be misleading in that
    it is not uncommon for the age range of pupils in a class
    in primary school to extend over six or seven years,e.g., pupils
    in class I can range from six to twelve years. Thus the number
    of primary school pupils in 1980 was the number of children aged
    between six and seventeen years who were attending primary
    school. This figure was equivalent to 87 percent of the
    estimated total number of children aged seven to twelve in the
    country.

13 This could be viewed as analogous to the situation of the
    use of Latin by the priests of the Catholic Church in order to
    retain control of the sacred texts.

14 It is common practice, at least in Bali, for primary school
    students to have three different uniforms. On Monday and
    Tuesday, an all white uniform; on Wednesday and Thursday, a
    grey and white uniform; and on Friday and Saturday, a brown and
    orange uniform. While this ensures that the children change
    their uniforms frequently, it surely adds considerably to the
    costs of educating children. Sports clothes are also often
    required for the children.

15 This takes into account differences in definition which led
    to many more women being included as economically active in the
    1976 Labour Force Survey, compared to the 1971 Census.

16 The WFS definitions were that 'folk' methods included herbs,
    uterus inversion, massage and others (abortion); traditional
    methods were abstinence, rhythm, withdrawal and douche.

17 These rewards include a trip to Jakarta to receive a certificate
    of achievement from BKKBN.

18 Geertz (1968:107-20) examined the attempts by a number of
    royal families in Tabanan, Bali, to preserve their power through
    economic activity since their political prestige had waned.
    Geertz noted (1968:123) that while these royal businesses were
    not run according to normal management principles, they may if
    they survive, provide employment and fulfil the purpose of
    maintaining princely power.

19 As described in Chapter 4, it was known that by the mid seventies
    fertility was quite low in Banjarangkan kecamatan, and
    there was no reason to believe that it had not been higher in
    earlier times.

20   It could be argued that very few areas would be typical of
      all Bali, only an island-wide sample could be claimed to be
      representative.

21   This is supported by the somewhat limited data on proportions
      ever-married for the village of Banjarangkan (Pop. 3,400),
      obtained from the 1980 Census.

22   The TFR's for the period 1971-75 were, from SUPAS I, 5.1,
      and from SUPAS II, 5.3, and 4.9 for 1975 using Last Birth method
      by Hull,(Cho et al., 1979:14).

23   The oldest age group in 1980 (50-54) were only 35-39 in the
      period 1961-65.   Hence there are no data for women aged 40+
      in that period.

24   The 1971 Census data provided TFR's for Bali (Rural) for
      the 1960s of 5.74 (1961-63), 5.84 (1964-66), and 5.95 (1967-70),
      (BPS,1976:6).

25   If the sets of proportions currently-married from SUPAS I
      or II were used to determine ASFR's from ASMFR's, the resulting
      TFR's for women aged 15-49 would have been 3.66 and 3.74
      respectively.

26   These data were obtained by looking back five, ten, and
      fifteen years in the women's pregnancy histories and estimating
      how many children they had given birth to up to that time.   At
      those times the women were, of course, one, two, or three five
      year age groups younger than in 1980.   This procedure also
      permits cohorts to be followed through a maximum of four
      consecutive five-year age groups (see Figure 5-H).

27   Before 1970, mean age at childbearing in Bali was almost
      certainly higher than in 1980, as indicated by the patterns of
      age specific fertility rates (Table 5.4). If higher mean ages
      at childbearing were employed in the calculations for earlier
      times, the Feeney method would give higher rates of infant
      mortality due to the positive sign of the coefficient of M in
      the regression equation (Table 5.9).

28   The mean of 5.0 for women 40-44 in the Census is probably
      too low for reasons of underreporting discussed in Chapter 4.

29   'Women who have no children are believed to go to hell, and
      lurid paintings and drawings abound which depict the barren
      women in hell with enormous hairy caterpillars sucking at their
      dry breasts' (Belo,1970:5).

30   Data from Yogyakarta indicate that mortality rates for
      single children are unreasonably low, suggesting that deaths to
      single children often go unreported   (McDonald and Sontosudarmo,
      1976:29).

31   See Chapter 2 for details of naming system and life cycle stages.

32   While 46 percent of the women who have completed primary school are 30 or over, some 70 percent of the 'no school' group were 30 years or over.

33   It could be argued that Bali in 1980 was no longer in 'the early stages of fertility transition', but with a TFR of over 6 some twelve or so years earlier, it could not yet be classed as a 'late transition' region.

34   The number of items possessed was multiplied by the weighting given each in direct proportion to its price. One unit of price was roughly equivalent to the price of the cheapest item on the list (a kerosene lamp at Rupiah 500 or A$0.70) at the time of the survey.

35   Generally speaking, the economic score of respondents increases with age (mean of 206 for ages 20-24 years to 310 for ages 35-39 years) as individuals accumulate more wealth, or take on responsibility for those items present within the compound.

36   Prior to standardisation the range was from 3.2 CEB (poor group, Rs.10,000-99,999) to 4.4 (wealthy group, Rs.150,000-449,999).

37   A further 129 couples own sawah but do not farm personally. Of these, 46 (35%) are Pegawai Negeri (Civil Servants), and 45 are labourers generally owning too little land to support a family by farming alone.

38   For land-owning farmers, the mean area owned is 29.1 Are whereas for land-owning Pegawai Negeri the mean area owned is 42.6 Are, reflecting the fact that many of the large plots of sawah are owned by people other than farmers.

39   This group will be seen in the next chapter to also have the highest level of family planning use.

40   Such a clustering pattern is not uncommon with members of the same caste apparently preferring to live together, possibly because this facilitates such interactions as marriage which is generally within caste boundaries, also for reasons of ceremonial and language convenience.

41   As described in Chapter 4, the survey covered women aged 15 to 54, but as women over 49 years would not normally be considered as 'exposed to risk' they will be excluded from much of the analysis, although seven of the eighteen said that they were using family planning at the time of the survey (six IUD's and one tubectomy).

42   Regarding the definition of Current Use of family planning some surveys ask 'Have you used family planning in the last week, or in the last month?' and take a positive answer as indicating current use, even if the respondent is not actually using anything at the time of interview. This survey asked only about status at the time of the interview, although recent practice could be determined from the family planning history.

43   This can be compared to the BKKBN Sistem Banjar data for the same villages at the same time, Banjarangkan = 71.4 percent, Tusan = 57.8 percent, and Bakas = 71.9 percent (See Chapter 4 for more detail).

44   A striking feature of the pregnancy histories of a number of older women was that many of proven fertility had stopped childbearing in their thirties while still cohabiting with their husband, but were practising no family planning, and apparently were not becoming pregnant. This pattern of early secondary sterility was said to be not uncommon by several doctors with whom it was discussed.

45   Women in the Banjarangkan area are not eligible to receive family planning until they have proved their fertility with a child.

46   A typical small shop might sell school supplies, stationery, children's clothes, shoes, soap, toothpaste, fruit, biscuits, tea, batteries, and precooked foods, cigarettes and incense for offerings, among other things.

47   Eighteen of the 24 female civil servants in regular employment are married to male civil servants.

48   Of the women wanting more children and using family planning, 93.9 percent were using the IUD, 2.6 percent the pill, and the remaining 3.5 percent were using condom, rhythm and even tubectomy.

49   Effectiveness is indeed high as 95 percent of segments of ever-use were either IUD, tubectomy or vasectomy.

50   These schedules result in marital TFRs of 9.9 for 1971-75, and 9.0 for 1976-80, compared to 10.7 for 1966-70.

51   In the survey some women claimed weight losses of 10 kilograms with one of 18 kilograms many of these could state their exact weights before and after receiving the IUD.

52   If the problem was loss of weight, the injection was usually Vitamin-B Complex, repeated weekly, to encourage the woman to eat more. If the problem was heavier menstrual periods, the injection was a single dose of Ergometrine with Vitamin K. And if the problem was white vaginal discharge with itch, she received a penicillin injection.

53   The Lange Handbook of Obstetrics and Gynecology advises
      that: 'if the IUD is removed because of pain or bleeding, one
      should substitute the next smaller size or another design'
      (1974:669).

54   In late 1979 the cost of bulk-packaged (without inserter,
      unsterilised) Lippes Loops was US$0.08-0.16 each, compared to
      US$5.00 for individually prepackaged sterile units with inserter
      (Population Council,1979).

55   Fawcett (1977) discussed the convergence between micro-economic
      and social-psychological theories on the subject.

56   There are exceptions, as with most things Balinese, where some
      hamlets base membership eligibility on having fathered a child,
      and some where a man, even if married with children, may not
      'have a voice' at council meetings until his father has stood
      down, for example when the youngest son marries and replaces the
      father.

57   A Balinese household is defined as a group of people who all eat
      food cooked in the same kitchen, usually a married couple and
      their children.   A son will usually set up a separate kitchen
      upon marrying.

58   The Indonesian word used in the question on aspirations for
      children's occupation was _diharapkan_ which could be interpreted
      as either 'expect' or 'hope for' which may imply variable degrees
      of realism in the replies.   The fact that about half the respon-
      dents aspire to the civil service for their daughters when only
      2.3 percent of the women are themselves civil servants suggests
      that either the question was understood to mean 'what job would
      you most want for your daughter if she had a choice of any job?'
      or else a great many of the respondents are under the impression
      that provided the children have sufficient education, then they
      have a reasonable chance of obtaining employment with the civil
      service.
          Some three-quarters of parents expect their sons, and two-
      thirds expect their daughters to go on to junior secondary
      school, which is sufficient to satisfy the requirements for a
      number of occupations within the civil service: for example,
      fieldworkers with the Family Planning Program need only to have
      completed this level of schooling.

59   Indeed these are not unrealistic goals as the intercensal growth
      of the workforce in Bali between 1971 and 1980 has been heavily
      concentrated in the service sector (89 percent increase in
      numbers of Service workers;   148 percent increase in Clerical and
      Related workers;   184% increase in Production, Transport and
      Related workers).   This is in contrast to a growth of only 2
      percent for Agricultural and Related workers - and this latter
      figure conceals a net decline of 6.3 percent in numbers of male
      agricultural workers.   Agriculture is, of course, still the
      largest single occupational category (BPS,1971, E14,Table 34;
      BPS,1980,S2,Tables 44.7 & 44.8).

60   In comparison with the rather static culture of Java, Balinese culture is strong and dynamic. The confidence of the Balinese in their culture is reflected in the openess to change, to experimentation in painting, dance and music, as well as other aspects of life. These arts are 'alive' and constantly changing but remain distinctly Balinese.

61   In the past a banjar leader usually received some benefit for undertaking the responsibility during his five years or so in office. Commonly some banjar land was made available for him to grow extra crops.

62   These figures are almost certainly overestimates, but the relative levels are instructive.

63   This is presented only as an 'example' of one possible approach to examining the role of the banjar in the acceptance of government programs. It is too small a sample, arbitrarily selected, to be conclusive.

64   I am grateful to Joko Affandi for raising this point.

BIBLIOGRAPHY

ABRAMSON, F.D., (1973), 'High foetal mortality and birth intervals', Population Studies, 27(2):235-42.

ADELMAN, I. and MORRIS, C.T., (1966), 'A quantitative study of social and political determinants of fertility', Economic Development and Cultural Change, 14(2):129-57.

ARNOLD, F., BULATAO, R.A., BURIPAKDI, C., CHUNG, B.J., FAWCETT, J.T., IRITANI, T., LEE, S.J., WU, T-S, (1975), The Value of Children - A Cross National Study: Vol.I - Introduction and Comparative Analysis, East-West Population Institute, East-West Center, Honolulu.

ASTAWA, I.B., (1977), Interview in Asian Population Programme News, 6(3):28.

_____., (1979), 'Using the local community - Bali, Indonesia', in Potts, M., and Bhiwandiwala, P. (Eds.), Birth Control - An International Assessment, MTP Press, 55-70.

_____., WALOEYO, S. and LAING, J.E., (1975), 'Family planning in Bali', Studies in Family Planning, 6(4):86-101.

ASTIKA, K.S., (1978), 'Social and economic effects of the new rice technology: The case of Abiansemal, Bali', PRISMA (English Edition), 10(1):47-56.

BALI, (1978), Bali Dalam Angka - 1976 (Bali in Figures), Statistik Tahunan - 4/75, Kantor Sensus dan Statistik, Bali.

BATESON, G., (1978), Steps to an Ecology of Mind, (2nd Edition), Paladin/ Granada.

BATESON, G., and MEAD, M., (1942), Balinese Character: A Photographic Analysis, New York Academy of Sciences.

BKKBN (Badan Koordinasi Keluarga Berencana Nasional), Bali. Laporan Trieulan, Sistem Banjar, (Quarterly Reports of the Sistem Banjar Family Planning Program).

_____, Jakarta. Monthly Statistics, Bureau of Reporting and Documentation.

_____, Contraceptive Use Effectiveness in Mojokerto Regency, East Java, Technical Report Series, Monograph No.9, Bureau of Reporting and Documentation.

_____, Ulusan Singkat Ciri-Ciri Akseptor.

BECKER, G., (1960), 'An economic analysis of fertility', in Demographic and Economic Change in Developed Countries, Universities-National Bureau Conference Series 11, Princeton, N.J., 209-31.

_____., (1965), 'A theory of the allocation of time', Economic Journal, 75(299):493-517.

BELO, J., (1970a), 'A study of the customs pertaining to twins in Bali', in Belo, J., (Ed.), Traditional Balinese Culture, Columbia University Press, New York, 3-56.

_____., (1970b), 'The Balinese temper', in Belo, J., (Ed.), Traditional Balinese Culture, Columbia University Press, New York, 85-110.

BENDESA, I.K.G. and SUKARSA, I.M., (1980), 'An economic survey of Bali', Bulletin of Indonesian Economic Studies, 16(2):31-53.

BERELSON, B., (1974), 'World Population: Status Report 1974', Reports on Population and Family Planning, Population Council, New York, No.15.

BERNET KEMPERS, A.J., (1978), Monumental Bali: Introduction to Balinese Archeology, Guide to the Monuments, Van Goor Zonen Den Haag.

BIRO PUSAT STATISTIK, JAKARTA, INDONESIA, (1971), National Census Report, Bali, Series E, No.14.

_____, (1976), Perkiraan Angka Kelahiran dan Kematian Di Indonesia Berdasarkan Senses Penduduk 1971, SP76-L02.

BLACKER, C.P., (1947), 'Stages in population growth', Eugenics Review, 39:81-101.

BLAKE, J., (1967), 'Income and reproductive motivation', Population Studies, 21(3):185-206.

_____., (1968), 'Are babies consumer durables? A critique of the economic theory of reproductive motivation', Population Studies, 22(1):5-25.

_____., (1974), 'Can we believe recent data on birth expectations in the United States?', Demography, 11(1):25-44.

BOON, J., (1977), The Anthropological Romance of Bali, 1597 - 1972, Cambridge University Press, Cambridge.

BOURGEOIS-PICHAT, J., (1967), 'Social and biological determinants of human fertility in non-industrial societies', Proceedings of the American Philosophical Society, 3(3):160-3.

BRASS, W., (1975), Methods for Estimating Fertility and Mortality from Limited and Defective Data, Occasional Publication, Laboratories for Population Statistics, University of North Carolina, Chapel Hill, N.C.

BRASS, W., (1978), 'Comments on comparison strategies for the evaluation of family planning impact', in <u>Methods of Measuring the impact of Family Planning Programmes on Fertility: Problems and Issues</u>, United Nations, Department of Economic and Social Affairs, ST/ESA/Ser.A/61.

_____., (1979), 'A procedure for comparing mortality measures calculated from intercensal survival with the corresponding estimates from registered deaths', <u>Asian and Pacific Census Forum</u>, 6(2):5-7.

CAIN, MEAD, (1977), 'The economic activities of children in a village in Bangladesh', <u>Population and Development Review</u>, 3(3):201-77.

CAIN, MELINDA L., (1981), 'Java, Indonesia: The introduction of rice processing technology', in Dauber, R., and Cain, M.L., (Eds.), <u>Women and Technical Change in Developing Countries</u>, West View Press, Boulder, 127-38.

CALDWELL, J.C., (1976), 'Toward a restatement of demographic transition theory', <u>Population and Development Review</u>, 2(3-4):321-66.

_____., (1980), 'Mass education as a determinant of the timing of fertility decline', <u>Population and Development Review</u>, 6(2):225-55.

_____., (1982), <u>Theory of Fertility Decline</u>, Academic Press, London.

CENTRAL BUREAU OF STATISTICS AND WORLD FERTILITY SURVEY, (1978), <u>Indonesia Fertility Survey: Principal Report</u>, 2 Vols., Central Bureau of Statistics, Jakarta.

CHANG, M-C., FREEDMAN, R. and TE-HSIUNG S., (1981), 'Trends in fertility, family size preferences, and family planning practice: Taiwan, 1961-80', <u>Studies in Family Planning</u>, 12(5):211-28.

CHO, L.J., <u>et al</u>., (1979), 'Fertility section of the Indonesia Panel Report', Committee on Population and Development, National Academy Press, Washington D.C., forthcoming.

_____., SUHARTO, S., MCNICOLL, G., and MDE MAMAS, S.G., (1980), <u>Population Growth of Indonesia: An Analysis of Fertility and Mortality Based on the 1971 Population Census</u>, Monographs of the Center for Southeast Asian Studies, Kyoto University, English-Language Series, No. 15, University of Hawaii Press.

CLELAND, J.G. and SINGH, S., (1980), 'Islands and the demographic transition', <u>World Development</u>, 8:969.

COALE, A.J., (1965), 'Factors associated with the development of low fertility: An historical summary', <u>United Nations World Population Conference</u>, Vol.2:205-9.

COALE, A.J., (1969), 'The decline of fertility in Europe from the French Revolution to World War II', in Behren S.J., et al.,(Eds.), Fertility and Family Planning: A World View, University of Michigan Press, Ann Arbor.

_____., (1973), 'The demographic transition reconsidered', International Population Conference, Liege,1973, International Union for the Scientific Study of Population, Liege, Vol.1:53-71.

_____., and DEMENY,P.,(1966),Regional Model Life Tables and Stable Populations, Princeton University Press, Princeton, N.J.

_____., and TRUSSELL, J., (1974), 'Model fertility schedules: Variations in the age structure of childbearing in human populations', Population Index, 40:185-201.

COOMBS, L., FREEDMAN,R. and NARAYANAN NAMBOTHIRI, D., (1969), 'Inference about abortion from foetal mortality data', Population Studies, 23(2):247.

COVARRUBIAS, M., (1974), The Island of Bali, Oxford University Press/ Indira, Kuala Lumpur, first published by Alfred A. Knopf, 1937.

CRAWFURD, J., (1856), A Descriptive Dictionary of the Indian Islands and Adjacent Countries, Bradbury and Evans, London, 197p.

DAROESMAN, R., (1973), 'An economic survey of Bali', Bulletin of Indonesian Economic Studies, 9(3):28-61.

DAVIS, G.J., (1974), 'Varieties in adaptation: Balinese migrants in central Sulawesi'. Unpublished paper presented to the American Anthropological Meeting, November 1974.

_____., (1976), 'Parigi: A social history of the Balinese movement to Central Sulawesi,1907-1974'. Unpublished Ph.D. thesis, Stanford University.

DAVIS, K., (1955), 'Institutional patterns favouring high fertility in underdeveloped areas', Eugenics Quarterly, 2(1):33-9.

_____., and BLAKE, J., (1956), 'Social structure and fertility: An analytical framework', Economic Development and Social Change, 4(3):211-35.

DEMENY, P., (1968), 'Early fertility decline in Austria-Hungary: A lesson in demographic transition', Daedelus, 97:502-22.

DUESENBERRY, J.S., (1960), 'Comment', in Universities-National Bureau Committee for Economic Research, in Demographic and Economic Change in Developed Countries, Princeton University Press,231-4.

EASTERLIN, R.A., (1969), 'Towards a socioeconomic theory of fertility: Survey of recent research on economic factors in American fertility', in Fertility and Family Planning: A World View, University of Michigan Press, Ann Arbor, 127-56.

EASTERLIN, R.A., (1975), 'An economic framework for fertility analysis', Studies in Family Planning, 6(3):54-63.

_____., (1976), 'The conflict between aspirations and resources', Population and Development Review, 2(3-4):417-26.

ECK, R.VAN., (1880), 'Een en ander over Bali', De Indische Gids, II:544-62.

EDMONDSON, J., 'Population adaptation and family planning in a Balinese village', mimeo, 18p.

EIJSINGA, VAN., (ND), Cited by Hanna, 1971.

EKANEM, I.I., (1972), 'A further note on the relation between economic development and fertility', Demography, 9(3):383-98.

EMMERSON, D.K., (1976), Indonesia's Elite: Political Culture and Cultural Politics, Cornell University Press, Ithaca.

FAWCETT, J.T., (1977), 'The value and cost of children: Converging theory and research', in Ruzicka, L.T., (Ed.), The Economic and Social Supports for High Fertility, Australian National University, Canberra, 91-114.

_____.,et al., (1974), The Value of Children in Asia and the United States: Comparative Perspectives, Papers of the East-West Population Institute, No.32.

FEENEY, G., (1976), 'Estimating infant mortality rates from child survivorship data by age of mother', Asian and Pacific Census Newsletter, 3(2):12-16.

FERTILITY-MORTALITY SURVEY PRELIMINARY REPORT, BALI, (1974), Indonesian Fertility-Mortality Survey, University of Indonesia, Institute of Demography, Economics Faculty, Jakarta.

FORGE, A., (1979), 'Balinese religion and Indonesian identity', presented at 'The Indonesia Connection' seminar series, November 1979, RSSS, Australian National University, Canberra, 23p.

FREEDMAN, D., (1963), 'The relation of economic status of fertility', American Economic Review, 53:414-27.

FREEDMAN, R., (1961-2), 'The sociology of human fertility: A trend report and bibliography', Current Sociology, 10/11(3).

_____., (1963), 'Norms for family size in underdeveloped areas', Proceedings of the Royal Society, B.159, Part 974:229-45.

_____., (1975), The Sociology of Human Fertility: An Annotated Bibliography, Irvington Publishers, New York.

_____., (1979), 'Theories of fertility decline: A reappraisal', Social Forces, 58(1):1-17.

FREEDMAN, R., and BERELSON, B., (1976), 'The record of family planning programs', Studies in Family Planning, 7(1):1-40.

_____., KHOO, S-E., and SUPRAPTILAH, B. (1981), 'Use of modern contraceptives in Indonesia: A challenge to the conventional wisdom', International Family Planning Perspectives, 7(1):3-15.

GARDINER, P., (1979), 'Mortality in Indonesia'. Unpublished seminar paper presented to the Indonesia Study Group, Australian National University, Canberra.

_____., (1981), 'Vital Registration in Indonesia: A study of the completeness and behavioural determinants of reporting of births and deaths', Unpublished Ph.D. thesis, Demography Department, Australian National University, Canberra.

GEERTZ, C., (1963), Agricultural Involution: The Process of Ecological Change in Indonesia, (2nd Edition 1974), University of California Press.

_____., (1966), 'Person, time and conduct in Bali: An essay in cultural analysis', Southeast Asia Studies, Yale University, New Haven, Connecticut.

_____., (1967), 'Tihingan: A Balinese village', in Koentjaraningrat (Ed.), Villages in Indonesia, Cornell University Press, Ithaca, New York, 210.

_____., (1968), Peddlers and Princes: Change and Economic Moderni-zation in two Indonesian Towns, (2nd Edition), University of Chicago Press.

_____., (1980), Negara: The Theatre State in Nineteenth-Century Bali, Princeton University Press, Princeton.

GEERTZ, H., (1959), 'The Balinese Village', in Skinner G.W., (Ed.), Local, National and Regional Loyalties in Indonesia, New Haven, Con-necticut, 24-33.

_____., and GEERTZ, C., (1964), 'Teknonomy in Bali: Parenthood, age grading and genealogical amnesia', Journal of the Royal Anthro-pological Institute, 94:94-108.

_____., (1975), Kinship in Bali, University of Chicago Press, Chicago and London.

GOLDMAN, N., and WESTOFF, C., (1980), 'Can fertility be estimated from current pregnancy data?', Population Studies, 34(3):535-50.

GORIS, R., (1960), 'The religious character of the village community', in Swellengrebel, J.L., (Ed.), Bali: Studies in Life, Thought and Ritual, van Hoeve, The Hague and Bandung, 77-100.

HAMID, M.D., (1980), 'An evaluation of hand-tractor leasing project in Indonesia: A case study in Kabupaten Badung, Gianyar, and Tabanan, the province of Bali'. Unpublished Master of Agricultural Development Economics, Development Studies Centre, Australian National University, Canberra.

HANNA, W., (1971), 'Too many Balinese', American Universities Fieldstaff Reports, Southeast Asia Series, Indonesia, 20(1).

_____., (1972), 'Population and rice', American Universities Fieldstaff Reports, Southeast Asia Series, Indonesia, 20(4).

_____., (1976), 'Bali profile', American Universities Fieldstaff Reports, New York.

HARRISON, P., (1978), 'And in Bali...Banjars show the way', People, 5(1): 14-17.

HAWTHORN, G., (1970), The Sociology of Fertility, Collier-MacMillan, London.

HELMS, L.V., (1882), Pioneering in the Far East, London, cited by Hanna, 1971.

HENRY, L., (1961), 'Some data on natural fertility', Eugenics Quarterly, 8(2):81-91.

HOBART, M., (1975), 'Orators and patrons: Two types of political leader in Balinese village society', in Bloch, M., (Ed.), Political Language and Oratory in Traditional Society, Academic Press, London, 65-92.

_____., (1979), 'A Balinese village and its field of social relations'. Unpublished Ph.D. thesis, SOAS, London University.

HOFFMAN, L.W., (1972), 'A psychological perspective on the value of children to parents: Concepts and measures', in Fawcett, J.T., (Ed.), The Satisfactions and Costs of Children: Theories, Concepts, Methods, 27-56.

_____., and HOFFMAN, M.L., (1973), 'The value of children to parents' in Fawcett,J.T. Psychological Perspectives on Population, Basic Books, New York, 19-76.

HUGHES, J., (1968), The End of Sukarno, Angus and Robertson, Sydney.

HULL, T.H., (1975), 'Each child brings its own fortune: An inquiry into the value of children in a Javanese village'. Unpublished Ph.D.thesis, Department of Demography, Australian National University, Canberra.

_____., (1978), 'Where credit is due'. Unpublished paper presented at the Population Association of America Meeting, April 1978.

HULL, T.H., and HULL, V.J., (1976), 'The relation of economic class and fertility'. Report Series No.6, Population Institute, Gadjah Mada University, Yogyakarta, Indonesia.

_____., (1977), 'Indonesia', in Caldwell, J.C., (Ed.), The Persistence of High Fertility, Department of Demography, Australian National University, Canberra, 827-96.

_____., and SINGARIMBUN, M., (1977), 'Indonesia's family planning story: Success and challenge', Population Bulletin, 32(6):1-52.

HULL, T.H., and SINGARIMBUN, M., 'The sociological determinants of fertility decline in Indonesia: 1965-76'. Unpublished paper.

HULL, V.J., (1975), 'Fertility, socio-economic status, and the position of women in a Javanese village'. Unpublished Ph.D. thesis, Department of Demography, Australian National University, Canberra.

_____., (1976), The Positive Relation Between Economic Class and Family Size in Java, Working Paper, Population Institute, Gadjah Mada University, Yogyakarta, Indonesia.

INDONESIA, BIRO PUSAT STATISTIK, (1976), Analysis and Evaluation of the First Year Results of the Sample Vital Registration Project, Technical Report Series, Monograph No.2, Jakarta.

_____, (1979), Analysis and Evaluation of the Third Year Results of the Sample Vital Registration Project, Technical Report Series, Monograph No.4, Jakarta.

JACOBS, J., (1883), Cited in Ploss et al., Woman, Vol.II, William Heineman, London, 1935:498.

JONES, G., (1976), 'Economic and social supports for high fertility: Conceptual Framework', in Ruzicka, L.T., (Ed.), The Economic and Social Supports for High Fertility: Proceedings of the Conference held in Canberra 16-18 November 1976, Department of Demography, Australian National University, Canberra, 3-47.

_____., (1977), 'Fertility levels and trends in Indonesia', Population Studies, 31(1):29-42.

KASARDA, J.D., (1971), 'Economic structure and fertility: A comparative analysis', Demography, 8(7):307-17.

KATZ, J.S. and KATZ, R.S., (1978), 'Legislating Social Change in a developing country: The new Indonesian marriage law revisited', American Journal of Comparative Law, 26(2):309-20.

KHOO, S-E., (1981), 'The determinants of modern contraceptive use in Indonesia: Further analyses of individual and aggregate level data'. Unpublished paper, East-West Population Institute, Honolulu, Hawaii.

KIRK, D., (1971), 'A new demographic transition?', in Rapid Population Growth: Consequences and Policy Implications, National Academy of Sciences, Johns Hopkins Press, Baltimore, 123-47.

KNODEL, J., (1977), 'Family limitation and the fertility transition: Evidence from the age patterns of fertility in Europe and Asia', Population Studies, 31(2):219-49.

KUSUMA, (1976), 'Berbagai aspek perbedaan pola perkawinan di Indonesia dewasa ini' (Several aspects of differences in marriage patterns in Indonesia today). The DemographicInstitute, Economics Faculty, University of Indonesia, Jakarta.

LANDRY, A., (1945), Traite de Demographie, Payot, Paris, 651p.

LANGE, (1974), in Benson, R., (Ed.), Handbook of Obstetrics and Gynecology, Maruzen Asian Edition.

LANSING, J.S., (1974), 'Evil in the morning of the world: Phenomenological approaches to a Balinese community', Ann Arbor Center for Southeast Asian Studies, University of Michigan.

LAURO, D., (1979), 'Life history matrix analysis: A progress report', in Pryor, R.J., (Ed.), Residence History Analysis, Studies in Migration and Urbanization No.3., Department of Demography, Australian National University, Canberra, 134-54.

LEASURE, J.W., (1963), 'Factors involved in the decline of fertility in Spain, 1900-1950', Population Studies, 16(3):271-84.

LEE, B.M., and ISBISTER, J., (1966), 'The impact of birth control programs on fertility', in Berelson B., et al.,(Eds.), Family Planning and Population Programs: A Review of World Development, University of Chicago Press, Chicago, 737-58.

LEIBENSTEIN, H., (1974), 'An interpretation of the economic theory of fertility: Promising path or blind alley?', Journal of Economic Literature, 12(2):457-79.

_____., (1975), 'The economic theory of fertility decline', Quarterly Journal of Economics, 89(1):1-31.

LEKKERKERKER, C., (1919), 'De geschiedenis der Christelijke zending onder de Baliers' (The history of Protestant missions among the Balinese), De Indische Gids, XLI, 835-52.

LESTHAEGHE, R. and VAN DE WALLE, E., (1976), 'Economic factors and fertility decline in France and Belgium', in Coale, A.J., (Ed.), Economic Factors in Population Growth, MacMillan, London.

LORIMER, F., et al., (1954), Culture and Human Fertility, UNESCO, Paris.

MANDELBAUM, D.G., (1974), Human Fertility in India: Social Components and Policy Perspectives, University of California Press.

MAULDIN, P.W. and BERELSON, B., (1978), 'Conditions of fertility decline in developing countries, 1965-75', Studies in Family Planning, 9(5): 89-147.

MCDONALD, P.F., (1979), Unpublished paper in Mortality Section of the Indonesia Panel Report, Committee on Population and Development, National Academy Press, Washington, D.C.

_____., (1982), 'Approaches to massive population growth: The case of Indonesia'. Unpublished paper presented to the Asian Studies Association of Australia, Fourth National Conference, Monash University, May 1982.

_____., and SONTOSUDARMO,A., (1976), Response to Population Pressure: The Case of the Special Region of Yogyakarta, Gadjah Mada University Press, Yogyakarta.

_____., YASIN, M., and JONES, G.W., (1976), Levels and Trends in Fertility and Childhood Mortality in Indonesia, (Indonesia Ferti-lity-Mortality Survey, 1973), Demographic Institute, Economics Faculty, University of Indonesia, Jakarta.

MCKEAN, P.F., (1978), 'Towards a theoretical analysis of tourism: Economic dualism and cultural involution in Bali', in Smith, V.L., (Ed.), Hosts and Guests - The Anthropology of Tourism, Blackwell, Oxford, 93-107.

MCNICOLL, G., (1980), 'Technology and the social regulation of fertility', Working Paper No.46, Center for Population Studies, Population Council.

MEARS, L., (1981), The New Rice Economy of Indonesia, Gadjah Mada University Press, Yogyakarta.

MEIER, G., (1979), 'Family planning in the banjars of Bali', International Family Planning Perspectives, 5(2):63-6.

MERSHON, K.E., (1937), Seven Plus Seven: Mysterious Life Rituals in Bali, Vantage Press, New York.

MEYER, P., (1981), 'The Value of Children in the Context of the Family in Java'. Unpublished Ph.D. thesis, Department of Demography, Australian National University, Canberra.

MILLER, B.D., (1981), The Endangered Sex, Cornell University Press.

MINCER, J., (1963), 'Labour force participation of married women', in Gregg Lewis, H., (Ed.), Aspects of Labour Economics, Universities National Bureau Conference Series No.14, Princeton University Press.

MISSEN, G., (1972), Viewpoints of Indonesia: A Geographical Study, Nelson, Melbourne.

MOORE, J., (ND), <u>Notices of the Indian Archipelago and Adjacent Countries</u>, cited in Hanna, W., 1971.

MUELLER, E.,(1976), 'The economic value of children in peasant agriculture', in Ridker, R.G., (Ed.), <u>Population and Development</u>, Johns Hopkins Press, Baltimore.

MUSTOFFA, S., (1981), 'Indonesia plans 10 years ahead', <u>Populi</u>, 8(1):14-17.

NAG, M., (1962), 'Factors affecting human fertility in non-industrial societies: a cross-cultural study', Department of Anthropology, Yale University, New Haven.

_____., WHITE, B., and PEET, C., 'An anthropological approach to the economic value of children in Java and Nepal', <u>Current Anthropology</u>, 19(2):293-306.

NITISASTRO, W., (1970), <u>Population Trends in Indonesia</u>, Cornell University Press, Ithaca, New York.

NOTESTEIN, F.W., (1953), 'Economic problems of population change', paper presented to the 8th International Conference of Agricultural Economists.

OKA, G.A., (1971), 'Agama Hindu Tidak Melarang Keluarge Berencana' (The Hindu religion does not forbid family planning), Parisada Hindu Dharma, Bali.

PEET, N., and PEET, D., (1977), 'Family planning and the banjars of Bali', <u>Cycle Communications</u>, Ford Foundation.

PERLMAN, J.E., (1976), <u>The Myth of Marginality</u>, University of California Press, Los Angeles.

PLOSS, H.H., BARTELS, M. and BARTELS, P., (1935), <u>Woman</u>, Vol.II, William Heineman, London.

POFFENBERGER, M., (ND), 'Fertility decline in Bali: Couple, community and religion'. Unpublished paper, 64p.

_____., and ZURBUCHEN, M., (1980), 'The economics of village Bali: Three perspectives', <u>Economic Development and Cultural Change</u>, 29(1):91-133.

POPULATION COUNCIL, (1979), 'Five intrauterine devices for public programs', booklet.

POTTER, J.E., (1977), 'Problems in using birth-history analysis to estimate trends in fertility', <u>Population Studies</u>, 31(2):335.

POTTS, M., KESSEL, E. and BHIWANDIWALA, P., (1977), 'Taking family planning to the world's poor', International Fertility Research Program, North Carolina.

POTTS, M., and BHIWANDIWALA, P., (1979), _Birth Control - An International Assessment_, MTP Press.

PUFFER, R.R., and SERRANO, C.V., _Patterns of Mortality in Childhood_, Pan American Health Organization, W.H.O.

PURBANGKORO, M., (1978), 'The special drive in East Java: An evaluation of an Indonesian Family Planning Program intensive campaign', mimeo, Jember University, Jember, cited by Freedman _et al._, 1981.

RAFFLES, SIR T.S., (1830), _The History of Java_, Oxford University Press, Kuala Lumpur, (2nd. Edition). First published 1817, London.

RAVENHOLT, A., (1973), 'Man-land-productivity microdynamics', _Population Perspective 1973_, Freedman, Cooper and Co., San Francisco, 216-26.

RIMBAWAN, I. DAYUH, (1982), _Perkawanan Dan Percerain Pada Masyarakap Hindu_, Gadjah Mada.

SCHULTZ, T., (1976), 'Determinants of fertility: A micro-economic model of choice', in Coale, A.J., (Ed.), _Economic Factors in Population Growth_, Proceedings of a Conference held by the International Economic Association at Valescure, France. MacMillan Press, London.

SINAGA, R., (1978), 'Note: Implications of agricultural mechanization for employment and income distribution: A case study from Indramayu, West Java', _Bulletin of Indonesian Economic Studies_, 14(2):102-11.

SINGARIMBUN, M., and MANNING, C., (1974), 'Fertility and family planning in Mojolama', Population Institute, Gadjah Mada University, Yogyakarta, Indonesia.

SINQUEFIELD, J.C., (1978), 'Estimating fertility from data on current pregnancy status of women', _Majalah Demografi Indonesia_, 10:25-39.

_____., and SUNGKONO, B., (1979), 'Fertility and family planning trends in Java and Bali', _International Family Planning Perspectives_, 5(2):43-58.

SOEDARMADI and REESE, T.H., (1975), _The Indonesian National Family Planning Program: A Cost-Effectiveness Analysis 1971/72-73/74_, BKKBN Technical Report Series Monograph No.10, BKKBN, Jakarta.

SOEDJATMIKO, (1976), 'Feasibility study Pengembangan Traktor Pertanian di Kabupaten Badung, Gianyar dan Tabanan, Propinsi Bali', Sub-Direktorat Mekanisasi Pertanian, Direktorat Bina Produksi Tanaman Pangan, Departemen Pertanian.

STREATFIELD, P.K., (1982), 'Fertility decline in a traditional society: The case of Bali', Ph.D. thesis, Department of Demography, Australian National University, Canberra.

_____., (1985), A comparison of census and Family Planning Program data on contraceptive prevalence, Indonesia', Studies in Family Planning, 16:342-49.

SUYONO, H., (1979), 'An interview with Haryono Suyono', International Family Planning Perspectives, 5(2):59-62.

_____., PANDI, S.H., ASTAWA, I.B., MOELJONO and REESE, T.H., (1976), 'Village Family Planning - The Indonesian Model, BKKBN Technical Report Series Monograph No.13, BKKBN, Jakarta.

SWELLENGREBEL, J.L., (1960), 'Introduction' in Bali: Studies in Life, Thought and Ritual, Selected Studies on Indonesia by Dutch scholars. W. van Hoeve Ltd., The Hague and Bandung.

_____., (1969), 'Non-Conformity in the Balinese family', in Bali: Further Studies in Life, Thought and Ritual, W. van Hoeve Ltd., The Hague, 199-212.

TEACHMAN, J., BOGUE, D.J., LONDONO, J. and HOGAN, D., (1979), The Impact of Family Planning Programs on Fertility Rates: A Case Study of Four Nations, Community and Family Studies Center, 155p.

_____., SUYONO, H, PARSONS, J.S. and ROHADI, (1980), 'Continuation of contraception on Java-Bali: Preliminary results from the quarterly acceptor survey', Studies in Family Planning, 11(4):134-44.

TJITARSA, I.B., WALOEYO S., WIRAWAN, D.N., WIADNYANA, G.P. and GUNUNG, K. (1975), 'Penelitian Kelangsungan Pemakaian Alat-Alat Kontrasepsi Akseptor Extra Drive di Bali' (An investigation of the use of contraception by Extra Drive acceptors in Bali), mimeo, Udayana University, Denpasar, Bali.

UNITED NATIONS, DEPARTMENT OF ECONOMIC AND SOCIAL AFFAIRS, (1967), Manual IV - Methods of Estimating Basic Demographic Measures From Incomplete Data, ST/SOA/Series A/42, New York.

_____, (1979), Manual IX - The Methodology of Measuring The Impact of Family Planning Programmes on Fertility, No.ST/ESA/Series A/66, New York.

USAID, (1980), 'Indonesia - Family Planning Program', U.S.Agency for International Development Office of Population, Jakarta, Indonesia.

WARE, H., (1974), Ideal Family Size, World Fertility Survey Occasional Paper, No.13.

WHITE, B., (1976), 'Production and Reproduction in a Javanese village'. Unpublished Ph.D. thesis, Columbia University.

WORLD FERTILITY SURVEY, (1976), listed under Central Bureau of Statistics.

GLOSSARY

A) TECHNICAL TERMS

Age Specific Fertility Rate: the age specific fertility rate (ASFR) for women of a given age (or age-group) 'x' is the number of babies born to women of that age (or age-group) per 1,000 women of that age (or age group) in the population in the middle of that year. Usually five year age-groups are used.

Age Specific Marital Fertility Rate: if the definition is restricted to births to married women only, then the resultant measure is the age specific marital fertility rate (ASMFR).

Crude Birth Rate: the crude birth rate (CBR) is calculated by dividing the number of births which occurred in a population in one calendar year by the size of the population at the middle of that year. The mid-year population is taken as an estimate of the average population during the whole calendar year.

Crude Death Rate: the crude death rate (CDR), like the CBR, equals the number of deaths occurring in a population during one calendar year divided by the size of the population at the middle of that year.

Family Planning Prevalence Rate: equals the number of married couples in a population currently using some form of contraception divided by the total number of currently-married couples in that population.

Infant Mortality Rate: the infant mortality rate (IMR) is defined as the number of deaths of infants under 1 year of age registered in a given year per 1,000 live births registered in the same year.

Natural Fertility: natural fertility, or fertility uncontrolled in any way, would be higher than has actually been experienced by any country's population. On the basis of an analysis made by Henry of fertility in a number of populations where little or no fertility control is practised, we may estimate a crude birth rate of about 60 as corresponding to conditions of natural fertility.

Parity: parity is the number of children previously borne. Zero-parity (childless) women are at risk of having a first birth, one-parity women of having a second birth, and so on.

Parity Progression Ratio: the parity progression ratio is the term used for the proportion of women of given parity (x children) who advance to the next parity (x+1 children).

Population Growth Rate: the annual population growth rate is obtained by dividing the increase in population during the year by the population at the beginning of that year, it is usual to use the exponential growth formula, rather than the compound growth rate formula, to calculate the growth rate.

Total Fertility Rate: despite the relatively convenient form of age-specific fertility rates when expressed in five-year age groups, there are occasions when a single figure index is desirable. What is required is a convenient formula for combining the individual age-specific rates. The simplest of these is the total fertility rate (TFR) obtained by adding together the age specific fertility rates for women of each age.

The total fertility rate thus represents the number of children that would be born (ignoring mortality) to a hypothetical group of 1,000 women who, as they pass through the reproductive ages, experience the particular age specific fertility rates on which the index is based.

The total marital fertility rate (TMFR) is calculated in the same way as the TFR but includes only births to married women.

B) INDONESIAN WORDS

The Indonesian words and terms frequently used in the text are presented below with their English translation. Most of these are also defined when they are used in the text.

ADAT   Customary or traditional law

ANGGOTA   member (e.g. of banjar)

AWIG-AWIG   written or oral set of regulations (e.g. for subak)

BALE BANJAR   banjar meeting hall

BALIAN   traditional healer

BANJAR   hamlet community of households

BEMO   4-wheel taxi van

BERAS   husked rice, either traditional (Bali) or High yielding variety (Baru)

BIMAS   Government program of 'mass guidance' (Bimbingan Masyarakat)

BRAHMANA   highest (princely) caste

BUPATI   administrative head of a kabupaten formerly regency or kingdom (8 in Bali)

CAMAT   administrative head of a kecamatan or sub-district (51 in Bali)

DADIA   a type of kin group

DESA   village, either administrative (desa dinas) or traditional (desa adat)

GABAH   harvested rice still on stalk (i.e. before threshing)

GENDAK   trial marriage

GENTENG   baked clay roof tiles

IUD   intrauterine device (also Lippes Loop; spiral)

LONTAR   traditional book with words or drawings scratched on palm-leaf pages

LUMBUNG   traditional household rice barn (less common now)

KAHYANGAN-
TIGA   set of three major temples in a village (desa adat)

KELIAN	administrative head of a banjar (kelian dinas) or traditional head of a banjar (kelian banjar) or person responsible for temple care (kelian pura)
MANIK	'gem', or traditional concept of ovum
MAPADIK	arranged marriage, particularly amongst high castes
NGEROROD	marriage by mock capture or elopement
OTON	period of 210 days, equal to six 35-day Bali months or thirty 7-day weeks.
PADI	growing rice (i.e. before harvesting)
PEDAGANG	travelling salesperson; hawker
PEDANDA	high priest, always from Brahmana caste
PEKARANGAN	houseyard, usually walled in Bali
PEMANGKU	village priest, may be from any caste
PERBEKEL	administrative head of a village
RAJA	traditional head of a kingdom, now replaced by Bupati as administrative head
Rp.	Rupiah 620 = US$1
SANGKEP	meeting of banjar council, normally every 35 days
SATRIA	second (princely) caste from which royal families come
SAWAH	irrigated rice fields
SEBEL	state of being polluted (e.g. a person or place)
SEKA	voluntary organisation or club
SENTANA	arrangement where son-in-law lives in household of wife's parents, when no natural son exists
SUBAK	irrigation society
SUDRA	term for casteless Balinese (some 90 percent of population)
TRIWANGSA	collective term for Brahmana, Satria and Wesia castes
WARIS	inheritance system
WARUNG	small street stall or shop
WERENG	leaf-hopper beetle, pest of rice crops
WESIA	third caste, formerly warrior and merchant caste